THE MAKING OF MODERN DRAMA SERIES

The Breaking String

THE PLAYS OF ANTON CHEKHOV

MAURICE VALENCY

SCHOCKEN BOOKS · NEW YORK

First published by Schocken Books 1983
10 9 8 7 6 5 4 3 2 1   83 84 85 86

Library of Congress Cataloging in Publication Data
Valency, Maurice Jacques, 1903–
  The breaking string.
  (The making of modern drama)
  Reprint. Originally published: New York: Oxford
  University Press, 1966. With new pref.
  Bibliography: p.
  Includes index.
  1. Chekhov, Anton Pavlovich, 1860–1904—
Dramatic works. I. Title.
PG3453.Z9D79   1982   891.72'3   82–3369   AACR2

Manufactured in the United States of America
ISBN 0–8052–0716–3 (paperback)

Preface to the Schocken Edition

In the seventeen years since the first publication of this study the application of the techniques of structuralism and semiotics to the plays of Chekhov has produced results that are certainly impressive, if not altogether illuminating. Nevertheless I am not impelled to alter in any substantial way the views advanced in the following pages. The critical methods now in vogue, and those that may be expected to succeed them, will doubtless deepen our understanding of Chekhov's patterns of composition and help us to chart the topography of his soul, but it is likely that the type of analysis with which I have endeavored to approach his work will be found of some use as long as his plays continue to be staged.

Chekhov's plays have the complexity of the utterly simple. For the curious analyst there is nothing more baffling than the limpid surface they invariably present. The characters he devised and the manner in which they are posed make the impression of a series of snapshots too ingenuous to require comment. It is depressing to realize that we shall never understand them. With the exception of *The Three Sisters,* which was eventually subtitled "A Drama," Chekhov insisted that his plays were comedies, vaudevilles, and farces. Yet, in spite of his many and frequent objections, the tendency from the time of Stanislavsky has been to emphasize not their comic aspects, but their pathos. On what basis can such a discrepancy be resolved?

It is disquieting to see a work of art manifest a mind of its own, and it could hardly have escaped Chekhov that occasionally his characters flatly refused to do what was expected of them. In any event, this is clear to us, and it is the source of some confusion. Of course, with the aid of a little psychological legerdemain it is generally possible for the critic to distinguish an author's conscious purpose from the unconscious tendencies which shape his work in spite of him. This sort of analysis, while comforting, has its drawbacks. If we assume that our author does not really know what he is about, we are led to the assumption that our critic really does. But critics, however astute, also have unconscious motives which subvert their judgment. There is no end to this. We may recall, in this connection, the sad case of Pirandello who, while blissfully unaware of what he was doing, wrote beautifully until Adriano Tilgher explained to him what he had in mind, after which there was nothing more to be said.

Happily, nothing of the sort happened to Chekhov. So long as he lived he continued to lament, even in the face of the most convincing success, that he was completely misunderstood and misrepresented on the stage. If this is so, the fault is hardly the fault of Stanislavsky; and it cannot be ours. In spite of all efforts to render them comprehensible, Chekhov's plays maintain their reserve. Even when it is interrogated with methods reminiscent of the gestapo, his drama refuses to commit itself or to name its accomplices.

It is, of course, the destiny of great artists to be misunderstood. That is, no doubt, the price they pay for greatness, for what can be defined is seldom great. It is disconcerting, certainly, to reflect that perhaps we admire Chekhov for the wrong reasons. But there is nothing more to be done about it. At this point Chekhov is what we have made of him. For us, given the psychologic temper of our age, Chekhov's plays, however we interpret them, cannot fail to convey the uncertainty that lies at the core of his work, a psychic malaise, tempered with humor, that quite exactly matches our own. His characters are people we get to know quite well, since they are none other than ourselves, though never well enough, never intimately. In general they elude our understanding, which is to be expected in the circumstances, and this perhaps accounts for their extraordinary vitality; for to understand is to destroy.

"On the way here," says Ivanov, who is on his way to commit suicide, "I laughed at myself, and it seemed to me that the birds and the flowers were laughing at me also." To Chekhov also it seemed, one imagines, that life was a practical joke in rather bad taste. In such cases it is usually best to join in the laughter, and generally he invites us to do so, but Chekhov cannot altogether disguise his disgust at the coarseness of the jest, and I cannot imagine that he intended us only to laugh.

I think if I were re-writing these pages, I should emphasize more strongly Chekhov's debt to Maeterlinck, not, of course, to the Maeterlinck whose style he spoofed in *The Sea Gull,* but to the author of *La Tragique quotidien,* the Maeterlinck who wrote of the art of the unexpressed, of stasis and mystery, and the dramatic use of silence. Chekhov invites us to think of himself as a naturalist and we fall readily into his trap; but he was frequently inclined to mysticism. Quite often in Chekhov's plays and his stories we are aware of something very like the Maeterlinckean *au-delà,* and there is the unmistakable sound of "*le chant mystérieux de l'infini,*" a song that readily dispenses with words. Like Maeterlinck, like Balzac, Chekhov manifests a sense of the oneness of life, a feeling that all that lives is informed with a universal idea, that "everything has a soul," as the young magistrate Lyzhin says, "one soul, one aim."

In Maeterlinck's works these intuitions are pervasive. They color everything. It is otherwise with Chekhov; he is not consistent in this, or in anything. He was too much the skeptic to follow a definite line. The ability to make explicit statements is admirable. Obviously it requires faith. To Chekhov, it would seem, nothing was so dear that it was worthy of faith. The Tao that could be said was not the Tao. For the honest writer there was only the possibility of uncovering for a moment an uncharted vision, which might be illusory, a psychic landscape which could perhaps be revealed momentarily by a gesture, by a sound perhaps, but never by words.

Chekhov was certainly not a symbolist in the sense that Blok or Bryusov or even Andreyev were symbolists. His symbolism, like Ibsen's was not doctrinal, but instinctive. It was the stuff of which poetry is made. In 1937 Giraudoux had no trouble in expressing his impatience with those who insist that plays should be understandable. In 1903 such a position would have been premature. It was then considered advantageous for drama to have clarity and message. Consequently, in Stanislavsky's theatre Chekhov was made clear. In our day such violence is no longer necessary. One cannot be sure that obscurity is the best way to excel in the theatre; but at least ambiguity can be tolerated, and even savored. If we can enjoy Chekhov without understanding him, by all means it should be done, for it seems wrong to clarify what he forbore to make plain. If we cannot manage, there is an alternative, though seldom a good one. But before we hazard an interpretation it may be well to remember what he wrote to Olga Knipper when she asked him to tell her what life is. "That is just like asking what is a carrot," he told her. "A carrot is a carrot, and nothing more is known about it."

1983 M.J.V.

Preface

When first I embarked on what was intended as an introduction to modern drama it seemed to me that it would surely be possible to describe in a single stout volume the shaping influences in the theatre of our time. But it soon became evident that it would be a very capacious volume indeed that would contain so ample a subject. Of the concise survey which I originally planned, the first part, *The Flower and the Castle,* advances the discussion no further than Strindberg. This is the second part. It principally concerns Chekhov.

On the subject of Chekhov

> Tant on li conteor conté
> Et li fablior tan fablé,

that it may well be questioned whether there is anything left to add. Perhaps there is. Many interesting studies exist of Chekhov in his various aspects, too many, indeed, to list; but I am not familiar with any in which Chekhov's work in the theatre is systematically considered in connection with the development of dramatic art generally in the West. It is to this end that the present study is directed.

Toward the end of the nineteenth century the great cultural tradition which binds our age to the world of the Renaissance began to give way. The theatre echoed with some clarity the premonitory sounds of the impending cataclysm. Along with Ibsen and Strindberg, three major dramatists—Chekhov, Pirandello, and Shaw—concerned themselves with the attendant phenomena. Of the three, Chekhov appears most clearly to represent the period. He is beyond doubt the most elusive of these writers, and the most difficult to interpret.

The difficulty of interpreting Chekhov has nothing to do with geography. Chekhov was Russian to the core, but one does not need to be Russian to take his measure or to feel his charm. A knowledge of the language in which he wrote certainly helps. But even this is not indispensable. His plays grew out of the same spiritual soil which nourished the rest of the European drama. He was in close touch with the literary currents of his time, and his work clearly reflects their power and pressure. Moreover, the universality of his genius and his enormous influence on the Western stage sufficiently demonstrate how keenly his mind was attuned to the intellectual tendencies of his day. All of his work has to do with Russia and the Russian predicament, but beyond this it has to do with man and the predicament of man; and if this is worth pointing out it is mainly because it is only in terms of the larger concept that it is possible to arrive at a sufficient comprehension of this singularly complex and beautiful spirit.

Since it is hardly possible to evaluate Chekhov's plays without taking account of the theatre for which they were written, it seems sensible to preface the discussion of his work with some description of the Russian stage and its development up to his time. Needless to say, there can be no question here of anything like a thorough survey of Russian drama. For my purpose, a few landmarks will serve to orient the reader as well as, or even better than, a wealth of careful detail; and for those who wish to explore the matter more curiously, there is no lack of guide-books and guides.

Chekhov's plays represent, of course, only a small fraction of his literary output. As he himself observed more than once, he found the drama a flashy, noisy, and tiresome mistress. His legitimate spouse was the short story. It was out of his skill as a storyteller that he developed his unique style in the theatre. It would make no sense, obviously, to attempt a detailed analysis of his plays without reference to the non-dramatic work which occupied him even during the years when he wrote principally for the stage. I have, accordingly, treated his plays and the relevant stories together as the product of a single line of thought, and I have tried, wherever possible, to illuminate the one through the other.

In the course of this discussion I have concerned the reader almost exclusively with primary materials. Many excellent critics have interested themselves in Chekhov. I have tried not to report what they have written, considering that it is more profitable to read their words in their proper context than to have them retailed at second hand. But the good things have a disconcerting way of turning up brightly in one's mind, and one takes hold of them with such gusto as may delude one into a comforting sense of originality when one no longer remembers their provenience. For such lapses as I may be guilty of in this respect, as well as for my other sins, may God forgive me. I am, in any case, deeply aware of the heavy debt I owe to the many gifted scholars whose labors in this field have made it possible to traverse the area with confidence. Some of my more special obligations I have indicated in the text and the notes; for the rest, I take this opportunity of expressing my gratitude to those without whose guidance a study of this sort would hardly be possible.

Any account of a body of literature in a language so far removed from English must depend ultimately on the accuracy of the textual interpretation. Chekhov has been fortunate in his translators. But, as every writer knows, translation must be reckoned high among the creative arts, and the better the quality of the work the closer it tends toward originality. Chekhov's Russian is extremely simple, but his style is a miracle of concision, so that it is virtually impossible to translate him without amplification. The result is that no one who compares versions of his text by different hands can fail to be impressed by their disparity. In these circumstances, a "do-it-yourself" approach to the subject seems least troublesome. Accordingly, with few exceptions, the translations in this volume are my own, as is also the responsibility for whatever ineptitude may be discovered in them.

Chekhov was, as I have said, a writer of great concision, and it would be pleasant to interpret his work in a manner appropriately concise. Unhappily, this is not possible. The materials from which he worked were not new, but in the drama he succeeded in transmitting a new sound, and it is only by sorting out its overtones with some care that one can represent him truly. In these circumstances, one aims not so much at brevity as at an acceptable signal-to-noise ratio. This has been my aim, and I can only hope that my shortcomings in this respect will inspire more talented technicians to achieve something better.

It remains only to write a word of thanks to my friends and colleagues. I am particularly indebted to Professor Ernest J. Simmons, who read the manuscript and made many valuable suggestions; to Dr. Toby Lelyveld, whose expert advice in matters of the theatre I have always found invaluable; to Mr. Sheldon Meyer, Miss Alison Bond, and Mr. John Begg of the Oxford University Press, whose kindness I cannot pass over in silence; finally to Janet Cornell, my wife, who came, as always, valiantly to my assistance when assistance was needed. The staff of the Columbia University Libraries has been helpful far beyond the call of duty. I am extremely grateful to the John Simon Guggenheim Foundation whose magnanimity in renewing my fellowship made it possible to complete this volume in half the time it would normally have taken, and to the Administration of Columbia University which made a generous contribution toward the cost of preparing the manuscript. Thanks are also due to the Citadel Press, New York, for permission to reprint extracts from Maxim Gorky, *Autobiography* (1949). For the rest, I thank heaven.

New York
April 1966

M.J.V.

Contents

THE BREAKING STRING

Chekhov's Theatre

IBSEN published *A Doll's House* in 1879. He does not appear to have had any strong conviction that he was doing anything new, and he was as surprised as anyone at the magnitude of the reverberation which his play aroused. But, though it served to indicate in striking fashion the newest tendencies of the contemporary stage, *A Doll's House* did not break with tradition. It was two years later, with *Ghosts*, that Ibsen definitely set the scene for the social drama of our time. *Ghosts* was published in 1881. It is not unreasonable to date our contemporary theatre from this point.

That year, in Moscow, Anton Pavlovich Chekhov finished what appears to have been his first play. He offered it for production to Maria Yermolova. It must have required courage. Yermolova was a famous actress, a mainstay of the Maly Theatre, at this time accounted one of the finest theatres in the world, second only to the Comédie Française. Anton Pavlovich was nobody in particular, a lad of 21 in his second year at the School of Medicine, tall, handsome, penniless, as busy as a bee, and quite as anonymous. One might wonder at his temerity in approaching so magnificent a person as Yermolova; but Russian students were not shy, and Chekhov less shy than most.

Everything indicates that young Chekhov troubled himself very little in these years with the philosophical and political excitements which exercised so many of his fellows at the university, and still less with current attitudes in the literary bohemia of Moscow. Judging by his letters, his thoughts at this time were principally of money.[1]

His family was large and, in a curious way, dependent on him. His grandfather had been a serf. His father was a ruined shopkeeper, without a shop, and with many children, a very absolute man who found it difficult to work for others, and impossible to work for himself. Anton's mother, his sister Maria, and even his older brothers counted heavily on the boy's success. Meanwhile, times were hard. The scholarship which supposedly maintained him at the university, a grant of 25 rubles a month from his native city of Taganrog on the Black Sea, was for a time the backbone of the family exchequer. After the failure of the elder Chekhov's grocery store, the family had moved hopefully to Moscow, and huddled into cramped quarters to await the turn of fortune. It was slow in coming.

For Anton, science was the sure way to success; but he had a turn for comic writing, and even before he came to Moscow, he had managed to sell some short pieces to the comic weeklies. There was not much future in this sort of writing. It was miserably paid. But Chekhov was not thinking of a literary future. He wrote to make money, and he signed his stories with a pseudonym, Antosha Chekhonte, so as not to sully the name which he hoped one day to sign to his scientific papers.

In these years the lure of the stage was strong and its rewards great, but the difficulties of getting a play produced were even greater. Nemirovich-Danchenko quotes the Russian saying—doubtless valid for all times and places: "To write plays you need talent, but genius to have them produced." At this time, young Chekhov was able to demonstrate neither talent nor the necessary genius, and Yermolova hastened to return his play with the regrets of the administration. Chekhov destroyed the manuscript. Evidently the time had not yet come for him to brave the rigors of the imperial stage.

The art of the theatre in Russia is of no great antiquity. In Chekhov's day, Russian drama was barely three centuries old, and by no means rich in masterpieces. But there were some; enough, at least, to establish a tradition.

From a historical viewpoint there is no reason to consider Russian drama apart from the general development of dramatic art in Europe. On the contrary, what is chiefly significant in its early phases is its dependence on external influences. Until relatively modern times there had been little enough in Russia by way of a native literature. Pushkin had taught the Russians to write in Russian. Griboyedov, Lermontov, Gogol had focused public attention on the Russian scene. The masters of drama in the later nineteenth century—Turgenev, Ostrovsky, Tolstoy—dealt exclusively with the Russian milieu, but all of them showed clearly the influence of the literary currents that were shaping the course of European art. What was chiefly original in the Russian drama was the Russian spirit; all the rest was borrowed or adapted from the literature of the West.

At the present time it taxes the efforts of the scholar to find anything of significance in the Russian theatre before 1750. Throughout a good part of the seventeenth century, the Tsars intensified their pious efforts to regulate their vast dominions in accordance with monastic practices; not only plays but, for a time, even songs were forbidden. About 1660, under Tsar Alexei Mikhailovich, whose second empress admired the English, a troupe of child actors was organized under pastoral tutelage to perform plays for the edification of the court. Peter, the son of Alexei, made efforts to establish at court a theatrical company that would add brilliance to his reign by performing a Western repertory and, more especially, a series of plays that would celebrate his victories. For this laudable purpose he built a theatre in the Red Square in Moscow; but it saw little use in his lifetime. In 1709, the court was moved to Petersburg, and the court theatre—such as it was—went with it. This theatre developed slowly, first under German influences, then under Italian; finally it became firmly French. In 1735 Francesco Araia introduced the imperial court to the marvels of Italian opera; some five years later, Jean-Baptiste Landé organized a *corps de ballet* along French lines. The national theatre as such made its debut about the middle of the century with a tragedy in Russian entitled *Khorev* (1749) by Alexander Sumarokov. It was composed in classic style, and was proudly imitative of the French.

Theatre in Russia was theoretically a state function, under direct state control. Peter I had organized his state as an army with himself at the head; he considered the theatre a cultural arm of the autocracy. In later years, the Russian theatre, like the French, was justified and supported as a medium of moral instruction, a school of manners, a convenient means for the dissemination of official propaganda, and an instrument for the control of public opinion. From beginning to end, therefore, all its productions were subject to official scrutiny, as well as to the control of the ecclesiastical authorities, and the secret police of the Third Department felt that it was intimately concerned in its operations and responsible for them. Russian drama thus developed in the teeth of the most resolute bureaucratic regulation; there was no time in which the theatre was wholly free from pressure, and its tensions were always in part attributable to the circumstances of production.

In 1773 the Empress Catherine built what was later called the Bolshoi, that is to say, the Grand Theatre, in Petersburg, and a half-dozen years later she established a dramatic school to provide the state with properly trained actors. As the imperial actors were civil servants, their professional careers were assured for life, but their dependence on the bureaucracy was absolute. Outside the imperial playhouses there existed a considerable number of private theatres supported by wealthy nobles, in emulation of the court, and staffed by companies of their serfs. The actors and actresses in these companies were, of course, completely at the disposal of their owners. They were bought and sold, or presented as gifts, and might be flogged if they failed to give satisfaction. Some of the greatest Russian actors came from these companies, the better part of which were absorbed by the imperial theatres after the Emancipation of 1861. There were also commercial theatres in some of the provincial cities, often operated under appalling conditions, and more or less independent of regulation, though nominally under the supervision of the government in Petersburg.

In the reign of Nicholas I (1825-55) three state theatres were active in Petersburg and two in Moscow, all financed by the court and administered by court officials. The Bolshoi in Petersburg–later called the Marinsky–was the principal home of the opera and the ballet companies. The Alexandrinsky, built in 1832 in neo-classic style, offered a varied repertory of drama directed primarily to the educated classes of the capital. At the head of this company in the 1840's was the great tragedian Vassily Karatygin, whose studied, "French" acting style left its mark, according to Stanislavsky, on the majority of Russian tragic actors throughout the century. The Mikhailovsky Theatre, established in 1833, specialized in the Russian classics, save for the periods during which it housed touring companies from abroad playing in French or German. As early as 1805 an imperial edict established two state theatres in Moscow. The Bolshoi in Moscow had two thousand seats. It offered a dramatic repertory until 1853; later its stage was devoted exclusively to opera and ballet. The Little Theatre, the Maly, was half this size, and became the centre of theatrical activity in Moscow.

Toward the middle of the nineteenth century, the Maly was dominated by the tragic actor Mochalov, a former serf. Mochalov's style was considered to be at the opposite extreme from that developed by Karatygin; he was an explosive actor, barely literate, who depended completely on the inspiration of the moment, and who incarnated the romantic idea of art as a divine enthusiasm which had no need of instruction. Shchepkin, his successor, was an actor of a different stamp. He too had been born a serf, but he was an educated man, basically a comedian, a specialist in the theatre of Molière, and the quiet, conversational style which he developed influenced many of the fine character actors of the latter half of the century. The distinction between the grandiose style which distinguished the Alexandrinsky troupe and the realistic manner of the Moscow Maly continued to be felt until the very end of the century. It was Shchepkin's thoughtful method which developed into the production techniques of the Moscow Art Theatre, and the style of acting which we associate with Chekhov's plays. Chekhov, in his last years, saw no essential difference between the style of production at the Maly and that of the Art Theatre, though he appears to have preferred Stanislavsky's actors as somewhat more sensible and conscientious than most.[2]

The repertory of the state theatres was replenished chiefly by a self-perpetuating group of playwrights closely associated with the Alexandrinsky and the Maly, who were expert in providing plays suited to the tastes and talents of the imperial players. The virtual monopoly of the state theatres enjoyed by such writers as Potekhin, Shpazhinsky, Krylov, and Karpov presented as great an obstacle to the development of Russian drama as did the official censorship which had, in a sense, created them. Nevertheless, a few outsiders were able to impose themselves either through influence or by the sheer weight of their talent. It was through these insurgents that the theatre raised itself gradually above the level of mediocrity that best suited its administration.

In spite of the enormous difficulty of carrying on private theatrical enterprises in either of the capitals, by the third quarter of the nineteenth century there were, it is estimated, some two dozen theatrical ventures operating more or less regularly in Petersburg and Moscow, while the provincial theatre had expanded quite out of proportion to the situation in the capitals. By 1882 the absurdity of maintaining a state monopoly which in fact did not exist was sufficiently manifest even in official circles to warrant an edict legalizing privately operated theatres throughout the empire.[3] As in the case of the analogous Theatres Act in England (1843), there was no immediate consequence; but in time, A. A. Brenko and, later, F. A. Korsh opened theatres in Moscow which attempted to compete with the Maly, and later still Suvorin opened a theatre in Petersburg which was intended to compete with the Alexandrinsky. All of these ventures rapidly degenerated into ordinary commercial enterprises, and until the 1890's the dramatic life of the empire continued to center on the imperial theatres which alone could afford to maintain a serious approach to the drama as art.

The development of realism on the Russian stage took place despite the censor. It was a slow process, the more so as in the initial phases there were no actors in Russia capable of playing a scene in any but the highly artificial style considered appropriate to the stage. The first play written in colloquial style was Denis Fonvizin's *The Minor* (1781), a play which is sometimes said to mark the beginning of the Russian theatrical repertory. This is a comedy composed along Terentian lines, involving the difficulties of a young girl who is being forced by her guardian into a disagreeable marriage for mercenary reasons. The story ends happily, but the play was promptly censored as an unflattering description of domestic life in

Russia. Nevertheless, some years later, in 1798, Kapnist was able to produce a far more controversial play, *The Slanderer*, which dealt with corruption in judicial circles. Thus, by the beginning of the nineteenth century, the outlines were already discernible of the type of comedy which was to become the specialty of the Russian stage; but it would have been a wise prophet who could have predicted from these modest ventures that in less than a century Russian social drama would be a major force in Western literature.

After the close of the Napoleonic wars, the Russian theatre began to reflect all the influences at work in Europe. In the first decades of the nineteenth century the vogue of the classic mode was seriously challenged first by Pushkin, then by Lermontov, both of whom came, like the French romantics, strongly under the spell of Shakespeare and Schiller. Romanticism was considered in official circles an unwelcome intrusion upon the culture of Russia, but in spite of the government's efforts to bolster up the classic tradition with its authoritarian attitudes there was found no effective way of insulating the reading public from the political and social ferments of this turbulent time. There were impressive literary repercussions. All the major Russian dramatists of the period—Pushkin, Griboyedov, Lermontov, and Gogol—were in some degree opposed to established authority, and all of them encountered resistance on the part of the censor. In these circumstances, it was normal for repressive measures to be intensified, and the result, as always, was a deepening of the gap that divided liberal from conservative opinion. In the grim and sullen silence of the Russian state, the theatre offered a unique opportunity for the sounding of progressive thought, and for this reason it was subject to constant police scrutiny. Accordingly, a chief outlet for the expression of public discontent in these years was the *comédie-vaudeville*, a semi-musical form originally imported from France, like most of the other Russian genres, for the amusement of the court, but very rapidly stabilized on a popular level along lines derived from operetta.

The vaudevilles, highly elaborated in France by Scribe, enjoyed the greatest popularity among the urban classes in Russia. They were generally short comedies centered on a love story, but their loose structure, and the musical *couplets* with which the dialogue was enlivened, gave ample opportunity for satirical comments on the current political and social scene. The vaudevilles therefore served precisely the same function in Russia as in nineteenth-century France in quite similar circumstances, and they were tolerated for much the same reasons. The atmosphere they generated was too cheerful and too hearty to be considered dangerous, and the police were persuaded that these popular trifles were not sufficiently serious to warrant their intervention. During the latter half of the nineteenth century these productions took on a clearer definition; they were elaborated, on the one hand, into true operetta, on the other, into satirical farce and comedy, often no more than a single act in length. In these forms the popularity of vaudeville continued, undiminished, until the very end of the nineteenth century, and even longer.

Gore ot uma (1824) is generally considered to be the first masterpiece of the Russian stage, and it is still a very useful play, one of the cornerstones of the classic repertory. It is a comedy in verse, one of the very last of this genre, for henceforth Russian comedy was written almost exclusively in prose. *Gore ot uma* means "The Misfortune of Having Brains," but, having once been translated with remarkable ineptness as "Woe from Wit," the play is now generally saddled with that title in English. Alexander Griboyedov, at that time a career diplomat, wrote it at the age of 29. It was his only significant contribution to Russian drama.

The language of this play has been extravagantly admired, and many of its lines have become proverbial. The dialogue is indeed exceptionally witty, easy, and pungent. Griboyedov took pains to represent the various levels of Russian speech, from the "sublime" Slavonic to the popular speech of the servant class, so that the effect is not only vivid and realistic, but also compendious, a lively cross-section of the language of the period. The verse has a strong iambic movement. It consists of lines of irregular length in a pattern of alternate rhymes which make the effect of linked quatrains in a very fluid poetic structure. Thus from the viewpoint of its versification, as well as in the energetic management of its plot, *Woe from Wit* recalls Lope de Vega's comedies of manners as well as those of Molière, who without doubt furnished its principal inspiration.

When it is recalled that this play was written in the time of Scribe, the contrast between the simplicity of Russian plotting at this time and the French passion for complexity becomes impressive. The narrative design of *Woe from Wit* is entirely innocent and completely conventional. What distinguishes this play is certainly not the plot, but the gallery of superb characters which it exhibits. These are comic types, easily recognizable as such, but not in the least abstract, and all eminently playable. One would have to look hard to find comparable characterizations among the masterpieces of Western comedy; possibly nothing better has ever been done along these lines.

The hero of *Woe from Wit* recalls the tradition of "The Malcontent," which Marston had made explicit in England, and doubtless Griboyedov had *Le Misanthrope* in mind when he framed his play. There are, however, important differences between the European conception and the Russian. Marston's hero stems from the traditional court-satire of the sixteenth century, but his pretended misanthropy has a certain universality. He hates everybody. Molière saw the whole world mirrored in the society of Paris. Alceste's contempt knows no bounds. It includes the human race; and the same may be said for Gulliver when he returns from the land of the Yahoos. But Chatsky, in Griboyedov's play, is conscious of a world outside Moscow, which is incomparably better than Moscow, and his misanthropic tendencies have, in consequence, a much more local character than those of his prototypes in France and England.

Nevertheless, this satire of nineteenth-century manners in Moscow has universal validity. Whether this was intended or not, what is said of the blockishness of the Moscow ruling class, the baseness of the social climber who cannot stoop too low in his avidity for medals and promotions, the indiscriminate adulation of foreign fashions, and the ways of getting on in general seems as readily applicable to life in our time as it was to the era for which it was originally designed. Certainly the enduring interest of this play is in great measure due to the proliferation in all times and countries of the various species of human reptiles it depicts—the Famusovs, Molchalins, Zagoretskies, Skalozubs, and Repetilins of the world.

The plot of *Gore ot uma* is no more than a convenient framework on which to hang the caricatures which chiefly enliven the hero's commentary. It concerns the efforts of Chatsky, a young nobleman of modest fortune, to win the hand of the beautiful Sophia, his childhood love, the daughter of the high government official Famusov. Chatsky has been away from Moscow for three years, seeing the world. Apparently he was never well adjusted to life in the Russian capital, and his absence has done nothing to improve his relations with the class to which he belongs. The play, framed within the unity of time, describes his adventures in Famusov's house from early morning until late at night, and, incidentally, affords a priceless glimpse into the daily routine of a wealthy household of the period.

Sophia has grown up during Chatsky's absence. She is now seventeen, superbly beautiful, and deeply involved with her father's secretary Molchalin, a needy young man who has schooled himself to endure insults in silence, and is now making his way rapidly up the ladder of success by ingratiating himself with everyone. But while this canny gentleman pays respectful court to Sophia, he is secretly wooing her maid Liza, who has also to withstand the advances of her master Famusov, and is herself much taken with the butler Petrushka. Since Chatsky has no inkling of these involvements, he is astonished at the cool reception he is given by his former flame, and he determines to discover who it is that has captured her fancy in his absence. At first his suspicions light on Colonel Skalozub, a pompous dullard who has won preferment through the fit of his uniform, his deep bass voice, and his single-minded absorption in military routine.

Chatsky is a liberal, enlightened and sincere, but by no means tactful, and he takes every opportunity to rail rhetorically at the stupidities of those who frequent the house of his host. The frankness of his utterance causes Famusov to stop his ears, but Skalozub, too stupid to get the drift, takes his savage sallies as compliments to the military profession. Only Sophia is angered by Chatsky's derisive comments on her beloved Molchalin, and to avenge herself she takes the occasion during the evening ball to set a rumor afoot that Chatsky has come back from his travels somewhat touched in the head. This bit of gossip makes the evening. It travels among the guests like wildfire, and when, at the end of the act, Chatsky launches into a full-scale tirade against the evils of the Moscow Establishment, he finds that long before he has finished, his audience is waltzing around the room.

The last act takes place in Famusov's front hall. The guests are leaving, but Chatsky's carriage is delayed, so that he is forced to stay after the others have departed, and stands unobserved in the vestibule. When, as she thinks, the guests are gone, Sophia sends Liza to fetch Molchalin to her room. The perfidious Molchalin, however, makes love to Liza, and his protestations are sufficiently loud for Sophia to hear. While she is upbraiding Molchalin for his baseness, Chatsky comes forth. He has heard everything, and now he laughs bitterly at Sophia's plight. Molchalin runs off in a panic, and at this point Famusov bursts in with candles and footmen and proceeds to put his house in order. Chatsky delivers himself of a final oration and at last flings off, vowing never to return to this city of fools. Thus he amply confirms Famusov in the impression that he is as mad as he is said to be.

Everything in the play indicates that Chatsky was meant to play a sympathetic role. He is noble and sincere, and he burns with the honest indignation of the Decembrists of 1825. But his nobility poses the same problem as that of Alceste in Molière's play. One sides with him completely, but he is not a pleasant man, and one can hardly blame Sophia for preferring Molchalin, who has the soul of a jackal, but the manners of an angel. Chatsky is indisputably right, but he is intolerable; and it is interesting that Griboyedov was apparently unaware that his hero is as ridiculous in his way as the people he mocks in theirs. Molière had made his point quite clear in the case of Alceste. But Griboyedov had no Philinte to point the way of the Golden Mean, probably because he was unwilling to admit the possibility of compromise with the dunces and hypocrites who graced the society of Famusov's Moscow. The jest, therefore, is not, as in *Le Misanthrope*, that an excess of probity is a lack of good sense, but that it is madness to be sane in a madhouse.

Gore ot uma was Griboyedov's only original work, and it was much admired. He spent a good part of his remaining years smoothing and polishing the verse, but he died young, and had no time to develop his style further. Nevertheless, with this play he inaugurated in Russia a tradition of bitter comedy with amusing characters very precisely drawn, and an unhappy ending, which was characteristically Slavic. Griboyedov had little hope for the Russia he depicted. He wrote:

"In my comedy there are twenty-five fools to one reasonable man, and that man, of course, is in conflict with all the society that surrounds him. Nobody understands him. Nobody forgives him for being superior to the rest."

The play was, of course, banned by the censor. Though it circulated widely in manuscript, for a time its publication was forbidden. It was first played in 1830 in Petersburg, the year after its author's death, but even then in a mutilated version which made Chatsky's behavior seem preposterous, and which therefore directed the satire principally against him, and not against his opponents. The first uncensored performance took place in 1869, and then had no great success; but the efforts of such weighty critics as Belinsky eventually brought the play into its proper place in public estimation. By Chekhov's time, *Gore ot uma* was firmly established among the Russian classics.

Griboyedov did not share the Aristotelian view that the narrative, and not the characterization, is the essential element in drama. As he saw it, a play was an album of portraits. "Portraits, and portraits only," he wrote his friend Katenin, "form the substance both of comedy and tragedy. These portraits, however, include certain traits common to many, and some which appertain generally to the human race." [4] In his view of the matter, dramatic technique was mainly descriptive; and it was in the accuracy and power of the description that the comedic artist best displayed his talent and his originality.

It was, in fact, as we have seen, not the narrative, which is entirely banal, but the superb characterization which makes *Woe from Wit* memorable. The types he caricatured—the pompous bureaucrat Famusov, the blimpish Colonel Skalozub, the fawning secretary Molchalin—trace their ancestry to Roman comedy, and have recognizable French kindred besides, but they are actually Russian to the core, and the vigor and aptitude of these portraits is such that their types and even their names have become proverbial in the language and the folklore of Russia. These roles in time became the staple of the character-actor; they were extensively studied in every acting school, and variant interpretations were diligently compared by theatregoers. A consequence was that in the future development of Russian comedy the emphasis was commonly placed on portraiture rather than plot, so that the comedic tradition that leads from Griboyedov to Chekhov exhibits a magnificent picture-gallery, but no great narrative ingenuity.

The attack on the classic modes which we associate with early romanticism was hardly felt in the Western theatre before 1812. A. W. Schlegel's *Vorlesungen* were published 1809-11; Stendhal's *Racine et Shakespeare* in 1823. It was in 1825 that Pushkin finished *Boris Godunov*. His *Essay on Shakespeare* came out in 1834, in the same year as Vigny's preface to *Chatterton*, and barely seven years after Hugo's *Préface à Cromwell*. Pushkin was therefore in the very forefront of European romanticism, and he opened a very different path for the Russian drama from that staked out by Griboyedov. Griboyedov was, at bottom, a classicist. The dark side of human nature horrified him. It fascinated Pushkin. For him, Shakespeare's tragic heroes were quite other than the bloodless abstractions of classic drama. They were "living beings, full of many passions and many vices," who evoked what Schlegel had called "the tragic tone of mind," that "feeling of inexpressible melancholy for which there is no other counterpoise than the consciousness of a vocation transcending the limits of the human mind." [5]

Pushkin was particularly impressed by the vigor and spaciousness of Shakespeare's histories, and also by their freedom and formlessness, and he fully shared the impatience with formal restrictions which characterized Russian drama after the advent of romanticism. To Pushkin the free movement of Shakespeare's line seemed vastly preferable to the restrained ingenuity of the French Alexandrine. The language of *Boris Godunov* is vigorous. "I am firmly convinced," Pushkin wrote, "that the folk tradition of the Shakespearean drama best befits our theatre, and not the court etiquette of Racinian tragedy." [6]

Boris Godunov was impressively Shakespearean, with mass effects, many scenes, and much movement in time and place, but Pushkin was not able to develop either in Boris or in the Impostor the sort of complex characterization he admired in Shakespeare's tragedies. His play has a number of interesting portraits, but his hero makes an operatic effect. Pushkin pointed the way: it remained for others to work out a characterization along the lines he advocated.

Pushkin's tragedy aroused even greater anxiety in official circles than Griboyedov's ironic comedy, which, after all, dealt with a less exalted aspect of Russian life. Soon after Pushkin began reading *Boris* to his friends, the Third Department evinced its interest, and Pushkin was directed to correct and purify his play. He refused. Five years later, the play was licensed for publication with "minor corrections," but it was not approved for production on the stage during the author's lifetime and, when at last it came before the public in 1870 at the Marinsky Theatre in Petersburg, its hour had passed, and it aroused no interest. It was only after the Revolution of 1917 that the play had any considerable success on the Russian stage. But long before that, in 1873, Moussorgsky had already made it the basis of the opera with which he revolutionized Russian music.[7]

The objection to romanticism in autocratic Russia is readily comprehensible. By emphasizing the unique character of the individual, the romantic writers widened the distance between the subject and the state. Since the state and the Tsar were theoretically synonymous, and the Tsar's partriarchal image was an essential part of the myth of government, the danger to the monarchy of an awakened individualism was all too clear. Throughout the century the government propagated with varying degrees of intensity the ideals of nationalism, orthodoxy, and autocracy, all of which involved an attitude of unquestioning obedience. The exponents of romanticism, on the other hand, dwelt lovingly on the dignity of the individual and his right to resist collectivization. The rebel, the outlaw, the malcontent, the dissident—in short, the *bêtes-noires* of the autocracy—were the heroes of the romantic writers, who insisted also on assailing the existing order by indicating at every opportunity the manifest disparity between the true worth of men and the marks of honor bestowed by the state on those who conformed with its policies. At the core of the romantic fervor of the nineteenth century there was clearly perceptible the spirit of the Great Revolution of 1789 with its terrifying onslaught on the established regime. Thus, as the antagonism between the state and the intellectual classes deepened from year to year, the ever-present sense of danger gave a peculiar glamor to every progressively minded writer, and books banned by the censor enjoyed a vogue which was often quite unrelated to their merits. The situation was thus not altogether different from that which obtained in France in the 1820's; but it lasted longer.

In literature—the political influence of which the Third Department perhaps overestimated—the classic modes, with their strict rules and their clear, if senseless, limitations, were thought to be of considerable value in the maintenance of order and discipline. The government therefore felt it had every reason to support the classic tradition in the schools and elsewhere. But in spite of all efforts to develop literature on an exalted and innocuous plane, the tastes of the literary classes—at first almost exclusively aristocratic—shifted inevitably toward the romantic and the realistic. The adulation of robbers and outlaws which characterized the literature of the early 1800's was soon followed by a wave of sympathy for the poor, the humble, and the wretched. It was an emotion very easy to motivate in a country in which the vast majority of the population lived in misery. Rousseauistic ideas of the beauty of poverty, and the idealization of peasant life, were of course widespread in this period, but at no time in the course of the century were the economically privileged wholly free from guilt-feeling with respect to the laboring classes which sustained them. These feelings became increasingly articulate toward the middle of the century, and crystallized into various forms of humanitarianism. The *narodniki* and, later, the Tolstoyans were especially influential in providing appropriate emotional outlets but, as the century wore on, the need of the cultivated classes to make self-sacrificial gestures was perceptible in every branch of Russian life and letters. It is not difficult to see in these psychic pressures an important predisposing cause for the March Revolution of 1917.

Russian romanticism found full expression in the life and work of Mikhail Lermontov. Lermontov died at 27. His masterpiece, *The Masquerade*, was written in 1835, when he was barely past his majority. His earlier play, *The Spaniards*, reflects an even earlier stage of development—it is obviously the fruit not only of his poetic temper but of his reading at the age of 16: it shows the influence of *The Robbers*, *Don Carlos*, *Hernani*, and the novels of Walter Scott, the basic books of the university youth of his day. In *The Spaniards* the hero has already the wild and moody aspect that the later Russian romantics were to find irresistible. He is a lonely soul, dark and daring, and utterly contemptuous of the paltry crowd he overshadows, in which are particularly discernible the representatives of the vain and selfish nobility, the hypocritical clergy, and the indolent landlords. Obviously, this Byronic hero is no very distant relative of Griboyedov's Chatsky, but the play makes a completely different effect from *Woe from Wit*. This play did not see the stage until after the October

Revolution, a full hundred years after it was written, nor did Lermontov's other early works—*Men and Passions* (1830) and *The Strange Man* (1831)—have any better fortune with the censor.

These plays, in spite of their romantic character, give a fair notion of the trend toward realism in Russia in the 1830's. Both plays are autobiographical in substance, and portray domestic tensions which the author himself had experienced, and both end in the tragic death of the hero. This hero is a fiery and embittered individual, consumed by an inner sorrow of unknown origin. His literary provenience is hardly in doubt. He is the Satanic young man of the early 1800's, more or less as Byron had conceived him. But he has a disconcertingly realistic nuance, which, without making him wholly credible, rescues him from the more obvious absurdities of French romantic tragedy.[8]

Unlike these two plays, *The Masquerade* is in verse. It was written in 1835, shortly after the poet made his debut in the capital as a young officer of hussars. The hero, Eugene Arbenin, is the character traditionally associated with Lermontov—a haughty and lonely young man, whose expression of disdainful indifference conceals the fiery passions that seethe within his breast. He is the obvious prototype of Solyony in Chekhov's *The Three Sisters;* but there is a difference. Solyony was intended to provoke a smile as well as a shudder. Arbenin was meant to be taken quite seriously, and he inclines one to reflection. Lermontov understood somewhat better than Byron the nature of the illness that deforms the Satanic character. The disease of the spirit gives way to love. It requires—in the absence of a qualified psychiatrist—the services of a pure girl to relieve its misery. But, unlike the heroes of romance, these characters are inclined by nature to be suspicious and vindictive, and are incapable of a healthy sexual relationship. In these circumstances it is chiefly the girl who suffers. The man is, in any case, incurable; and his demonism—

an irresistible compulsion to do harm—defies solution. It must be conceded that so long as neuroses were conceived along metaphysical lines, nothing more could be done with such a situation. Lermontov's description is both accurate and impressive. For all their theatricalism, his characters foreshadow more or less clearly the neurotic hero of our time, the modern counterpart of the tragic protagonist of Sophocles.

In the course of time, the inexplicable demonism of *l'homme fatal* of the nineteenth century was to be turned into useful channels. There is no inkling of this development in Lermontov, and none in Chekhov; but in Turgenev's Bazarov, and in Shaw's Satanic heroes—Dick Dudgeon, for example, and Andrew Undershaft—demonism is seen to be a superior human trait. The smoldering passions of the Byronic hero now become moral fervor. The rebel turns his destructiveness against the evils of society. This is perhaps the last stage in the development of the Satanic character. His appearance, indeed, does not change—he remains lofty and defiant. He retains, and even cultivates, his Mephistophelean grimace; but now he is defiant to some purpose: his destiny becomes a sort of providence. In this guise, the individualist is revealed as a socialist; the enemy of society is seen to be a humanitarian; the enemy of God becomes a friend to man. The danger of the early romantic hero was that in overturning the old order he brought about merely disorder; he took pleasure in destruction, and turned readily to nihilism. Shaw, though professedly anti-romantic in the extreme, carried the romantic hero to his logical conclusion. The result is the eminently eligible Jack Tanner of *Man and Superman*, a far cry indeed from Eugene Arbenin.[9]

In *The Masquerade*, the Russian *beau monde* is seen to be a conspiracy of scoundrels, cheats, intriguers, and débauchés. The play presents an interesting gallery of rogues. *Woe from Wit*, with which *The Masquerade* is certainly in some relation, is, by comparison, a miracle of self-restraint. But while

Lermontov was visibly affected by Griboyedov, he had a very different aim; he wished to write a tragedy of jealousy, not a social comedy, and, at this stage of romanticism, tragedy meant dark passions and bloody deeds. The influence of Shakespeare on *The Masquerade* is stronger than that of Griboyedov.

The Masquerade was submitted to the censor in 1835. It was promptly rejected as a "eulogy of vice," with the recommendation that it be given a happy ending. Lermontov compliantly added a fourth act in which an Unknown—presumably the censor—tells Arbenin that the wife whom he has murdered was in fact guiltless. The censor did not fancy this outcome either. The third version was given a still happier ending—this time Arbenin does not poison his wife at all. In this form the play was licensed for publication; but the gruesome panorama of Russian life was not relished by the Third Department, and the license for performance was indefinitely withheld. The play was finally produced in 1852 in a diluted version. Ten years later the full four-act version was performed. As usual, the belated production had no success. It was actually not until 1917, in the last days of the empire, that the play was successfully performed. By that time its social implications had become painfully clear to most people.

During the long and heavy reign of Nicholas I, the most popular of all dramatic genres was melodrama. The *mélodrames* of Pixerécourt and Ducange, which had enjoyed spectacular success in Paris in the early years of the century, were speedily adapted for the Russian stage and furnished roles which were marvellously suited to the talents of the Russian tragic actors. They had mysterious plots which could hardly be rationalized, but they appealed mightily to the imagination. Their language was beautifully bombastic, and the action involved broad theatrical gestures well calculated to impress an impressionable audience.

Melodrama, during this period, often bordered on romantic

tragedy—these genres were not always clearly distinguishable. The most successful of the romantic dramatists in Russia was Nestor Kukolnik, the author, among other things, of the celebrated tragedy *Prince Michael Skopin-Shuisky*, a prime favorite of the provincial tragedians of the period. This play includes a climactic scene in which Prokopy Lyapanov forces the evil Catherine to drink the poison with which she has killed the good Michael Skopin: "Drink," he cries, "drink under the knife of Prokopy Lyapanov!" This speech is said to have brought down the house with unfailing regularity, and Kukolnik was compared in the press with Alexandre Dumas, whom he was held, perhaps with justice, to have far surpassed as a dramatist.[10]

Although *Julius Caesar* had been, quite understandably, in the official repertory almost from its inception, it was Polevoy's translation of *Hamlet* that definitely established Shakespeare on the Russian stage. Polevoy had spent most of his life as a journalist. In his last years, he repaid Kotzebue, who of all the dramatists of his time had most impressed him, by writing thirty-eight plays in the manner of this master. Among these was his version of *Hamlet*, a very Russian conception of the tragedy of the melancholy Dane.

Polevoy had some difficulty in getting his *Hamlet* produced. The play was most irregular in form, and when Polevoy first offered it to Mochalov at the Maly, the great tragedian refused the part on the ground that Shakespeare was unsuited to the Russian taste. Nevertheless in 1837 Mochalov was persuaded to play the role. Shchepkin played Polonius. Their success astounded them. In Petersburg, Karatygin hastened to rival the Moscow production with his own. From that time on, Polevoy's tragedy became a fixture of the Russian repertory, and Hamlet became as familiar a stereotype as Famusov or Skalozub. With the overwhelming success of *Hamlet*, the goal marked out by Pushkin and Lermontov was at last achieved, and the course of Russian drama changed significantly. Henceforth, romantic writers took the lead; the classic repertory began to dwindle—it was no longer Corneille and Racine, but Shakespeare and Schiller who shaped the norms of Russian taste.

In Polevoy's version, Hamlet was, in fact, a very apt creation, a typical Russian dandy of the 1830's, futile, world-weary, introspective, morbidly sensitive, and extremely articulate. It requires no special insight to recognize in him an early version of the "superfluous man" of Turgenev, who so assiduously haunted the Russian stage in the following generations, the man who is *de trop* everywhere, a nuisance to himself and to everyone around him. The influence of this melancholy figure on the Russian drama of the later nineteenth century is indeed impressive. Evidently, Hamlet realized for the Russian mind a psychic posture that was more familiar, and much more acceptable, than that of Lermontov's Arbenin or Byron's Manfred. All of Chekhov's plays in some way make use of Hamlet; but the character after whom Ivanov was modeled, and with whom even Lopakhin laughingly compares himself in *The Cherry Orchard*, was not the Hamlet of Shakespeare. It was the Hamlet of Polevoy, and this fact in itself involves some measure of irony.

The line of social comedy which leads from Griboyedov to Chekhov reached its zenith with Gogol.

Nikolai Vasilevich Gogol (1809-52) came to Petersburg at 19 and tried to become an actor, but failed his audition. He then entered the government service, and, after a brief experience as a clerk, began contributing stories and essays to the periodicals. By the time he was 25, he was famous as a short-story writer, and his professed interest in the Middle Ages won him an appointment to the chair of History at the University of Petersburg, a post for which he was hardly suited, and which he resigned without delay. His first attempt at the theatre was *The Vladimir, Third Class*, a satire of bureaucratic life, which he never finished. A comedy called *The Marriage*, a realistic account of middle-class family customs, fared little better; and when, after nine years of effort, he finally saw it performed at the Alexandrinsky (1842), it was hissed off the stage. It was *The Revizor* that made his fortune as a dramatist.

The plot of *The Revizor*—in English usually called *The Inspector General*—closely resembles that of a comedy by G. F. Kvita-Osnovyanenko, written in 1827 under the title of *The Newcomer from the Capital* and published in 1840. It is usually said, however, that Gogol took his subject from a personal anecdote related to him by Pushkin in response to his plea for a "genuinely Russian theme." In any case, *The Revizor* represents a considerable literary investment. Gogol wrote the play in 1835 and produced it the following year; but he continued working on it until 1842, and it is obvious that his novel, *Dead Souls*, begun immediately after *The Revizor*, is closely related to it—they are, in a sense, counterparts. His plan for *The Revizor* was ambitious. He wrote Zhukovsky in 1847: "I resolved to put together everything bad that I knew, and in one breath to laugh at it." In fact, the theme of the play is not broad. Gogol pokes fun principally at the administration of a provincial town; but the implications have a certain universality. Conceived in the classic tradition, though in a freer form, *The Revizor* has no sympathetic characters. The plot belongs to the order of Latin comedy that involves the efforts of a young gentleman and his clever slave to hoodwink a group of credulous people. It tells the perennial story of the country yokels and the city slicker, but the development is extremely original, and the caricature is unsurpassed by anything the Western stage has produced in the line of ironical portraiture.

The type of comedy from which *The Revizor* was derived principally develops the intrigue, and it is the *ingenio* of the scoundrel who turns the necessary tricks that is usually exhibited for the admiration of the audience. In Roman comedy the *personae* are often interesting; but the degree to which character is subordinated to plot need hardly be pointed out —these plays can be acted by puppets. *The Revizor* is of a different stripe. Gogol's characters are evidently drawn from life; they are typical, but marvellously individualized. On the other hand, the action is not especially ingenious. The young gentleman from the capital, with his few miserable tags of French, is a most unlikely hero, and it is in the highest degree absurd that he should be mistaken for the Inspector General. Unlike Scapin, or the intriguers in *The Beaux's Strategem* or *The Relapse*, he does not devise the intrigue; he is devised by it. Khlestakov is not a wit, like Aimwell. He is a fool; and his servant Osip is more dull-witted than he. Left to themselves, this wretched pair would be no more than a mouthful for the provincial wolves among whom they have fallen. But the provincial gentry outwit themselves. Blinded by their fears, trembling with guilt, they insist on localizing their terror in the first likely object, and, in their eyes, the miserable little clerk from the capital is magnified into an angry god who must be placated at any cost.

The dramatic reflex is equally interesting. As the local officials magnify the little *chinovnik* in their minds, he inflates obligingly in accordance with their expectations. His dream of grandeur thus parallels their sense of awe in a mad progression, until at last he can bear no more, and he makes off in sudden panic. But the moment this image collapses, another takes form. At the acme of their disenchantment—as the town officials are gloating over each other's discomfiture, and bitterly savoring their own—the gendarme suddenly announces the arrival of the real *revizor*. The implication is, accordingly, that all the time these scoundrels were going through their paces, the true inspector was inspecting them; the hidden eye—as in *Tartuffe*—was upon them from the start. But even this outcome leaves a lingering doubt. There is no guarantee that the new inspector will prove any more authentic than the first.

Thus, these shrewd, strong men — and, in particular, the *gorodnichy* of the town, a ruthless, sceptical, and vastly experienced rogue–are completely outwitted by the most ineffectual person imaginable, a very young, very thin, most unpracticed imposter who can hardly keep his mind on his business. The result is a play of considerable depth. On the surface it appears to be a humorous sketch, at the most, a satire of minor corruption in provincial circles. In reality, it affords a penetrating glimpse into the nature of authority.

The suggestion that authority is an illusion maintained by those who are subject to it was hardly calculated to find favor among those whose every official act was intended to enhance the patriarchal image of the autocrat. It was only after the most stubborn opposition that the play was finally performed, on April 19, 1863, at the Alexandrinsky Theatre. Nicholas I graced the performance with his presence; and since the Tsar was seen to laugh heartily, the puzzled audience concluded that the play was a farce, and that it was proper to enjoy it. But its dangerous facets were soon recognized, and it aroused a spirited controversy in both capitals. It was attacked very generally in the press on the ground that it was a scurrilous libel upon Russian life and Russian character. Gogol took these attacks to heart, and left in a huff for Italy, declaring that his play now disgusted him. But Belinsky praised both *The Revizor* and *Dead Souls* extravagantly; his lead was soon followed by others, and by the time the critical storm had subsided, both *The Revizor* and *The Marriage* had become landmarks in the Russian theatre, *Dead Souls* had won an important place among Russian novels, and the unhappy Gogol was firmly installed as the father of Russian realism.

No more than fifty years separate Gogol from Chekhov. This period was distinguished by three important dramatists

—Ostrovsky, Turgenev, and Tolstoy. In Russia, as elsewhere in Europe, it was a time of great social ferment, and of very rapid artistic development. The disasters of the Crimean War made the ineptitude of Nicholas's government painfully manifest. After the fall of Sevastopol it was impossible to control the spread of liberal ideas. Alexander II inaugurated the "age of great reforms," but the emancipation of the serfs in 1861—the focus of the hopes and efforts of the best minds in Russia—brought about a period of disillusion reminiscent of the despair that attended the failure of the Great Revolution of 1789 in France. The obscure and exorbitant provisions of the Emancipation Law, the *Polozhnye*, the harsh and hasty reorganization of the judiciary, the over-zealous imposition of forms of local self-government without regard for existing conditions and the obvious unreadiness of the country to govern itself at this time, resulted in the most widespread dissatisfaction. The predictable consequence of the wave of social protest that followed Alexander's reforms was a progressive renewal of the despotic policies of his predecessor.

In the meantime a partial relaxation of the censorship furnished a unique opportunity for public discussion. Liberals, led by the exile Alexander Herzen in London, Slavophiles like Ivan Aksakov, and radicals of the type of Chernyshevsky were for the first time given a public hearing. The press and the drawing rooms resounded with expressions of opinion, and the nation became increasingly aware not only of its problems, but of the presence of a large group of classless intellectuals—the *intelligentsia*—which was destined to play a certain role in defining the national future. The frontiers which divided the old from the new Russia were already taking shape; traces were visible in a long line of literary works from Griboyedov to Turgenev. Turgenev's young nihilist Bazarov, for whom everything was rubbish that the older generation held sacred, formulated, and in some degree caricatured, the radical youth of the 1860's. To many, the type was shocking.

The attempt on the emperor's life in 1866 initiated the official reaction. The result was an oppressive policy which brought about a more defiant organization of the radical movement. Young intellectuals in various states of moral exaltation began in the early 1870's to "infiltrate among the people," sharing the life of peasants, and laboring first to educate them, and then, under the influence of Bakunin and others, to activate their discontent along revolutionary lines. The police countered by arresting large numbers of these enthusiasts and exiling them to Siberia and elsewhere. A series of planned reprisals followed. There were waves of terrorist activity, which culminated in the assassination of the Tsar in 1881. The following two decades, the period of Chekhov's principal works, were a time of severe repression. The consequence, in the year after Chekhov's death, was the revolution of 1905.

In 1884, under Alexander III, an imperial edict destroyed the autonomy of the universities; at the same time a number of famous professors were dismissed because of their liberal leanings. The higher education of women was discontinued. The censorship was tightened. The reign of Nicholas II was equally disagreeable. Until after 1905 there was no slackening of the reign of terror.

Important changes, however, were taking place which made the governmental policy lamentably inappropriate. The Russia of the early 1800's had been, in theory, a completely integrated nation firmly centered on the capital at Petersburg. In reality it was a loose agglomeration of independent estates, isolated villages, and a few great towns, with very little industry, and surprisingly little intercommunication among the various districts and provinces. The Emancipation of 1861 brought about a rapid disintegration of the landowning class from which the military and bureaucratic establishment was principally drawn, together with the displacement of the gentry by middle-class bankers and merchants. A new group of industrialists came to power. Under its influence the growing demand for factory workers brought about an influx of peasants to the cities. The consequent exploitation of labor, shameless and unregulated, resulted in the familiar phenomena of labor organization, with its usual concomitants. Under these conditions, traditional police methods, designed for the maintenance of a semi-feudal economy, proved to be completely unsuitable and, as always, the less effectual they proved, the more zealously they were intensified. In this situation the aristocratic regime strove desperately to perpetuate itself in a world to which it no longer had relevance. As the century ended, the end of the autocracy was forseeable. It was equally forseeable that the attendant ceremonies would be agonizing.

These turbulent years form the background of Chekhov's life and works. The world with which he was concerned as an artist was a world of changing values and of great spiritual and social stress. He faced this world with a mind avid for impressions. It was his pleasure to fix the passing moment. He was entirely aware of its ephemeral nature, and this predisposed him to be accurate; but his landscapes and his portraits were manifestly provisional. He did not presume to speak for the ages, but for his time. He portrayed this time with greater accuracy, perhaps, than anyone else then living, but there is no reason to believe that the world he left us is of such nature as to form the basis for a historical survey.[11] Chekhov reflected and represented many of the aspects and attitudes of his day; he was extremely informative; but he portrayed life as an artist, not as a historian. Works of art may be expected to superpose a certain unity and consistency of form upon the amorphous stuff of experience. Chekhov set his stamp upon the changing times through which he lived, defining and formulating his world according to his personal lights and his temper. This world now exists only because he, and a few others, gave it form and substance. But there is evidently no point in pretending that Chekhov's world represents anything more than an artistic reality. The writer's world is ultimately his own creation. It is a fantasy guided and corrected by observation; nevertheless, it is a fantasy. Chekhov's world is the world of Chekhov.

If it is worthwhile repeating these truisms, it is because one needs occasionally to remind oneself that the languid figures who people Chekhov's Russia must have borne a very similar relation to the outward reality as the swan-necked figures of Modigliani's Paris, or the strange people who animate Utrillo's street. If, from the manner in which he depicts its inhabitants, we try to deduce the "reality" of Chekhov's world, we are certain to be confused. His world, for all its seeming transparence, remains as enigmatic as the man.

Chekhov's biography is richly detailed and amazingly well-documented. With curiously business-like efficiency, he filed in chronological order all the letters he received. The letters he sent were, on the whole, carefully preserved by his correspondents. We know all about him, his comings, his goings, his plans, his moods, the condition of his bowels and the state of his finances from day to day. His philanderings have been studied, weighed, and published in minute detail—nothing is hidden from us, nothing, that is, except what we need most of all to know. The more we learn about Chekhov, the more we see that the heart of this jolly, generous, and companionable man was completely sealed off from his companions, even the most intimate. Nobody really knew him in his lifetime. Nobody knows him now. His smile is charming and entirely inscrutable. What lies behind it can only be deduced from his work, and here it is entirely a matter of conjecture as to what is represented and what is not.

The dramatic tradition which Chekhov inherited was deeply influenced by the work of Ostrovsky and Turgenev, and to a certain extent by Tolstoy. Ostrovsky was 58 at the time

Chekhov offered his first play to Yermolova. He was firmly established at the Maly. It was in a sense his theatre, and fully reflected his viewpoint and his style.

Ostrovsky was the first Russian dramatist to devote himself exclusively to the theatre. By 1881, in spite of the most resolute bureaucratic opposition, he was generally recognized as the dean of the Russian playwrights, and it was he who initiated the theatrical reforms in the period immediately preceding that of Chekhov's ascendancy.

Ostrovsky was very much the realist; indeed, he is often called the father of Russian realistic comedy, a genre of exceptionally widespread paternity. Ostrovsky did not, however, follow in the footsteps of Gogol. The Gogolian tradition was developed chiefly by Alexander Sukhovo-Kobylin, a writer of astonishing gifts whose talents have received only the tardiest recognition. Sukhovo-Kobylin's comedy *Krechinsky's Wedding* (1854), and its sequels *The Lawsuit* and *Tarelkin's Death*, form a grim trilogy in which Russian upper-class life is very thoroughly examined from a standpoint which makes it progressively more grotesque until it reaches the verge of madness.

Ostrovsky was a more impressive figure than Sukhovo-Kobylin, and his influence was vast, but it is difficult to evaluate his importance outside the literary context in which he worked. Aside from *The Storm*, his work is barely known outside of Russia, and even this masterpiece has rarely been accorded the admiration it deserves. The reason is, perhaps, that Ostrovsky's plots are neither ingenious nor striking, his situations are firmly rooted in the local soil, and his dialogue, pungent and flavorful in the original, does not survive the ordeal of translation.

Griboyedov's phrase, "portraits and only portraits," serves to characterize a good part of Russian drama. Ostrovsky, like Gogol, specialized in portraiture. His range was wide, but his gaze was fixed primarily on the middle and lower classes, and he was the first to examine with an appreciative and critical eye the ways of the Moscow merchants, in whose curious customs and rich folklore he found a wealth of subject matter for the stage. Ostrovsky's literary career was based on the assumption, widely shared by contemporary French and German dramatists, that the everyday life of the middle class was the proper field for the drama of the time, and that the ordinary incidents of middle-class life would be found quite as absorbing in the theatre as the spectacular events with which tragedy and melodrama were more often concerned. This was a point that Diderot had made more than a century before, and it had already borne fruit in France and, after Lessing, in Germany. But Diderot was nothing if not sentimental; his portraits might have been painted by Greuze, who was, indeed, his favorite painter, and his followers shared his tastes. In the early years of the nineteenth century, the bourgeois *drame* dripped with sentimentality.

Toward the middle of the century, François Ponsard, whose tragedy *Lucrèce* (1843) had been found sufficiently dull and sufficiently correct to stem the flood of romanticism of the 1830's, won great honor with a series of *drames* in verse in which he extolled the heroic virtues of businessmen and stockbrokers: *L'Honneur et l'argent*, acted in 1853, put him among the Immortals of the Academy. The youthful Augier cannily followed his example with *Gabrielle* (1849), and then far surpassed it with his prose comedy *Le Gendre de Monsieur Poirier* (1854), which is generally accounted the chief ornament of this genre. Ostrovsky, however, had no idea of catering to the vanity of the Russian middle class. On the contrary, his comedies to some extent anticipated the vogue of the French social drama of the 1860's and 1870's, which took up critically the more sordid aspects of the bourgeois character. In France, indeed, the reaction had been swift. In such plays as *Le Gendre de Monsieur Poirier*, the worthy bourgeoisie had been found more noble than the nobility. Under more sober scrutiny, however, it appeared somewhat less than beautiful, and its little customs and habits were exposed with ruthless candor in such plays as Augier's *Les Effrontés* (1861) and *Le Fils de Giboyer* (1862). In the following wave of naturalism, the followers of Zola, particularly Becque and Brieux, handled it very roughly indeed.

Ostrovsky's merchant plays were, in fact, excellently timed. They reflected, on the one hand, that interest in common people which is an important aspect of European romanticism; more particularly, they accorded with the special interests of the literary circle of the *Moskvityanin*, a periodical deeply concerned with native poetry and folklore. It was under such auspices that Ostrovsky published his first plays. From the beginning to the end of his career his interest in the middle- and lower-class life of Moscow never wavered, and he was fortunate in being able to count on the support of an increasingly influential group. The Theatre Administration, however, had no interest in developing this aspect of Russian drama. It put every possible obstacle in Ostrovsky's way, so that in time he felt he must turn his talents in other directions in order to survive. In consequence, in his later years he tried his hand at plays treating of the Russian nobility; comedies dealing with the acting profession; and historical drama, a field in which he was not singularly gifted. Nevertheless, two of his historical plays, *The False Dmitry* and *Vassily Shuisky*, won a secure place among the masterpieces of the nineteenth century, and his fairy-play, *The Snow Maiden* (1873)—the only example of his departure from realism—inspired excellent music.

Ostrovsky was by no means a subtle writer. His plays have a strong melodramatic tone, the result of his habit of juxtaposing extreme types in situations designed to demonstrate the triumph of virtue and the inconvenience of vice. The Russian stage in the 1860's was not yet ready for subtlety. It dealt in extremes, and the acting styles of the period were all in some degree based upon strong contrasts and a bold separation of tonal qualities. In developing the drama of everyday life, Ostrovsky may be said, with some justice, to have furthered considerably the ascendency of soap-opera in the modern Russian theatre. But his eye was accurate and keen. He was the most percipient dramatist of his age, and he unfolded a panorama of Russian life that nobody before him had thought to exhibit. In this manner he collaborated mightily in the process of self-examination which marks the Russian awakening in these years, and through him the nation saw itself for the first time "as it was." This was Ostrovsky's primary contribution to the Russian drama. Chekhov levied magisterially on Ibsen, whom he accused repeatedly of not being a dramatist, and he greatly admired Hauptmann, whom he did not copy at all—but it was Ostrovsky who showed him the way to the drama of "life as it is," and the relatively plotless fable.

Ostrovsky's first play, *The Bankrupt*, was published in 1850. It was a comedy depicting the fleecing of a wealthy merchant of exceptional stupidity by a pack of scoundrels of quite ordinary attainments. The theme had been a favorite in Western drama from the time of Ben Jonson. In Russia, however, this theme was found objectionable. Ostrovsky's play centered on the smugness and self-importance of the rich man who is, so to speak, flattered to death by his parasites. The censor saw in this a veiled attack on the Tsar and his courtiers. As a result, Ostrovsky lost his position as clerk in the office of the Court of Conscience, and his name was placed on the police roster of subversive subjects. The play was, of course, forbidden. Three years later, his comedy *Don't Seat Yourself in Another's Sleigh*—that is, "Don't go where you don't belong"—had great success in Moscow, and the year after, he had another success with *Poverty Is No Disgrace* (*Byednost nye porok*). It was then thought wise, in view of his growing popularity, to license *The Bankrupt* for production, though under another title—*Between Relatives No Accounts Are Needed* (*Svoyi lyudi sochtyomsya*).

Poverty Is No Disgrace deals with the same subject as Gogol's *The Marriage*. It involves a case of parental tyranny in which a despotic father tries to force his daughter into an unwelcome marriage purely to satisfy his own sense of power. The girl loves a poor but handsome apprentice, and is saved through the mediation of her worthless uncle who unmasks his brother's egotistical motives in forcing the match. *The Storm* (*Groza*) was produced six years later, in 1860, and is usually accounted Ostrovsky's masterpiece. It deals with another and more tragic aspect of parental tyranny. In *The Storm* an extremely suggestible young woman, completely dominated by the matriarch to whose pallid son she is married, sins briefly, in her husband's absence, with a handsome lad of the neighborhood. Her sense of guilt is extreme; it is whipped up into a hysterical frenzy by a thunderstorm in which she feels the wrath she has aroused, so she thinks, in the heavenly father. Her terror is such that she confesses her guilt. There are immediate reprisals. The poor girl forestalls further punishment by seeking in the river a refuge from the hostile and incomprehensible world into which she was born.

Ostrovsky did not preach. His plays usually involve a moral lesson; but he did not insist. With respect to the social and religious implications of *The Storm*, for example, or *Poverty Is No Disgrace*, his raisonneurs are singularly tactful—the plays speak for themselves. Though it was impossible to dwell consistently and often on the subject of domestic economy without implying some criticism of the domestic economy of the state, the analogy between the brutality of the domestic despot and that of the imperial autocrat is not in the least explicit in any of Ostrovsky's plays. There is not even a veiled reference to the terrorism of heaven in *The Storm*. The censor, like the public, was expert at ferreting out analogies: Ostrovsky won the favor of Nicholas's successor Alexander, but he was never free of police suspicion. In *The Storm*, God appears to be quite as unreasonable as everyone else, equally mysterious, and much more terrible, and the wretched child who suffers his anger seems entirely justified in preferring death to a life made unbearable by the real and imaginary bugaboos which infest it. The gloomy spectacle of life in such circumstances is so poignant that one can only applaud the censor's broadmindedness in licensing the play.

In addition to the ideological objections of the Theatre Administration, Ostrovsky had to overcome the traditional snobbishness of the imperial theatres which for years found his plays too crude and too vulgar for presentation. The actors, however, were exceptionally sensitive to applause. Ostrovsky's plays were enormously successful whenever they were shown, and at last both the Maly in Moscow and the Alexandrinsky in Petersburg were forced to capitulate. The Maly became the "House of Ostrovsky," and for more than a generation he supplied it with plays. In the course of his tenure he had more than eighty productions, and he explored every branch of the drama.

It was inevitable that so productive a writer should borrow extensively. As he said, dramatists do not invent plots: "All our themes are borrowed. They are supplied by life, by history, by a friend's story, or at times by a newspaper article. I, at any rate, have borrowed all my plots. The thing that happens cannot be invented by the playwright. It is his business only to describe how it happened or could have happened, and that is all he has to do." [12]

The type of dramatic portraiture in which Ostrovsky specialized necessitated the collaboration of highly skilled character-actors. Russian actors trained in the 1840's were extremely proficient in character portrayal; but they knew nothing of the sort of people that Ostrovsky desired them to portray. At the Maly, the great Shchepkin, trained in the tradition of Molière, did not feel that his style was at all suited to the roles offered by Ostrovsky's plays. He had, however, imported from the provincial theatre Prov Sadovsky, who lent himself splendidly to the interpretation of Ostrovsky's characters.

The Maly had so far prided itself on its ensemble. Ostrovsky was an individualist. In his view it was the actor, and not the regisseur, who must be considered the essential element of the theatre. When he saw the Meininger perform *Julius Caesar* in 1885, he was impressed by the mob scenes. For the rest, the famous company seemed to him to make the effect of soldiers on parade. It was, he said: "an excellently disciplined company of mediocre actors and wailing actresses. Everywhere one sees the stage-director. The leading actor acts by command and according to plan."

In line with his notion of the importance of the individual, Ostrovsky did much to raise the social prestige of a profession which had never been highly regarded in Russia. He organized an actor's guild, and enhanced the status of the dramatists. In his famous memorandum of 1881 he pointed out to the Theatre Administration that the scale of remuneration of Russian authors had not changed in fifty years. In France, he wrote, authors' royalties ranged from ten to twelve per cent of the gross receipts for comedies in prose. Italian authors received at least ten, and as much as fifteen per cent of the gross. In Russia the playwright's royalty was no more than four and a half per cent. If there was to be a Russian theatre, he added, Russian dramatists must be encouraged financially to devote themselves to it. His efforts bore fruit. The result of his memorandum was the publication in 1882 of the "New Regulations for the Internal Administration of the Imperial Theatres," which, among other reforms, ended the government monopoly, and countenanced the organization of a Society of Authors and Composers patterned upon the *Société des auteurs* which Scribe had organized a half-century before in France. Thus, by the time of Chekhov, the theatre in Russia offered a very promising livelihood to a man of talent, provided he could get his plays produced, and provided the censor approved them.

By the time Ostrovsky died, in 1886, the Russian theatre had already enjoyed—at least in theory—a comfortable renovation. In fact, save for the broadening of the repertory and the amelioration of professional conditions, not too much had been accomplished. The significant fact was that an effort had been made to bring the Russian theatre abreast of the times. The current was running now in the direction of greater and greater realism. In France, the development of realism in the theatre had been a very gradual process. Efforts in that direction had started in the time of Balzac. By 1875 Zola had given the movement definition and a theoretical basis, as well as a certain practical course to follow. In this form, the new realism was dubbed naturalism, and had no immediate success; but by the time of the Russian theatre reforms of 1882, the *Théâtre-Français* was at last persuaded to perform Becque's *Les Corbeaux*, the first masterpiece in the naturalistic manner. The play failed, precisely as had been predicted, but the need for a new type of play and a new style of acting was beginning to manifest itself unequivocally in dramatic circles. In France this impulse resulted in the foundation of Antoine's *Théâtre Libre*, in 1887, the year after Ostrovsky's death.

Antoine formulated his theatre as a departure from the artificiality of the well-made play. In Russia, plays were rarely well-made, even when they were directly imitated from the French. The new movement proceeded nevertheless along much the same lines as in France. The question of truth and realism was at that time very much in the air in Russia. Dostoevsky and Tolstoy had amply demonstrated to what heights Russian genius could rise in the psychological novel; and it was evident to many that the time had come for something new in the drama. There was no lack of talented playwrights. Satiric comedy was developed further along Gogolian lines by Saltykov-Shchedrin; Pisemsky wrote a fine peasant tragedy. But neither was able to propagate a new wave; nor for that matter did Turgenev. There was plenty of discussion, but nothing happened of sufficient importance to induce the administration of the Maly Theatre to take cognizance of the new artistic tendencies of the time. Thus when Chekhov offered *The Sea Gull* in 1895, there was no theatre in Russia capable of producing it, and no audience ready to appreciate it. Yet, once the play was performed, and failed, almost at once a theatre was devised and an audience formed to receive it. It was as if nothing more were needed to crystallize the elements which had been so long inert, and the astonishing rapidity with which the Russian theatre accommodated itself to the new situation is one of the truly dramatic events of a period which is by no means lacking in drama.

Turgenev's career in the theatre was relatively short. In 1840, when he was 22, he completed his first serious play, *The Bachelor*. Ten years later, in 1850, he wrote *A Month in the Country*. Both plays were works of genius—the theatre-pieces he wrote in the interval seem trivial in comparison. Shchedrin produced *The Bachelor* in 1849. Turgenev followed it up at once with *A Month in the Country*. But the censor handled this play so roughly that a complete text could not be published until 1869, and there was no performance until 1872, ten years after the publication of *Fathers and Sons*. By that time Turgenev had decided he had no talent for the stage, and wrote nothing more for it.

The Bachelor is a comedy. It has to do with the problems of a middle-aged jurist who is charged with the duty of marrying off his young ward, a charming girl. He ends by marrying her himself. The play is said to show the influence of Gogol. The relation seems clearer to Dostoevsky's early novel *Poor Folk* (1845). Gogol's *The Marriage* is a bitter farce; but plays like *The Bachelor* have few sharp edges. They are kindly works which take a relaxed and humane view of human nature; their humor differs widely from the acerbity of the type of social comedy in which the world is seen as a wilderness inhabited by jackals and kites. In Chekhov it is easier to see Turgenev than Gogol.

A consequence of the idea that realism and idealism are contrary attitudes is the expectation that the first will invariably disparage humanity, and the second will flatter it. But there certainly exists a considerable body of idealistic literature which takes society to task, more or less fiercely, for its shortcomings; and many examples come to mind of a type of realism which finds in the limitations of humanity a source of understanding, compassion, and hope. It is to this category that the work of both Turgenev and Chekhov belong. This is obviously a very different realism from the noncommittal, "scientific" sort, in which the author pointedly refrains from making judgments and taking sides. Turgenev took sides. He left no doubt as to where his sympathies lay; but he did not quarrel; he forebore to argue; and this aristocratic posture Chekhov also found congenial to his temper.

In *The Bachelor*, the young clerk Vilitsky, Masha's suitor, is not especially sympathetic. He is evidently a snob, and not overly bright; but Turgenev does not despise him. He understands his psychic predicament, and he sees the comic side of his Hamlet-like state of indecision. The kindly lawyer Moskvin, also, lends himself easily to caricature. A man of fifty who courts a young girl is traditionally out of his depth, but Turgenev's treatment of his middle-aged lover is a miracle of tact and sympathy. Similarly, in *A Month in the Country*, Turgenev tells the truth regarding his characters. None of them is especially admirable. But the author is courteous; there are neither heroes nor villains in his play, only men and women, subject to the impulses of nature, like all living things.

In *A Month in the Country* the portraiture could hardly be more realistic. Islayev is a good-natured man, simple, but no fool. He has long been cuckolded by his best friend; this is, after all, not an unusual state of affairs and, since the matter is never brought to his attention, it does not harm him in the least. Natalya is not only unfaithful to her husband, but also to her lover; when she realizes her passion for the young tutor, Belyayev, she becomes cruelly jealous of her ward, who also loves him, and in general she behaves abominably with respect to everyone. Yet she does not forfeit our sympathy; on the contrary, she arouses compassion. From a moral viewpoint, Rakitin, her lover, is doubtless much to blame, but he preserves his nobility. Even the scoundrelly old doctor Shpigelsky is drawn with understanding. What gives charm and depth to what might be considered a sordid situation is, evidently, the warm and delicate characterization, but there is more than this—it is, above all, a question of tone. The story is told from the viewpoint of one who has no idea of being censorious, but who desires chiefly to demonstrate the intricacy of human character. Unlike Stendhal, whose bitterly indignant novel *Le Rouge et le noir* perhaps suggested the situation in *A Month in the Country*, Turgenev seems to be at peace with the world he created.[13] It makes a difference. The play is warm and wise. It is a comedy which leaves one with a feeling of sadness, but also with a feeling of strength. This was precisely the effect at which Chekhov aimed. Before he achieved it, however, he had to study Turgenev.[14]

Turgenev's plays made use of a mode of characterization which as yet had no great currency in the theatre, and which was not clearly defined until Strindberg gave it memorable formulation in the Author's Foreword to *Miss Julie*. Characterization in the French drama of the period was generally based on a static concept of personality, vaguely related to the theory of humors and similar physiological notions derived from the ancients. According to these ideas, character was predicated on the *faculté maîtresse*, the dominant trait which shaped the man. All that was necessary to fix a character for stage purposes was to identify this trait; an individual's behavior could then be motivated and justified in whatever circumstances the plot required. This system, which could be referred to such weighty authorities as Aristotle and Theophrastus, had the additional merit of convenience. It vastly simplified the definition of character, and made it possible to differentiate human types quite easily by means of identifying symbols which served the same purpose as the masks of the ancient stage or the *commedia dell'arte*. Moreover, the wealth of information handed down through the centuries with regard to human types distinguished in this manner was always readily available for the guidance of the actor, and, once he was given a clue with regard to the character—often the name was enough—he could invest himself with the role as if it were a costume.

This system, delightfully simple at bottom, was capable of considerable elaboration. It was conceivable that a dominant trait, no matter how masterful, could be nullified or transformed through a sufficiently powerful experience. Characters could thus be "developed" by means of plot, and a play could become an auto-educational experience, an exercise in self-revelation. Thus a coward, under stress, might discover that he was in fact brave, a generous man could be made to see his own stinginess, an ascetic might learn that he was at heart a lecher, or a pirate that he was in reality a sentimentalist. Unmaskings of this sort were, of course, by no means foreign to the classic concept of character. What was involved was a special sort of agnition, the sudden discovery, not of a physical but of a spiritual identity, accompanied by a psychic peripety. This could take place in an instant. It was therefore a very convenient device for the stage, and was in fact a favorite with authors from Farquhar to Shaw.

Turgenev's characterizations are not of this sort. For his

people, life is a process of self-realization. They neither know themselves from the start, nor do they stumble upon themselves suddenly in the end. They discover themselves little by little, and are constantly surprised at the things they feel and do. The result is that we gain insight into their natures step by step as they do themselves, and are quite unprepared for the turns and contradictions in their behavior. The effect of this kind of development is extraordinarily lifelike.

Turgenev forebore to analyze. He did no more than to suggest, and since it is not always quite certain what it is that he suggests, the spectator's mind is not trapped in the author's labyrinth, but quite free to consider and to reflect. This technique is one of exploration and not of definition. Each suggestion is offered as temporary and provisional. In the end, the characters retain the enigmatic quality of people. The author makes no attempt to explain them beyond the point where they have explained themselves. This is the technique of impressionism.

In *A Month in the Country*, at the inception of her scene with Vera in act three, Natalya Islayeva has no certainty as to her feelings for the handsome young tutor. At the most she has a vague premonition, and she has no idea of what she is going to do, if anything. It is her behavior that defines her passion in her mind. When she realizes her motives, she is shocked, and still more when she sees how badly she is behaving. But she cannot help herself; it is as if she were possessed, and no one is more astonished than she when she recognizes this trace of evil in a nature that has so far revealed nothing but its kindliness.

In comparison with this sort of characterization, the classic methods are likely to seem summary and unvital. The idea that we do not know ourselves until our behavior forces us to a recognition is by now in the nature of a truism, but no dramatist before Turgenev—save perhaps Shakespeare in *Measure for Measure*—had thought to formulate a character in such terms. This technique, in fact, does not belong to the stage. The characters of drama are traditionally simple and whole, and completely submissive to the exigencies of the plot. Turgenev's methods belong to the novel. It was by way of Pushkin, Stendhal, and Balzac that Turgenev learned how to emancipate his characters from their story. Russian actors, whose ideas of characterization were formed mainly along classical lines, could not be expected to play these "over-delicate" pieces in which characters had no certain outline and quite defied definition; and Turgenev's awareness of the inappropriateness of his method very likely motivated his acceptance of the suggestion that his plays were not suited to the stage but might be read profitably as novels. At any rate, he acquiesced in this view and, after 1850, forebore to trouble the players with his subtleties.

Upon the faults of Turgenev, Chekhov founded his church. What was revolutionary in *The Sea Gull* was the irrationality of the characters and the inconsequentiality of their behavior; what was new in *The Three Sisters* was the development of a novel on the stage. One has only to compare Turgenev's plays with Chekhov's to see that the very things which caused Turgenev to fail brought about the overwhelming success of Chekhov.[15]

The critical reception of Dostoevsky's first novels demonstrated, however, that even among novelists these psychological innovations were disconcertingly advanced for the time. The idea of personality as process was not consistent with the Renaissance world-view. Traditionally, the soul was an entity which might move toward or away from its creator in accordance with its moral condition. Its moral worth varied, but the soul was essentially an identity, the ultimate being of which did not change, and it was therefore capable of responsibility. It was only when the age-old system of archetypes disintegrated that the romantic idea of human character took form, and the impressionistic view of life which this idea implied.

When Turgenev, as a young man, hit upon his extraordinary dramatic technique, it was still too early for it to be useful in the theatre. He was merely thought to be inept. But the age was moving rapidly in the direction of impressionism in every branch of art, and even in science. By the time Chekhov was 40, it was possible to make an audience sense, at least in part, what was involved in a play like *The Three Sisters.* When Chekhov was making his first steps as a dramatist, the audience was not yet ready, and he himself had not yet progressed so far. Chekhov did not begin where Turgenev left off. It took him half his life to reach that point.

Platonov

THE manuscript which Chekhov took to Maria Yermolova no longer exists; but after his death, a manuscript was discovered which doubtless represents an earlier version of the play. It is a much corrected copy in four acts, about three times the length of *The Cherry Orchard*. Since this manuscript lacks a title page, it has been published under various titles, and in several versions, representing the efforts of editors to improve what evidently stands in some need of improvement. This is the play which generally passes under the name, *faute de mieux*, of *Platonov*.[1]

Platonov is a very poor play, but it repays study. It indicates, among other things, that at this stage of his career, at least, Chekhov had no idea of doing anything new. The theme he settled on was the most popular theme of the day. In developing it he followed assiduously the practice of successful playwrights. For a beginner, he was as sensible as could be. *Platonov* is entirely conventional. The Administration of the Maly Theatre had no reason for rejecting it other than its lack of merit.

What Chekhov had in mind was a depiction of the spiritual plight of the landowning class during the period of transition following the emancipation of the serfs. It is substantially the theme of *The Cherry Orchard*. Unlike *The Cherry Orchard*, of course, *Platonov* is full of plot and artifice. It is more than generous in theatrical effects, and is obviously journeyman's work. But the importance of the theme for Chekhov may be inferred from the persistence with which he returned to it throughout his dramatic career. For Chekhov, Platonov was a character of exceptional significance.

Platonov is a country schoolmaster, a witty man whom life has beggared. When he went to the university, he was a wealthy landowner. He made a failure of his university career. Subsequently he failed at everything else, until he was ruined. He has now degenerated into the local Don Juan. His wife Sasha is a devout and extremely innocent girl, the daughter of an army colonel, and the sister of the local doctor Triletsky. She has borne her worthless husband a son, to whom she is devoted. Such is the initial situation. The consequent action is very complicated. It concerns the final stages of the decline and fall of Platonov, a process which takes place with some celerity.

Five years before, while at the university, Platonov was in love with Sonia, a fellow student. She has since married Sergei Voynitsev, a wastrel who is being systematically fleeced by a pair of usurers. Anya, the widow of Sergei's father, is a lusty woman who, having depleted the sexual resources of the local gangster Osip, is now casting lascivious glances at the attractive schoolmaster. Anya has a Satanic tinge: "I am an immoral woman, Platonov," she tells him. "The reason I love you is, I suppose, that I am an immoral woman." In the face of such forthright avowals, Platonov puts up only the feeblest resistance—before long, he becomes Anya's bedfellow.

His former flame Sonia, however, is on the side of the angels, and her drunken husband disgusts her. In these circumstances she finds Platonov's renewed advances difficult to withstand, and the idea of beginning with him a new life of work and usefulness to society stirs her pulses. But once she too becomes his mistress, their relations begin to deteriorate.

Platonov has doubts as to his ability to make a fresh start. He has neither much desire to work nor any wish to be useful. Instead, he deliberately involves himself with yet another girl. This time it is the young science student Maria, a girl who is both susceptible and aggressive, so much so that when Platonov kisses her, somewhat brutally, she prefers charges against him and has him summoned to court. In the meantime, the thief Osip, at Anya's instigation, has informed Sasha that her husband is deceiving her with another, a piece of news which impels Sasha to throw herself under a train. But she does not die. Osip saves her, vowing to avenge her honor at the first opportunity.

In the third act, Platonov is packing his valise preparatory to eloping with Sonia, when Anya comes to cajole him into staying where he is. She is, indeed, so persuasive that Platonov is on the point of resuming his relations with her. At this moment, however, Osip rushes in to kill him. Sasha intervenes in the nick of time. Their child is ill. She asks her husband point-blank what he has been up to. He confesses his adultery with Sonia. Sasha is outraged, and she leaves him, as she says, forever.

The last act begins inauspiciously. Anya informs her stepson Sergei that, as a result of his bad management, their estate has been sold at auction. They are penniless. Meanwhile Osip has been exterminated by the peasants he has so long terrorized. His body is lying unburied by the well where he was killed. In the midst of these developments, Platonov appears, ill and in a bad mood. He insults first Anya, then Sonia. Dr. Triletsky interrupts this scene with news that Sasha has taken poison, and is on the point of death. But before Platonov can go to his dying wife, Sonia implores him once again, on her knees, to go away with her. He refuses. Then, left alone for a moment, he attempts to shoot himself. But his nerve fails him, and when Maria comes to tell him that she has withdrawn her complaint, he takes her viciously into his arms. She whispers that she loves him. And now he reveals his own Satanism: "They all love me!" he cries. "When I get well, I'll make a whore of you! Once I was kind, but now I'll make whores of you all!" But before he can further these ambitious plans, Sonia runs in with a pistol. She shoots once, misses, then shoots again and wounds him fatally. In his agony, Platonov exhibits great charm. He asks them to give the old bailiff who brought Maria's summons three rubles for his trouble. Then he dies.

Obviously this play, such as it is, has many romantic elements; indeed, it has as much in this line as a play could possibly have. There are two Satanic characters, one male, one female; there is the woman who is resolved to ruin her lover, and the one who is determined to save him at all costs; there is the innocent wife, and the no-nonsense type of girl who is really more vulnerable than the rest; finally, there is the irresolute, impulsive, and introspective hero, by turns brutal and masochistic, who attempts to sum up in himself the illness of the age. One might say that from the standpoint of characterization, Chekhov covered the ground.

Platonov is indeed a compendious character. He is a hero out of Lermontov's mold, beautiful and damned, unstable, moody; there is, in addition, something of Chatsky in him; finally, he shows the influence of Hamlet. The Hamlet in question is, of course, the Hamlet of Polevoy, an ineffective youth, with a sense of thwarted vocation, and inexplicable accesses of brutality. Platonov speaks darkly of his destiny. "Fate," he tells Sonia, "has played me a trick I could never have foreseen in the days when you saw in me a second Byron." Like Chatsky, he is infuriated by the swinishness of the world around him; but he knows he can do nothing about it. He can only express the despair of his generation: "Nothing will come of us, the luckless of the earth! We are lost! We are completely useless!" Glagolyev, the neighboring squire, sees in him the symbol of the fallen youth of the period: "He is an admirable example of the uncertainty of our time!"

Platonov thus has unexpected universality. He speaks not only for the lost generation of the 1880's, but for all those who periodically find it possible to rationalize their ineptitude in terms of a tragic sense of the world's absurdity. If he speaks badly, it is because Chekhov did not as yet know how to make him speak well; but it is not difficult to see in Platonov an early example of the angry young men of a later age.

If it is worthwhile dwelling at some length on this immature work, it is because *Platonov* so clearly represents the matrix from which so much of Chekhov's later drama was drawn. Its protagonist was, in fact, surprisingly well conceived. It is in the telling of the story that Chekhov demonstrated his lack of skill. Platonov compensates for his failure as a man by exerting his power over women. His Don Juanism is the sign of his weakness, and the principal symptom of his disease, and it is fitting that it should be the cause of his death. He is, to use the Freudian phrase, neither *arbeits-* nor *liebesfähig*, and he is socially dangerous. In the circumstances there is nothing much to be done about him but to have him shot.

Ivanov, in Chekhov's later play, is evidently much the same man. Though shorn of the excessive sexuality of his predecessor, he has the grace to shoot himself. Uncle Vanya is a much later development. In his first version, he too shoots himself. But in *The Cherry Orchard* it is quite unnecessary to shoot Gayev. He is ineffectual, but no longer dangerous. He has retired gracefully from the fray, and taken refuge in a dream. In the evolution of this character it is perhaps possible to gauge with some accuracy the development of Chekhov as a realist.

His lack of success with *Platonov* does not appear to have damped his spirits, but it was a long time before Chekhov had another try at the stage. During these early years he vastly increased his output of humorous anecdotes and articles. He was now contributing a regular column on the current scene in Moscow to the humorous weekly *Fragments*, which N. A. Leikin published in Petersburg. At the rate of a kopeck a word, hard as he worked, his earnings did not keep pace with his expenses. In August 1883, during his last year at the medical school, he wrote to Leikin apologizing for the paleness of the column he was sending him: "I write under the most wretched conditions... In a neighboring room a relative's child is howling... In another room Father is reading aloud to Mother... Someone has wound up the music box and is playing *La Belle Hélène*... My bed is occupied by a relative who is talking to me about medicine..." In December he wrote him again: "I am extremely weary, spiteful, and ill... The devil knows where I get the time to work—that is why I didn't send you a story for the last number... And in addition to the fatigue, hemorrhoids." [2]

In 1884, Chekhov passed his final examinations, and was admitted to practice. But he had no real taste for medicine and, in any case, it brought in little money. At the end of 1884 he suffered a sudden hemorrhage from the throat. It was a disquieting symptom. He brushed it off with characteristic levity. "No doubt," he wrote Leikin, "the cause is some broken blood vessel." In the meantime he was writing at a furious pace. During the four years he spent at the university, he published some 300 short pieces in the magazines, most of them stories, and nearly all hack work. Leikin insisted that he make his pieces funny and keep them brief. For a time, whatever Chekhov wrote that exceeded a thousand words was rejected. He protested that there were sad and serious things to be written, and that it was inhuman to ask him to limit his pieces mechanically. But Leikin was obdurate. Willy-nilly, Chekhov learned the technique of concision.

It served him well. In a period when fine writing was diffuse and elegant in the manner of Turgenev, or involved and involuted in the manner of Dostoevsky, Chekhov was simple and brief. He became a master of the short story at its shortest.

Moreover, his apprenticeship to the comic weeklies liberated him in great measure from whatever tendency toward sentimentality he may have had at this time. He taught himself to look for what was humorous in the pathetic, for the grotesque in the tragic, for the wry comment with which one could redeem a lapse into sentiment. In this stern school, his tales acquired a characteristic outline, and for the rest of his life, brevity, humor, and self-restraint defined his style. In after years he was often surprised to find that what he thought was funny was considered by others to be tragic: this discrepancy in attitude was the source of infinite misunderstanding when he came to deal with such resolute intermediaries as Stanislavsky and Nemirovich-Danchenko. It was also perhaps partly a consequence of his intensive early training that even when he attempted, in his later life, to write at considerable length—as in *My Life*, *Three Years*, or *The Duel*—the effect was, in general, episodic. He was never quite equal to a long sustained effort. In his art, as in his life, he was by nature and habit a man of intense energy, and of short breath.

The turning point in Chekhov's life came toward the end of 1885 when, as the guest of his publisher, for the first time he visited Petersburg. Chekhov felt at home only in Moscow. He arrived in Petersburg under the impression that he knew nobody there, and was entirely unknown. To his immense surprise he found not only that he was widely read in the capital, but that his work was beginning to be discussed seriously in literary circles. It was in some ways a dispiriting thought. In January 1886, after his return to Moscow, he wrote Leikin's secretary, Bilibin: "Formerly, when I did not know they read my stories and passed judgment on them, I wrote serenely, the way I eat pancakes; now when I write, I'm frightened."

He was standing, as a matter of fact, on the very brink of fame. The novelist Grigorovich had been deeply impressed with Chekhov's short story *The Hunter*, recently published in the *Petersburg Gazette*, and had mentioned the story to Suvorin, the influential publisher of *New Times*, the most widely read newspaper in Russia. The two decided to discover Chekhov. Toward the beginning of January 1886, Chekhov received an invitation to contribute to *New Times*, and in February his story *The Requiem* appeared in Suvorin's paper. Suvorin paid him handsomely and set no limit to the length of his pieces. For the first time Chekhov saw some possibility of earning a living as a writer. So far he had consistently avoided using his true name for his stories. He was still writing under the name of Antosha Chekhonte. Suvorin persuaded him to sign his new pieces Anton Chekhov. He began to think of himself no longer as a part-time hack, but as a writer whose work might some day be accepted by one of the "thick" journals, the literary publications in which important works were published.[3]

A few months after his return from Petersburg, he received a letter which formally marked his elevation from the ranks. It was from Grigorovich. This was a man of real distinction, a celebrated author well past middle age, who was accorded the highest consideration in the cultural community. Grigorovich wrote at length in a tone of solemn exhortation. He assured Chekhov that he had talent, "a talent which places you in the front rank among the writers of the new generation," and he admonished him to write slowly and carefully, to avoid the pornographic nuances with which young writers strove to attract attention and, finally, to print under his own name the book of stories which he was then preparing for publication. For Chekhov it was as if the heavens had opened and God had spoken to him in person. He answered with becoming modesty. Nobody, he said, had so far taken his work seriously; he himself had not properly respected his gift. But now he felt the need to develop his talent: "All my hopes lie entirely in the future. I am only 26. Perhaps I shall manage to do something . . . "[4] And he asked Grigorovich for his photograph.

Chekhov's correspondence for the next few months amply reflects his excitement and his pride in this semi-official recognition of his abilities. But his jubilation was tempered by a sobering fact. It was fully two years since he had suffered his first throat hemorrhage. Now once again he was spitting blood. He was unwilling to consult a doctor; but he had a good idea of what it must be. Tuberculosis ran in his family on his mother's side. His talent and his illness had come to light simultaneously. One would say he was the victim of a practical joke. He was a genius and he was doomed. It was a romantic stereotype.

In the case of so vivid and so joyous a nature as Chekhov's it would be a mistake to assign to his illness a weightier role than is necessary in the development of his genius. Everything indicates his growing physical discomfort in these years, and his gnawing sense of the brevity of life. From the time he was 24 his life was punctuated by attacks of dysentery, hemorrhoids, and bronchitis. The taste of blood was often in his mouth, and after 1884 he suffered serious lung hemorrhages once or twice a year.[5] In such circumstances, a less cheerful nature might well have come to consider life a burden. But Chekhov's capacity for enjoyment was boundless. The world delighted him. He loved the city, was enchanted by the country. He took pleasure in people, boisterous talk, travel, good company, laughter, music, wine, pretty women. He was a passionate fisherman. In his youth, at least, he was rarely sorry for himself and seldom complained. He avoided doctors. He disliked discussing his health. No man was ever less subject to hypochondria. But after 1887, the sombre undercurrent of his thoughts became increasingly apparent. His expression showed no sudden change, his buoyancy was unfailing; but little by little his features composed themselves into that smile of amused resignation which henceforth represented him to the world. Behind that smile, obviously, there was something that did not smile.

With Chekhov the transition from youth to age was accomplished before he was 35. It is possible that he hardly noticed the change. As he grew older, he began to suffer from the pathological restlessness that characterized his later life, and made it difficult for him to endure any place or any company for very long. People were a necessity for him. He could not bear solitude. But these people, whose company he invited, crowded his life and prevented him from working. He complained incessantly of intrusion, yet obviously he welcomed it. He knew many women intimately, but felt comfortable only with his sister. He was generous to the point of extravagance with all who came to him for aid, but his help was abstract. It was obvious that, for all his friendliness, he had no real warmth for anyone. The consequence was that he remained reserved and solitary all his days, a desperately lonely man surrounded by a throng of friends.

The growing recognition of his talent, though flattering, was, as he had already intimated to Bibilin, in some sense disturbing. He was being asked to grow up. He hastened to comply. But this compliance meant an end to the carefree days when all he had to worry about was money. Now great things were expected of him. He had somehow incurred an obligation not only to his family but, so it seemed, to all Russia, to all the world. Now that he was said to have genius, it was necessary for him to demonstrate it. If he was, as they said, greater than Korolenko, he must prove himself greater than Korolenko. It came to him, quite suddenly, that genius is a burden.

The second half of 1886 found him in a mood of despondency, the extent of which he very likely exaggerated. He wrote to Maria Kiseleva, his favorite correspondent during this period, in pompous phrases which recall the epistolary style of Petrarch: "Life is a nasty business for everyone. When I am serious it seems to me that people who nourish an aversion to death are illogical. So far as I can understand the order of things, life consists exclusively of horrors, cares, and banalities that succeed and pile up one on the other." [6]

Now that he was taking himself seriously as an artist, he was faced with problems. There was, first of all, the question of style. So far he had written, easily and thoughtlessly, whatever came into his head. Now he began to formulate theories; and also to counsel others, beginning with his brother Alexander, regarding the mysteries of the craft.

In the 1880's the standards of prose style in Russia were mainly set by Turgenev. Turgenev was a master of description, detailed and elegant. He was not personally popular in Russia, but his reputation in the West was very great. He held an enviable place in Russian letters. This was the master whom Chekhov chose to rival.

It is unlikely that Chekhov undertook this competition with any seriousness in the beginning. In the eyes of the lowly medical student, the great Turgenev, noble, rich, and famous, must have seemed infinitely remote. But young Antosha Chekhonte was not above impudence. His story *The Hunter*, which first attracted the attention of Suvorin, was a five-page sketch intended as a parody of Turgenev's famous story *The Rendezvous*. In itself, of course, this meant nothing. Chekhov's early work was full of parodies and imitations. But *The Sea Gull* leaves us no doubt that Chekhov had Turgenev very much in his mind in the middle years of his life; and in his correspondence there are occasional disparagements of Turgenev that indicate his admiration more clearly than praise.[7]

Turgenev's stories are works of high finish, with long ceremonial introductions and meticulously detailed backgrounds. Chekhov, on the contrary, cultivated an abrupt and incisive attack. He took leave of the reader with equal abruptness.

The Rendezvous begins with a long legato passage. In *The Hunter* Chekhov composed his scene in sharp strokes, dry and terse: "A hot and stuffy afternoon. Not a cloud in the sky. The sun-scorched grass has a sad and desperate air. Even if the rain comes it cannot be green again . . ." Turgenev's country landscape is stylishly self-conscious; his tableaux recall the Barbizon painters, Corot, Daubigny. Chekhov makes one think of the early Impressionists, of Manet, of Signac.

The Steppe showed him what he was about. He began writing this piece at the beginning of January 1888, during the period of spiritual malaise which followed the success of *Ivanov,* the first of his plays to be produced. He felt now that he had come to a crucial point in his career, and that the success or failure of this story would decide his fate once and for all. He was full of doubts as to its merit. "It is my *chef d'œuvre,*" he wrote his friend Lazarev-Gruzinsky. "I cannot do better." [8] In February 1888, he sent the story to Pleshcheyev, the editor of *The Northern Herald,* one of the "thick" periodicals, with a desperate letter: "For God's sake, friend, don't stand on ceremony. Write me that my story is rather dull and awful, if such is the case. I need terribly to know the truth." The truth, when he learned it, was better than he had hoped. *The Steppe* was attended by a storm of applause. It was his first real success as a writer, and it established him not only in the opinion of others, but also in his own opinion, as a man of genius.

And now he saw where his power resided. He had, more or less unconsciously, already developed a simple style in accordance with the contemporary tendencies which he felt and shared, but so far he had tried to display the sophistication of the professional humorist. In *The Steppe,* he had dropped this pretense. The story described life candidly, as it appeared to the eyes of a child. For the first time he had succeeded in freeing himself from the accumulation of literary rubbish which ordinarily stands between the writer and the world around him. It had required courage, and an exceptional effort.

The Steppe describes the journey of a nine-year-old boy who is seeing the world for the first time. He has reached the age when he must go to school and, in the company of his uncle, he makes his way across the plains toward the distant town where he is to live. For Yegorushka the steppe is alive and sentient, tense with mystery, and vibrant with unimaginable beauty. After his long years of hack work, it must have given Chekhov intense pleasure to realize that he could still see the world with the vividness and innocence of childhood. He had succeeded in evoking within himself a being so simple and fresh that nature appeared to him in much the same colors as once it had appeared to Wordsworth. But it was not romanticism that Chekhov discovered. It was impressionism.

The discovery was not altogether new. He had made conscious use of the little tricks of the impressionist for some time. As early as 1886, he had written his brother Alexander, who was also ambitious to be a writer: "You will get an effect of moonlight if you write that on the dike of the mill-race there sparkled like a bright little star the fragment of a broken bottle, and there passed, rolling like a ball, the dark shadow of a dog or a wolf." [9] This was a favorite example, to which he returned more than once in his writing, but it was, after all, no more than a trick of optical reduction, an effect which indicates at the most the painterly character of his method at this time. *The Steppe*, however, clearly revealed his analytic habit of mind, and the true nature of his literary affiliations. He was, on the one hand, close enough to Maupassant to be mistaken for a naturalist. But he was not at all a naturalist. He was a poet; an impressionist, and a symbolist, as close to Hofmannsthal and Rilke as he was to Maupassant, and perhaps closer.

Grigorovich's letter had been, as Chekhov wrote, "better than a diploma." [10] But it was *The Steppe* that really initiated

Chekhov's life as an artist. Now for the first time he began to assert himself, to take positions on general questions, or to refuse to take them. On October 19, 1888, he was awarded the Pushkin prize for his third book of collected stories, *In the Twilight*. Five years later he felt that in some ways he had already gone beyond Turgenev. In 1893 he wrote that in Turgenev, "The descriptions of nature are beautiful, but I feel we have already lost the habit of this sort of description, and that we must find something else." So far as Chekhov was concerned, the necessary departure would bring the writer closer to the soil than Turgenev had come. It would involve a type of metaphor that was not elegant but strong, not learned but spontaneous and naïve, something that belonged to life and not to literature. Thunderstorms were a favorite subject for descriptive elaboration. In *The Steppe* Chekhov had written:

> To the left someone seemed to scratch a match against the sky; a pale and phosphorescent streak lit and went out. Then somewhere, far away, there could be heard someone walking on a zinc roof, no doubt barefoot, for the zinc gave forth a long dull groan.

Turgenev did not write like this; nor did Maupassant. It was Yegorushka who taught Chekhov how to write in this style. He became a specialist in the apt and homely phrase, the earthy, non-literary comparison in which Gorky also specialized, though without Chekhov's vividness. The essence of Chekhov's style, as he himself said more than once, was brevity and simplicity. "Do not give too much space," he advised his friend Shcheglov, "to an overinsistent image . . . To emphasize the poverty of a beggarwoman it is not necessary to speak of her miserable appearance, it is enough to remark in passing that she wore an old rusty cloak . . . A single detail is enough." [11] "One should fix on small details and group them in such a way that when the book is closed a picture forms before the eyes." [12] This technique of suggesting large effects through small details, of characterizing by means of a word or a gesture, became an essential element of his dramatic method. All of his plays are small in scope. They deal with insignificant people and inconsiderable events, but the effect is immense; the suggestion inescapable; the significance cosmic. Obviously, no technique, however skilful, could achieve such an effect in itself. Chekhov said little of the essential qualities of the artist—the depth of his insight, his sensibility, his intuition. But perhaps about things of this sort, there is nothing that warrants discussion. They are simply indispensable.

When the burst of applause attending the publication of *The Steppe* had subsided, Chekhov expressed his own dissatisfaction to Grigorovich. He had failed, he thought, to synthesize his material. "Instead of a general artistic representation of the steppe, I offer the reader an encyclopedia of the steppe . . . It is in spite of myself that I sin; obviously, I do not yet know how to write a long narrative." [13] In fact, he did not know, and never learned, how to write a long narrative. *The Steppe* is a succession of episodes, and so it is with the greater part of his long pieces. With the possible exception of *The Duel*, none of his long stories has the type of unity we ordinarily associate with the novel of the period. His mind formulated life in brief vivid scenes. He was never able to develop the long lines of a novelist in a manner satisfactory even to himself.

When he understood his limitations in this respect, he very sensibly adjusted his method to them, and made a virtue of necessity. The Chekhovian story centers on a strong effect. Sometimes there is a series of such effects. It is by means of a flash, or a succession of flashes, that he illuminates his subject, not through a carefully modulated interplay of lights and shadows. It was only when he understood that this was the way in which he wrote best that he became a master. His novels are frankly in each case a sequence of related episodes which serve to define a character, but rarely to develop a narrative pattern. His plays, beginning with *The Sea Gull*, consist also of a sequence of scenes, arranged in a meaningful way, but conspicuously lacking in the formal development which was in that day considered essential to the drama. They dispense almost entirely with intrigue, complication, climax, and denouement, in short, with all the machine of the theatre. It is in this artlessness of construction that the special art of Chekhov consists. Doubtless this effect was consciously arrived at. In all his great plays, even the last, it is possible to discern, if one wishes, the vestiges of the intrigue around which the narrative at first took form; and in each case it is impossible not to admire the fortitude with which its outlines were erased. The immediate consequence was, of course, to weaken the action, but the ultimate effect was to transform the story into a poem.

Along with the question of style came the question of substance, and this was even more vexing for a writer who found himself suddenly called upon to define his position. The publication of *The Steppe* by no means ended Chekhov's days as a hack writer, but it gave him literary status. The time had now come to consider what it was he stood for, and what he meant to say. The literary tradition in Russia was uncompromisingly didactic and argumentative, and had been so from the beginning. From Gogol to Korolenko, all the major Russian writers wrote as teachers, and derived their strength from the spirit of opposition. In the drama, especially, every work was justified along didactic lines. In spite of his impressionism, Chekhov too was a teacher. In the Russian climate of letters, the pedagogical attitude was inescapable. But aside from the most general notions of right and justice, he had no readily definable position, and he found it impossible to engage himself wholeheartedly in any movement. In a period of resolute partisanship, he was neither a liberal, nor a conservative, a Westernizer, nor a Slavophile. He prized, above all, his neutrality.

It is customary to say that Chekhov was primarily an artist and a realist, and that in representing life he had no other aim than to represent life "as it is." With regard to this notion, enough has been said, perhaps, already; but it is necessary to add that Chekhov himself was primarily responsible for its currency. Almost from the beginning of his career, he associated himself as a writer with Balzac and Zola. "Literature," he wrote Maria Kiseleva, "is called artistic because it depicts life as it actually is. Its aim is truth, unconditional and honest . . . A man of letters must be as objective as a chemist, he must abandon worldly subjectivity and realize that dunghills play a very respectable role in a landscape, and that evil passions are as inherent in life as good ones." [14] "In this world," he had written the year before, "it is indispensable to remain indifferent." [15]

At that time he had been reading Marcus Aurelius. The indifference to which he referred was of venerable ancestry. It was that stoic *apatheia* to which the Antonines gave the compassionate and humane coloring which brought Stoicism so close to Christianity. But, as we see in such revealing stories as *Ward No. 6* and *The Exile*, this classical posture did not entirely accord with Chekhov's temper. Objective as he might wish to be, he could not manage to remain indifferent. Life troubled him. He desired to feel himself a part of it, and not only with respect to his time and place, but to all times and all places. He wished to live as widely and as deeply as possible. At bottom he had a kind of enthusiastic piety, a devout feeling with regard to nature and living things which was never well defined, but never far below the surface of his thoughts. His life was short, and perhaps he knew it was to be short; but it was exceptionally wide and deep. He felt that he shared the life of plants and trees, that he participated in a universal impulse, and he took greater pleasure in his garden, when he had one, than in his writing. Possibly the stoic indifference of which he spoke was more than a pose, but it expressed only a part of his nature. This nature was complex. However simple the man appeared, he was at the same time detached and deeply engaged, and this ambivalence was the source of some confusion to him, and a good deal of misunderstanding. He cultivated, as a writer, the clinical courtesy of the physician who observes without undue sentimentality the symptoms of a world that is far from well. But he was himself ill; and the ills of the world were never far removed in his mind from his own discomfort. To be an artist, he felt, was to be primarily an observer. Yet, in the nature of things, it was difficult for him to remain neutral. It was equally difficult for him to take sides.

Essentially, no doubt, he was inclined toward skepticism. He took readily to a type of relaxed Pyrrhonism, and suspended his judgment, at least nominally, with regard to everything he did not know as fact. He often balanced conflicting viewpoints, but, as in *The House with a Mansard*, avoided a conclusion, for like Ibsen, he had a horror of being limited by a principle. It gave him claustrophobia to be classified. In the years 1886-88 he was especially sensitive in this regard, and in most others as well—these were difficult years for him. He wrote Pleshcheyev: "I am afraid of those who look between the lines for tendencies, and who want to label me precisely a liberal or a conservative. I am not a liberal, nor a conservative, nor an evolutionist, nor a monk, nor am I indifferent to the world. I should like to be a free artist, and that is all—and I regret that God has not given me the strength to be one. I hate lies and violence in all their aspects . . . My holy of holies is the human body, health, intelligence, talent, inspiration, love, and the most absolute freedom—freedom from violence and falsehood in whatever form they may be expressed. Such is the program I would hold to if I were a great artist." [16]

He knew very well, nevertheless, how much empty rhetoric there was in such statements, and it made him uncomfortable that he believed in nothing, and could find nothing in which to believe. In a letter to Pleshcheyev, written the same week, he defended himself—apropos of the story *The Name-Day Party*—against the charge of having no sympathies and no direction. "But, indeed, in the story, do I not protest from beginning to end against lying? And, in truth, is this not a direction?" [17] In truth, as he must have known, it was not a direction. He had, it is clear, a generally liberal, healthy attitude toward life and society. He detested constraint and compulsion and, perhaps for this very reason, he insisted on his neutrality at every opportunity. "The artist must not be the judge of his characters," he wrote Suvorin, "or of what they say, but only an objective observer." [18] But it is not easy for an author to be an objective observer of his characters. The characters he observes are not external to himself. They are the creatures of his fancy. They are himself; and the fact of their creation indicates the nature of his commitment to them. To observe is to select. To select is to judge. In spite of all the rubbish he felt obliged to write from time to time concerning his artistic objectivity, Chekhov knew very well what it is that an artist does:

> The artist observes, selects, guesses, combines; all this presupposes an initial problem. If one had not posed oneself a problem from the beginning, there would be nothing to guess and nothing to select. To put it briefly, I will use the language of psychiatry: if one denies that creative work involves any problem or purpose, then one must assume that an artist creates without either premeditation, or intention, but simply as the result of an aimless impulse; for this reason, if an author boasted to me of having written a story without any preconceived

> idea, but simply on a sudden inspiration, I should say he was mad.[19]

And he added:

> ... You confuse two things—the art of finding the solution to a problem, and the art of posing a problem correctly. For the artist, only the second is obligatory...

Many of Chekhov's stories, in fact, pose problems. A very troublesome one is posed in *The Lights*, a short story he wrote in the same year as *The Steppe*. It has to do with a young man who spends a night in the construction hut the railway engineer Ananyev shares with a student from the city. The student is a typical highbrow of the period. He has nihilist views of which Ananyev disapproves, although he shares them; for in his opinion such ideas are appropriate to age but not to youth. Ananyev then tells a sad little story to prove his point. He prefaces it:

> I was no more than 26 at the time, but I knew perfectly well that life was aimless and meaningless, that everything was a deception and an illusion ... I fancied at the time that my intellectual horizon had neither beginning nor end, and that my thought was as boundless as the sea. Well, as far as I can judge, the philosophy of which we are speaking has something alluringly narcotic in its nature, like tobacco or morphine ... Our generation has carried this dilettantism, this playing with serious ideas, into science, into literature, into politics, and everything which it is not too lazy to go into, and with its dilettantism has brought in also its coldness, its boredom, and its one-sidedness ...

It develops that Ananyev came to realize his moral emptiness as a consequence of his shameful treatment of Kisochka, an unhappy girl whom he had amused himself one day by seducing with false promises and protestations of love. But he had repented quickly of his perfidy, and this repentance has been of importance in his life:

> My mental health, so it seems to me now, dates from the day when I began again from the A, B, C, when my conscience sent me flying back to the town of N–, when, without philosophic subtleties, I repented and asked Kisochka to forgive me, like a naughty boy, and we wept together...

The nihilist, Ananyev indicates, must take account of facts like anyone else. Conscience is a fact. The inner voice is categorical. In the never-ceasing flux of experience there is at least this fixed point, and the skeptic Kant had balanced the universe on it. Ananyev does not go so far, but he has now a very definite sense of what is right, and this is derived from experience. Thus, he says, there is a great difference between the pessimism of youth and the pessimism of age.

> In the first place, the old are not dilettantes. Their pessimism comes to them, not casually from without, but from the very depths of their brains, and only after they have studied exhaustively all the Hegels and Kants, and have suffered, and have made no end of mistakes—in short, when they have climbed the whole ladder from the bottom to the top... Secondly, the pessimism of mature thinkers does not take the form of idle talk, as it does with you and me, but of *Weltschmerz*, of suffering: with them it rests on a Christian basis, because it is derived from love of humanity, and humane thoughts, and is quite free from the egotism of the dilettante. You despise life because its meaning and its object are hidden from you, and you are afraid for yourself, while the real thinker is unhappy because the truth is hidden from everyone, and he is afraid for all men... [20]

This statement substantially represents Chekhov's viewpoint. It is the basis of his two masterpieces in the long story form, *Ward No. 6* and *The Duel*, and is the shaping principle of his celebrated short novel, *A Dreary Story*. It is the idea that underlies most, if not all, of his later plays. In Chekhov's view the realization that life is absurd is a source of spiritual disintegration in a superficial nature, and can lead to every sort of viciousness and brutality. But it is also a liberating principle. In the mature and sensitive individual, it can motivate powerful and positive social impulses, and is a most useful concept for the betterment of mankind. This sensible notion perhaps defines Chekhov's world-view as well as anything; but there is always something in Chekhov that resists formulation. In *Ward No. 6*, his strongest story, a good deal is said on both sides of the question he raises. Between the apathetic Dr. Ragin and his excitable patient Ivan Dmitrich it is difficult to say who speaks for the author. The scales are certainly weighted on the side of the madman; but the intimation is that both are mad, and those who put them in the madhouse no less mad than they.

It is not a comforting thought. Chekhov is not a comfortable writer. He poses distressing questions, and he has no answers for them. Perhaps in his view, the answer is that there is no answer. It is a viewpoint which is by no means rare in the literature of the time. In his autobiography, Gorky attributes to a carpenter at Nizhni sentiments which echo Tusenbach's speech in the second act of *The Three Sisters:*

> Once there was a crow, and it flew across the fields and over the hills, and from frontier to frontier, and it lived past its time, and the Lord finished it. Now the crow is dead and dusty. What's the meaning of it? No meaning whatever. Just get some sleep; soon it will be time to go to work.[21]

Ward No. 6 ends, like so much of Chekhov's work, with a question. *The Lights* does not go so deeply into the matter;

it ends with a shrug. The young narrator leaves the engineer's hut in the dawn no wiser than he came:

> I began saying goodbye . . . A great deal had been said in the night, but I carried away with me no answer to any question, and in the morning there remained in my memory, as though in a filter, only the lights, and the memory of Kisochka . . . As I got on the horse, I looked at the student and at Ananyev for the last time, at the hysterical dog with the lustreless, tipsy eyes, at the workmen moving to and fro in the morning fog, at the embankment, at the little nag straining with its neck, and I thought: "You can make neither head nor tail of anything in this world."
>
> . . . a little later, I saw nothing before me but the endless gloomy plain and the cold overcast sky. I recalled the questions which had been discussed in the night, and I pondered. And all the time, the sun-scorched plain, the immense sky, the oak forest, dark on the horizon, and the hazy world in the distance seemed to be saying to me:
>
> "No, you can make neither head nor tail of anything in this world." [22]

Indeed, *The Lights*, like *Ward No. 6*, is strangely, almost, one would say, perversely, non-committal in its conclusion. As the story is framed, the parable is convincing. The engineer is clearly right; the student is wrong; and the narrator seems strangely mulish in his refusal to take sides. The young author Leontiev-Shcheglov, in fact, reproached Chekhov for ending his story in this manner. It was the function of the artist-psychologist, he suggested, to come to some conclusion. At least he must try to analyze the soul of his hero. In reply Chekhov affirmed the artist's God-given right to be confused. "The psychologist should not pretend to understand what in fact nobody understands . . . Then we shall not be charlatans, and we shall declare frankly that one can make neither head nor tail of anything in this world. Only fools and charlatans know everything and understand everything."[23]

Between knowing everything and knowing nothing there is, it would seem, some little space in which an honest man may perhaps set up his tent. For some time Chekhov sought a foothold in this area; in this effort he veered further and further away from skepticism. It was certainly not his skepticism which impelled him to make the back-breaking trip to Sakhalin in order to study the penal colony, nor was it skepticism that forced him to exhaust himself during the cholera epidemic of 1892-93, nor to quarrel with his lifelong friend Suvorin over the reactionary policy of *New Times* with regard to Dreyfus. In a measure, one conjectures, his skepticism was rather deliberate and professional. It permitted him to preserve his neutrality in situations in which it was best to express no opinion. He was nevertheless a brave man, and when he felt the necessity to speak, he could be outspoken. In general, when he expressed an opinion, he was on the side of the angels. He was reasonable, if somewhat neurotic. His sympathies were liberal; his impulses, generous; his viewpoint, modern. Both he and his best characters were devoted to the gospel of work. But with all this, there seems to have been a voice in his heart that insistently murmured, *vanitas vanitatum*, and it seems always to have had the last word with him.

The 1880's were obsessed with the idea of change. For a time, so it seemed, the world had stood still, changeless in mutability, with all things tending toward their perfection through the cycle of time. But in the nineteenth century, things seemed to be changing with unprecedented rapidity, and these changes were accompanied by a wave of hysteria which the art of the time amply reflects. "*Ce siècle est fait pour tout confondre!*" Stendhal had written in 1830. "*Nous marchons vers le chaos!*"

He had also written at that time: "*Les Russes copient les*

mœurs françaises, mais toujours à cinquante ans de distance. Ils en sont maintenant au siècle de Louis XV."[24] In Russia after 1861 there was much talk of progress, and also much talk of despair. All was seen to be in flux—truth, God, morality, society, the individual, and even the landscape. In the West, while the academic painters redoubled their well-intentioned efforts to fix permanently on canvas everything that was impermanent in reality, the artists of the new generation emphasized the only truth which inspired them with confidence—the ever-changing aspect of the surface, under which they posited no permanent substrate. In literature the first manifestations of impressionism were followed by a reaction. Then came a wave of mysticism. The aim of those who propagated this newer impulse was to reveal the true nature of that substrate, the very existence of which the materialists denied. In this, the symbolists hardly succeeded; but they succeeded in giving a new direction to art and letters, a direction which led, unhappily to periodic outbursts of spiritual debauchery, and at last ended in despair and Dada.

For Schopenhauer, the ever-driving Will was aimless. Influential though he was, his views could not establish themselves firmly in an age which was still basically teleological. After Darwin and Spencer, however, change acquired a sense of direction, and the world regained, if not stability, at least a semblance of form. Evolution, together with relativism, its poor relation, now became concepts of primary literary interest. All the major dramatists of the succeeding age were forced in some way to come to terms with these ideas—Ibsen, Strindberg, Shaw, Pirandello.

As a scientist, of course, Chekhov was more or less committed to an evolutionary attitude. In his day, anything else would have seemed eccentric. But as an artist, he found it not altogether simple to affirm a positivistic conviction. Like many other skeptics of his time he had a deep desire for God, and the impossibility of giving credence to any sort of religious belief depressed and discouraged him. His stories and his letters unfailingly affirm his devout faith in progress, but, as in *Ward No. 6*, this faith often takes an equivocal turn. The gesture of affirmation is overly theatrical; the circumstances of avowal strangely vitiate the force of the declaration.

The progressive attitude, it has been remarked, is clearer in Gorky than in Chekhov, yet even in Gorky there is sometimes apparent an undercurrent of black despair against which his vigorous optimism has difficulty in reacting. The squalor of life in Russia filled both of them with disgust, and Chekhov was more squeamish than Gorky. Yet he too felt that life must be exhibited in all its sordidness, for reasons which had therapeutic as well as artistic validity. He shared with Gorky also, and with the Slavophiles, a curious belief in the mysterious spiritual power of Russians to transcend what was brutish in their nature and to achieve, in time, a moral regeneration, and with it, a glorious future existence. The depth of his belief in this future paradise is perhaps open to question, but his attitudes, during his middle years, certainly invite comparison with those which Gorky later expressed:

> Often, recording such atrocious memories of our bestial Russian life, I wonder whether there is any point in recalling them. And with revived assurance I tell myself: "The point is that this continues to be the actual, loathesome fact to this very day, that this fact must be traced back to its source, and uprooted from our memories, from the souls of our people, from our confined and squalid lives."
>
> And there is another point in recording these brutalities. Repellent though they are, and though many beautiful souls are crushed to death by them, yet the Russian remains spiritually so young and sound that he can and does transcend them. In this extraordinary Russian life not only does our animal self thrive and fatten, but along

> with it, and despite it, grows a brilliant, creative, wholesome human type which encourages us to seek our regeneration, and a future of peace and humane living for all.[25]

For Chekhov's characters, however, faith in the glorious future of mankind serves only too often as a pretext for doing nothing at all in the present. His characters chatter, and they also complain that they chatter. They often speak of work. But, with rare exceptions—there is one in *My Life*—they do nothing to the purpose, or else—like Irina in *The Three Sisters*—they are soon tired. For the rest, Chekhov often affirms not only the impossibility of attaining happiness in this world, but—as in *Gooseberries*—the vulgarity of being happy in a world full of misery.

Chekhov himself took a healthy interest in living, and his viewpoint was consistently reformatory and active. The world was obviously in a mess; it was necessary above all to tidy it up. We owed our posterity the duty of handing forward a better world than we received. No one had the right to withdraw from life in order to cultivate his gooseberries in peace. In this respect, Chekhov differed radically from Voltaire. One owed society the courtesy of being indignant. The narrator says in *Gooseberries:*

> I reflected how many satisfied, happy people there really are! What a suffocating force they represent! You look at life—the insolence and idleness of the strong, the ignorance and brutishness of the weak; incredible poverty all about us, overcrowding, degeneration, drunkenness, hypocrisy, lying . . . Yet all is calm and still in the houses and streets; of the fifty thousand living in a town, there is not one who would cry out, who would give vent to his indignation aloud . . . Everything is quiet and peaceful, and nothing protests but mute statistics: so many people gone out of their minds, so many gallons of vodka drunk, so many children dead of malnutrition

> ... and this order of things is evidently necessary, evidently the happy man only feels at ease because the unhappy bear the burden in silence, and without silence happiness would be impossible ...

Here, as in *An Attack of Nerves*, the hero feels the need of an opiate in order to bear the thought of the world's injustice. These characters, of course, do not necessarily speak for the author; but the stories are too strong not to have been deeply felt. Doubtless they express, at least in some degree, that sense of guilt which periodically sent the writer into a neurotic depression, or caused him to engage in an orgy of disinterested activity which left him ill and exhausted. In his later years, especially, Chekhov rather fancied himself as the man with the hammer to whom he refers in *Gooseberries*, whose function it would be to disturb people when they were contented. As a man and a physician he had, in addition, more immediate obligations. There was so much to be done in the way of sanitation and education; the establishment of schools and hospitals, the relief of famine, the endless fight against disease, the conservation of natural resources, reforestation. The list of necessary reforms was formidable; the difficulties immense; and there were always so many who needed help. He did what he could. But beyond such practical matters, he found it difficult to go. Speculation bored him. He must have felt very keenly the need for a consistent world-view like that of Tolstoy, a simple and far-reaching program with a memorable slogan; but after his brief Tolstoyan period, he was able to find nothing that would do, and he never formulated any but the vaguest sort of philosophic conception.[26]

A Dreary Story (1889) indicates, however, the extent to which Chekhov attached importance to what he called "a general idea," that is to say, a consistent philosophical viewpoint. At this time he was obviously distressed that he could produce nothing of the sort with which to defend himself against those of his critics who said his work had no meaning. Gorky speaks scornfully of a philologist who refused to let him express an opinion until he had defined his principles. This man, "putting a patriarchal look on his womanish face, lectured me a whole hour on the responsibilities of criticism. 'Only a belief in some basic truth can give you the right to criticize—what is your basic truth?' "[27] Chekhov, however, was more vulnerable in this respect than Gorky. It took him a long time to reconcile himself to the fact that he was unable to arrive at a basic truth, and many of his characters express his discomfort as a skeptic.

His religious position was also not simple. He denied repeatedly that he was anything but a materialist; but he had been brought up in a deeply religious atmosphere, and it is more than likely that important vestiges of his boyhood faith remained operative in his psyche long after his intellect had rejected them. Some indication of this comes out in *The Beauties*, in which he describes a very complex sensation, the indefinable sadness of beauty. The narrator, in the company of his grandfather, had visited an Armenian farmer, whose daughter was extremely beautiful. He was surprised to find that her loveliness made him sad:

> It was a sadness vague and undefined as a dream. For some reason, I felt sorry for myself, for my grandfather, and for the Armenian, even for the girl herself, and I had a feeling as though we four had all lost something important and essential to life which we should never find again... Whether it was envy of her beauty, or that I was regretting that the girl was not mine and never would be, or that I was a stranger to her; or whether I vaguely felt that her rare beauty was accidental, unnecessary, and, like everything else on earth, of short duration, or whether perhaps my sadness was that peculiar feeling which is excited in man by the contemplation of real beauty, God only knows.[28]

That hope for the future of mankind which he expressed over and over up to the time of his last published story, *The Betrothed*, has something in it of this same wistfulness. It is a mood of nostalgia for a lost Eden, the details of which can be only dimly surmised. It is nevertheless an entirely secular and practical hope, the basis of which is not Providence, but science. What his characters look forward to is a time when the moral side of man shall have developed equally with his intellectual faculty, and society as a whole will be at last free from want, injustice, and fear. In *The Betrothed*, the heroine exclaims: "Oh, that this new brighter life might come quickly, when it will be possible to look one's destiny boldly in the face, and know oneself to be right, and be happy and free!" And such a life surely will come, she feels, sooner or later.

It would come, in Chekhov's usual phrase in "three or four hundred years"—"two or three hundred years, or a thousand years, if you like—it doesn't really matter how long—" [29] That this pious hope echoes in some measure a childish confidence in the second coming of the Messiah, is entirely possible, though Chekhov ordinarily put the matter in very different terms. "Modern culture," he wrote Diaghilev in 1902, in reply to a letter soliciting his support for a religious cause, "is the beginning of work for a great future, a work that will continue for tens of thousands of years in order that, even if only in the remote future, humanity may come to know the truth about the real God: not guess at it, that is, nor look for it in Dostoevsky, but know it clearly, as it knows that twice two are four. Modern culture is the beginning of this work, but the religious movement in question is a survival, almost the last trace of something that has ceased, or is ceasing, to exist." [30]

From Chekhov's letters in his later years one may conclude that if he had any sort of faith, it was faith in the capacity of man to reach the divine principle through the exercise of his rational faculties. He expressed no belief in the religious tradition of his fathers. But it is difficult to suppose that a man without a deep-seated spiritual sense could have written *Easter Eve* or *The Student*. Chekhov did not believe in God, but he believed in man; and in man's persistent belief in God he found something profoundly significant and touching. The search for God was in itself a divine principle.

In *The Student* the young intellectual from the city tells the story of Good Friday to a group of simple village people. They are moved to tears. The student also is deeply moved; he realizes that

> The story he had just told had some relationship to the present, to this desolate village, to himself, to all men. The past was linked to the present by an unbroken chain of events proceeding one from the other. And it seemed to him that he had just seen both ends of the chain; he had touched one, and the other had stirred. The truth and beauty which had guided human life there in the high priest's courtyard had continued without interruption to this day and had, clearly, always been the chief thing in human life, and indeed in the whole world.

The religious overtones which sound so frequently in Chekhov's stories and plays doubtless reflect also a certain depth of mysticism which it is by no means easy to reconcile with his professedly naturalistic views. It is true that the mystical nuances he occasionally gave to his work also happened to be very much in fashion in literary circles at this time. There is no trace of the charlatan in Chekhov, but he was a professional writer, and he kept abreast of the changing literary scene. It is clear that he did not approve of the reaction against naturalism, but he was well aware that contemporary literary currents were strongly influenced by the antagonism of the generation of 1885 against the school of Zola and all it implied.

In France, by the middle of the decade, naturalism had had its day. Its opponents held it to be an obscene propaganda, the object of which was to denigrate humanity to the point where decency, order, and authority must give way, together with all the finer spiritual values. Under a storm of abuse, the naturalists hastened to retreat to more tenable artistic positions. The most influential literary trend of the day was, in fact, symbolism—the symbolism of Verlaine and Mallarmé, and in the drama the symbolism of Villiers de l'Isle Adam and Maeterlinck. All this symbolism flourished in the shadow of Baudelaire, the true prophet of the new aestheticism.

Baudelaire had advocated, above all, a defiant withdrawal from the hurly-burly of life into the more serene landscape of art. The aestheticism of the 1880's was correspondingly passive in its social outlook. Its adherents looked with indifference upon programs and reforms, and took a purely noncommittal stand with regard to the issues of the day. Since it was agreed that in nature all was relative and all in flux, the only sensible attitude for symbolists was a relaxed hedonism, and the only fit subject for contemplation was the world of art, that is to say, the ideal world of fantasy, the human substitute for the chaos of nature, and the only reality we could ever truly know or rely upon.

Chekhov's attitude toward society was, as we have seen, far removed from this sort of aestheticism; and he had nothing but contempt for its pallid reflection in the passivity of the disillusioned Russian intelligentsia of the 1880's. But it was impossible for him to avoid wholly the concept of *l'art pour l'art*. His purely receptive posture as an artist, his tendency toward a primarily lyrical interpretation of experience, his sense of the transitory nature of beauty, his yearning for a life which is not of this world, but which in certain lights this world reveals, these, together with his manifest reverence for the more sensual aspects of religion, its music and ceremony, and even its faith, show Chekhov to be a child of his time.[31]

But these symbolist trends could not and, of course, do

not wholly define him. Chekhov never wholly adopted naturalism, nor did he ever relinquish it. From beginning to end, he insisted on the scientific nature of the artist's observations, and even more strongly on the social usefulness of the artist. He disagreed violently with the anti-naturalist doctrine of Bourget's *Le Disciple*, which in 1889 was appearing in installments in *New Times*.[32] The social ideal of the *fin de siècle* was the elegant dilettante. Chekhov detested dilettantism. The idea that art is an end in itself, the finest product of existence, and, indeed, a pattern for life, was the fundamental tenet of the *décadence* in France. The decadent was professedly and proudly *de trop* in the society of his time: he all but seceded from the state. This superfluousness was the outward token of that complete withdrawal from useful activity which was one of the consequences of romantic disillusionment. For the dilettante the world of art was the only possible refuge from the horror of life. But in Chekhov's eyes this decadence was an illness. Work was his remedy for both the ills of the soul and the ills of the world; moreover, it was man's only defense against the ever-threatening ennui of existence. This sensible view he never relinquished. For Chekhov, as for Goethe and Carlyle, it is in work, and only in work, that we find our health, our justification, and our salvation. We work because it is in our nature to work. We work because we have nothing better to do in this world; we work even though we do not understand too well what it is we are working for or towards, simply for the pleasure of working, because work is our life.

Far from seeking in art a refuge from the senseless drive of the Will, as Schopenhauer had counseled, Chekhov looked upon art as a prime expression of the Will. Life was painful, and it was senseless; that much was evident. But it was also evident that it is our duty as humans to work toward the improvement of life, just as it is the duty of the farmer to improve the soil from which he draws sustenance. A lifetime of service to the cause of humanity was, in Chekhov's eyes, the only rational solution to the problem of existence. Unhappily, one occasionally grew tired of humanity and even, occasionally, of existence. And work, for all its glamor, was in the long run, exhausting. It is out of such reflections, doubtless, that characters like Ivanov took shape.

Ivanov

THE *Steppe* had been the product of a month's intensive work at the beginning of 1888. When it was published in March of that year Chekhov could feel that he had at last justified himself in the eyes of those who had expressed faith in his talent. *The Steppe*, however, was a descriptive piece, and did not in any way touch social issues, nor did it do anything to clarify its author's political or philosophical standpoint.

The year before, Chekhov had made an effort to write something long and impressive, something that could be considered important. In October 1887, he had written his brother Alexander that he had a novel in hand, and had given him some notion of the subject. This proved to be abortive, and he destroyed the manuscript. In the meantime he was thinking once again of the stage. In January 1887, he had adapted one of his stories, *Kalkhas*, written the year before, into a one-act vaudeville afterwards called *Swan Song*. It had taken him, he boasted to Maria Kiseleva, an hour and five minutes to write, and he had at once begun another such piece, but had not found time to finish it. Later that year, the producer F. A. Korsh asked him to write a full-length play for his theatre. "I answered, 'With pleasure.' The actors assured me that I would write a good play because I am able to play on people's nerves. I answered, '*Merci.*' And, of course, I will not write a play . . . I want nothing to do with the theatre or with the public. The devil take them!"[1] Three weeks later he had finished the four-act play, *Ivanov.*

In a letter dated 10-12 October, he wrote his brother Alexander that *Ivanov* had taken him less than a fortnight to write. It was already in Korsh's hands. "Of the merits of the play I cannot judge. It worked out suspiciously short. Everyone likes it. Korsh hasn't found a single mistake or fault in it so far as stage technique is concerned, which proves how good and sensible my critics are. It is the first time I have written a play, ergo, mistakes are unavoidable. The plot is complicated and not stupid. I end each act like a short story. All the acts run on peacefully and quietly, but at the end I give the spectator a punch on the nose. My entire energy is concentrated on a few really powerful and striking scenes; but the bridges joining them are insignificant, dull, and trite. Nevertheless, I am pleased, for however bad the play may be, I have, I think, created a type of literary significance . . . a part which only such a talented actor as Davydov would undertake, a part in which an actor has room to move about and show his talent . . . "[2]

Korsh accepted the play without making any difficulty, and offered Chekhov a royalty of eight per cent of the gross, an arrangement which assured the author at least 600 rubles. The great Davydov was to play the leading role. Chekhov was in raptures. Late in October he wrote his brother a letter in which confidence and misgivings were about equally mixed:

> Our modern playwrights stuff their plays exclusively with angels, villains, and buffoons—go and find these types in all Russia! . . . I wanted to be original—there is not a single villain or angel in my play (though I could not resist the temptation of putting in a few buffoons). I have not found anyone guilty, nor have I acquitted anyone. Whether I have succeeded or not, I do not

> know . . . The play will most certainly be a success—Korsh and the actors are quite sure of that. But I am not sure. The actors do not understand their parts, they talk a lot of nonsense, insist on playing parts for which they are in no way suited; but I am fighting them, for I am convinced that the play will be a failure if it is not cast as I wish . . .[3]

What Chekhov was affirming as original in these letters was, of course, nothing more than the usual naturalistic attitude of the period. Louis Deprez's *L'Évolution naturaliste* had appeared in 1884. Antoine's theatre had just opened. The idea that a play was written for the sake of a few climactic scenes was one of the most frequently discussed notions of the new theatre in France. It had resulted, among other things, in the dramatic capsule, the *quart d'heure* in which Antoine specialized, and it was an idea that accorded very well with Chekhov's special talents as a dramatist.

The question of stock-characterization had been gone into even more thoroughly. In 1888, Strindberg summed up the naturalist doctrine with regard to characterization in the Author's Foreword to *Miss Julie*. On the stage, Strindberg wrote, a character "had come to mean an actor who was always one and the same, always drunk, always comic, or always melancholy, and who needed to be characterized only by some physical defect such as a club foot, a wooden leg, or a red nose, or by the repetition of some such phrase as 'That's capital!' or 'Barkis is willin'.' This uncomplicated way of viewing people is still to be found in the great Molière. Harpagon is nothing but a miser, although Harpagon might have been not only a miser but an excellent financier, a fine father, and a good citizen. . . . So," he added, "I do not believe in simple stage characters. And the summary judgments that writers pass on people—this one is stupid, this one, brutal, that one jealous, this one is stingy, and so on—should not pass unchallenged by the naturalists, who know how complicated the soul is, and who realize that vice has a reverse side that looks very much like virtue." [4]

From a theoretical standpoint, therefore, Chekhov showed that he was aware of what was going on in enlightened theatrical circles abroad. But his pride in not having made "a single mistake" in stage technique indicates to what an extent he was not yet an original playwright. It was hardly to be expected that at this stage of his career he would be sufficiently experienced to be careless of his stage management, and his concern about getting his actors on and off at the proper time, and with the proper *brio*, is entirely understandable. So too is the evident astonishment with which he viewed his sudden and surprisingly easy conquest of the theatre. He wrote his friend the novelist Yezhov in terms so complacent that they might well have elicited a smile: "If I am to believe such judges as Davydov, then I know how to write plays. It seems that instinctively, because of some kind of flair, and without my being aware of it myself, I have written an entirely finished piece without making a single stage error." [5]

His complacence, luckily, was not destined to last. The rehearsals went badly. He had been promised ten. There were only four, of which, he complained, two were wasted in useless argument. The great Davydov disappointed him. In general, he had a hard time with the cast, and at last he went so far as to ask Korsh to withdraw the play. Korsh "had a fit." When Leikin advised the disgruntled author to stop interfering with the rehearsals, Chekhov answered with considerable heat: "The author is the owner of the play, and not the actors; everywhere the casting is the obligation of the author if he is within reach... If the author's participation is to be eliminated entirely, then the devil knows what will happen!" [6]

What happened is a matter of opinion. Chekhov wrote his brother Alexander an amusing account of the proceedings on the opening night, but it is clear it was not an altogether happy occasion: "From the very first words I do not recognize my play. Kiselevsky, from whom I expected so much, did not utter a single word correctly. He just invented his dialogue as he went along . . ." The last act was evidently a shambles, and the play ended in turmoil. There was applause, and also hisses and stamping of feet. In the refreshment bar a fight broke out; students were arrested in the gallery. Chekhov's sister came near to fainting, and his friend Dyukovsky developed palpitations and rushed out of the theatre. As for Chekhov, on the whole, he was pleased.[7] In a subsequent letter to Alexander which he signed "Schiller Shakespearovich Goethe," he boasted that there had been no other occasion at Korsh's theatre when the author had to take a bow after the second act. After all this excitement, the reaction of the Moscow press seemed anti-climactic, and it was not altogether favorable. One of the reviewers went so far as to write that the play was "essentially immoral and repulsive, a highly cynical libel on contemporary life and people."[8]

Chekhov began to feel the reaction: he grew irritable and weary. But at the end of November, the lure of the stage reasserted itself, and he went to Petersburg to see if he could arrange a production there. He had taken the precaution to send a copy of the play to *New Times*, and on his arrival he found his friends "in raptures."[9] But he was not satisfied that anyone in Petersburg understood the play, and he returned to Moscow full of thoughts for improving the plot and clarifying the characters.

The publication of *The Steppe*, and its happy consequences, put the play out of his mind for almost a year. It was not until October 1888 that he took it up again. The revision took some three months: there were important changes in the second and fourth acts, and a new monologue for Ivanov in the final scene. Chekhov was full of enthusiasm. Two of his short pieces—*The Bear*, a vaudeville written in February 1888, and a farce called *The Proposal*—were enjoying spectacular success on the stage. He was full of projects. "Subjects for one-act plays," he wrote Suvorin, "gush out of me like oil from the soil of Baku." [10]

Ivanov had obviously not yet made its point. This, Chekhov felt, must be the fault of the characterization; the plot he considered to be beyond reproach. As a matter of fact, he had hit on a very interesting situation. *Ivanov* centers on the unhappy consequences of a misalliance. Ivanov is an impoverished landowner, a cultivated young man who has married a girl called Sarah, the daughter of wealthy Jewish parents, probably in the expectation of receiving a rich dowry. But in order to marry him, the girl has entered the Orthodox church, and changed her name to Anna. As a result, her parents have cast her off. Ivanov's financial state is now worse than ever, and he has been forced to mortgage his lands heavily to the Lebedevs, his miserly neighbors. After a brief period of happiness, Ivanov begins to tire of his wife who, in the meantime, has developed an illness of the chest. In these circumstances, he suffers dreadfully with ennui, and runs off frequently to the Lebedevs to escape the boredom of his home.

The local doctor Lvov, a man of compulsive nature, has diagnosed Anya's illness as tuberculosis, and prescribed a warmer climate; but Ivanov does not wish to go away with his wife, and he cannot afford to send her off by herself. Instead he becomes involved with Sasha, his neighbor's daughter, who ardently wishes to save him from whatever it is that ails him. The matter is brought to a head in the second act. During a party at the neighbor's house, Anya comes unexpectedly upon her husband at the very moment when he is passionately embracing Sasha. Anya swoons, and the curtain falls on what is evidently a critical situation.

Two weeks later, when Sasha comes to visit Ivanov at his home, Anya flies into a towering passion. She accuses Ivanov of having married her for her money, and then of having turned against her when she was disinherited. And now, she says, he is courting Sasha in order to avoid paying the Lebedevs the mortgage money—all his motives are mercenary. Ivanov is infuriated, calls her a Jewess, and when she retaliates with further insults, brutally informs her that the doctor expects her to die. Deeply shocked at this news, Anya staggers off tragically, leaving Ivanov full of remorse.

Act four takes place a year later. The scene is laid at Lebedev's house. Anya is dead. Ivanov is about to marry Sasha, and the family is getting ready to go to church to attend the wedding. But the idealistic Dr. Lvov is much troubled, and he informs the audience in a soliloquy that he is an honest man, and that it is his duty to open people's eyes to the rascality of Ivanov. He is resolved, therefore, to unmask this knave before it is too late, and then to leave the country forever. Directly Lvov has left the stage, Ivanov comes in, greatly excited, and demands to see Sasha. He is bored, depressed, exhausted, and ill, and he tells Sasha that he cannot go through with the wedding: the marriage must be broken off. Sasha, however, refuses to release him. She insists that he come at once to the church. In the midst of this discussion, Lvov bursts in, full of wrath, and informs Ivanov that he is a worthless scoundrel. But Ivanov does not challenge him to the duel he is attempting to provoke. On the contrary, when Sasha tries presently to propel him once again in the direction of the church, he produces a revolver, and shoots himself.

Chekhov made in all seven versions of this play, so that ultimately he came to loathe it.[11] In the first version Ivanov did not shoot himself; he suffered a heart attack as the result of his inner tensions. It was on the advice of his friends in Petersburg that Chekhov decided to ennoble his hero by having him commit suicide, after reciting an appropriate monologue. In this form Chekhov sent his play to Suvorin in December 1888, with a request that he transmit it to the Alexandrinsky Theatre: "I have finished Bolvanov and am sending it to you along with this letter . . . I give you my word I shall never write such rotten intellectual plays again." Now, he felt, his character was intelligible. The finale still did not satisfy him, but after all the form was not yet final; he could change it, if necessary.[12]

Ivanov was accepted but, to Chekhov's disappointment, the comments he received along with its acceptance made it clear that his hero was still not tragic. Ivanov was taken to be either a scoundrel or the traditional superfluous man, and Suvorin wondered what it was that made Dr. Lvov so great. In reply Chekhov wrote Suvorin a careful analysis of each of his characters. He added, despairingly, "If they have emerged on paper lifeless and indistinct, it is not their fault but my own lack of ability to convey my ideas. It seems as though I took up playwriting too soon." [13]

Evidently the rigors of dramaturgy had taken some of the starch out of his ego. In Petersburg, at the beginning of the year, he confided to Pleshcheyev, that to make over a bad play was as difficult as trying to turn a soldier's old trousers into a dress coat. Fiction, he wrote, was his legal wife, but the theatre was "a showy, noisy, impertinent, and tiresome mistress." [14]

The forthcoming premiere of *Ivanov* in Petersburg frightened Chekhov beyond measure. The great Savina was to play Sasha. The part had to be built up to suit her. Davydov could not understand what Chekhov was getting at with his revisions, and threatened to resign the role of Ivanov. The play opened January 31, 1888, under the most inauspicious conditions. To Chekhov's astonishment, it turned out to be a huge success. The characterizations were thought to be original and lifelike; the acting was said to be brilliant; the play was compared to *Woe from Wit*. Chekhov was overwhelmed, and even embarrassed. "Not even Shakespeare had to listen to the speeches I heard," he wrote.[15] The day after the opening he left Petersburg as furtively as a thief. It was very difficult for him to bear this success.

The truth is, no doubt, that in his heart he knew *Ivanov* did not deserve to succeed. It is a play put together like a pudding, with a ludicrous climax, and a desperate end. The ballroom scenes at Lebedev's, in the second act, are embarrassingly childish. The comic characters Borkin, Shabelsky, and Madame Lebedev are no more than stock caricatures. Chekhov had much to be ashamed of. But with all its drawbacks, *Ivanov* had elements of greatness, and the fact that these were not properly appreciated at any time by anybody might well have added to the author's discomfort.

His characters, he had written Suvorin, were not "born in my head . . . by chance. They are the result of observation and the study of life." [16] The Ivanov-Anya entanglement may, in fact, have been suggested to him by an affair he himself had lived through with a Jewish girl, possibly Dunya Efros. For a time he had kept his Petersburg friend Bilibin in close touch with this rapidly developing situation. "Yesterday," he wrote Bilibin, "while accompanying a certain young lady home, I proposed to her. I'd like to jump from the frying pan into the fire." [17] Not long after, he wrote, "When I speak of women I like, I usually restrain my words . . . a trait I have preserved since my schooldays. Thank your fiancée for her regards and concern, and tell her that my marriage is probably—alack and alas! the censor does not permit the word. My *she* is a Jewess. For a wealthy Jewess to accept Orthodoxy and its consequences, courage is necessary—well, it is not necessary and not needed. We have already quarrelled over this. Tomorrow we'll make it up, and in a week fall out again. She is vexed that religion is a problem, and has broken several pencils and a photograph on my table—this is characteristic of her. A terrible spitfire. I shall undoubtedly leave her within a year or two after I marry her."

Some weeks later, he wrote again to Bilibin: "I am still not married. I've parted finally with my fiancée. She broke it off. But I've not bought a revolver, and I don't keep a diary.

Everything in the world is changing, mutable, approximate, and relative." The communiqués regarding this affair were officially terminated in a letter of 11 March, 1886, and the correspondence with Bilibin on this subject came to an end. It was more than a year later, in September 1887, that Chekhov devised, overnight, the plot of *Ivanov* which deals also with a wealthy Jewess who is a spitfire, but who accepts Orthodoxy with its consequences.[18]

By contrast with Anya, who is violent, passionate, and vulnerable, Sasha is a pale character. It is easy to see that, in her determination to save Ivanov at all costs, she bears some resemblance to Sonia in Chekhov's first play. It is also not difficult to see that Ivanov is a later version of Platonov, and that he suffers from a similar indisposition of the soul. Like his dramatic progenitor, Ivanov has failed at everything. For reasons which he tries to make convincing, he finds himself exhausted long before he is old. Ivanov says—it is his swan song:

> IVANOV: . . . I used to be young, sincere, enthusiastic, intelligent; I used to love, hate, and believe in a way most people could not even imagine; I did the work, and had the dreams, of ten men; I tilted at windmills, and ran my head against brick walls. I knew neither my strength nor any weakness, I neither thought nor knew anything about life, and so I took up too heavy a load, and broke under the strain. I did everything to extremes; I drank too much, I worked too hard, I was constantly excited, I did not spare myself. Well, what else could you expect? We are so few and there is so much to be done, so much! And see now how cruelly life avenged itself, which I fought against so bravely! I'm finished. At thirty-five, I am old. I drag myself around, with a heavy head and a lazy mind, weary, useless, discouraged, without faith, without love, without purpose; I wander like a shadow among my friends, and I don't know who I am, or why I live, or what I want. And it seems to me

> that love and love-making are absurd; work and play, a waste of time; and the most passionate of speeches is just so much drivel. And wherever I go, I bring nothing but sadness, weariness, boredom, disgust with life. Completely and hopelessly ruined! Before you stands a man who at thirty-five is exhausted, disillusioned, and crushed by trifles, ashamed of his failure and scornful of his weakness... Oh, how my pride rebels against it, how my anger chokes me! (*He staggers*) Ah, I'm staggering! I've no more strength... Where is Matvey? Tell him to take me home.[19]

This monologue is usually said to describe the generation of the 1880's, and to reflect the disillusionment that followed the liberal reforms of Alexander II. But it seems to have a more general application. Chekhov evidently had in mind a type of Russian intellectual of no special period, but of a special temper, the sort of highly inflammable nature that is soon extinguished. He wrote Suvorin:

> His past was wonderful, and this is true of the majority of educated Russians. There is not or, at least, there is scarcely a single landed Russian gentleman or university man who at one time or another has not boasted of his past. Why? Because Russian enthusiasm possesses one specific quality—it is quickly followed by fatigue. A man who has only just left school assumes in his unbounded enthusiasm a burden he has not the strength to carry... thus, no sooner does he reach the age of thirty or thirty-five than he begins to feel tired and bored... and he is already willing to deny the usefulness of the Zemstvo, scientific farming, science, and love...[20]

In the light of Chekhov's analysis one can hardly wonder that Davydov was confused by the part he was now required to play. In Moscow he had played Ivanov in the tradition of

Turgenev's Rudin, a readily comprehensible and familiar character-type. This character now acquired tragic overtones. It was not easy to explain what happened to him between acts three and four in the new version to make him so unexpectedly heroic, but, whatever it was, it necessitated a revision of the entire conception if the character was to have consistency. Ivanov's boredom could be accounted for on the basis of his spiritual exhaustion; but his brutality, his repentance, and his moral rehabilitation required a more detailed analysis than an actor could be expected to undertake without substantial assistance from the author.

Ivanov's neurasthenia hardly needed to be generalized into a cultural characteristic of the Russian upper class, nor did he need to be justified on the ground that he had burnt himself out before he was 30. His disenchantment and his melancholy, as well as his occasional lapses into sadism, were recognizable symptoms of a romantic malady which had been given the fullest development in Western literature in the course of the century. They needed no special etiological amplification. The source of the difficulty was the composite nature of Ivanov. In part he was Rudin; but he was also an exotic specimen, a poor relation of the French Satanic heroes of the 1830's. It was to them that he owed his cruelty, as well as his tendency to partake, albeit frugally, of *les délices qu'il y a dans la trahison et dans l'adultère.*[21]

Platonov was a cruder and more brutal version of this character. In *Ivanov*, Chekhov brought him up to date; but he was not content to exploit him purely along romantic lines. He saw him as a pathological type who must be analyzed, and the analysis of this world-weary figure inevitably led to his association with a world-weary generation, which was itself a romantic creation. It was only when this exiguous figure was found lacking in the kind of magnitude appropriate to the Russian theatre that Chekhov thought of Ivanov's sudden moral rehabilitation, and caused him to discover in himself that spark of the "old Ivanov" which makes it possible for him to shoot himself heroically in the finale.

Ivanov suffers from ennui, the romantic equivalent of that medieval *accidia* which was one of the cardinal monastic sins. Its predisposing causes in the nineteenth century were doubtless complex, but it is usually associated with the general disenchantment of the intellectual classes following the high hopes, first of the Great Revolution, and then of the Commune. From this viewpoint, boredom would be specifically a vocational hazard of the leisure class, a protest against the monotonous stability of life, a reaction against the ordered security of an aimless existence.[22] But certainly this is an oversimplification. In nineteenth-century literature, all classes appear to have suffered from ennui. Hedda Gabler blames her mischievousness on her boredom; *The Three Sisters* is one long, desperate yawn; and for Gorky boredom was a miasma which poisoned all Russia:

> The breath of boredom, frost, and poverty exhaled from everything, from the earth sheeted in rags of stained snow, from the gray lid of ice on the roof, from the brick walls, red as chapped flesh. From the chimneys, boredom floated in thick gray clouds and crawled over the low, leaden, vacant sky. In boredom, toiling horses steamed, and men sighed . . . I could see how the burden of boredom was crushing them; the only explanation I could find for their sadism, for their habit of victimizing one another with senseless horseplay, was that they were in a hopeless struggle with their overpowering boredom . . . [23]

It is, in any case, far from certain that the *mal du siècle* of the nineteenth century was essentially different from the boredom of other centuries; ennui appears to have surprising universality. What is certain is that the form of spiritual distress from which Ivanov suffers became associated quite early and quite closely with romanticism. After Baudelaire, it became a mark of distinction, indispensable to the dandy, who customarily fancied himself

> loin du regard de Dieu,
> Haletant et brisé de fatigue, au milieu
> Des plaines de l'Ennui, profondes et désertes...[24]

Whatever may be said of the special character of Russian boredom in the time of Chekhov, its literary manifestations were certainly not unusual. Russian decadence was not intrinsically of native origin. It was a cultural import. Pushkin's Onegin, Lermontov's Pechorin, Turgenev's Rudin, were ill-adjusted, but not decadent. Nevertheless, the political condition of the country after 1861, the decay of the gentry, and the rapid development of a classless intelligentsia with nihilist tendencies provided a fertile ground for the propagation of a type of decadence which the latest novels from France were already endowing with a certain glamor. In the West, such refined natures as were caricatured in *A Rebours* suffered from fatigue, overcultivation, hypersensitivity, an inability to love or to work—all the symptoms of Ivanov's disease; and they shared with him also that romantic weariness and longing for death which the song of the nightingale aroused in Keats.

For the decadent, as for the earlier romantic, life was an abyss *tout plein de vague horreur;* the flesh was sad, and all the books were read. But while the imitators of Baudelaire and Verlaine could accept this state of mind, and even glory in it a little, Ivanov finds it intolerable. The psychic state he describes in his final monologue is precisely that condition which the French decadent proudly claimed as his. But Ivanov is a Russian. For him, life on these terms is a horror from which he finds it ultimately imperative to escape. It is not his feeling of guilt with regard to Anya that chiefly troubles him. Her death does not appear to weigh unduly on his mind. It is the sense of his progressive attrition as a man that kills him.

Had Chekhov intended to portray in *Ivanov* the half-comic plight of a decadent intellectual in a Russian provincial setting, the play would probably have offered no difficulty to anyone. But Chekhov realized his character only in part, and an essential component of the characterization rests on quite other grounds than the hero's spiritual illness. *Ivanov*, for all its ineptitude, has a very solid and carefully planned structural basis. It is, to begin with, a study in illness. Both Anya and Ivanov are ill; both suffer from a wasting disease which eventually proves fatal. Anya has tuberculosis; Ivanov is wasting away spiritually. Her death is accelerated by the shock of learning that she is expected to die; his, by the realization of the conditions under which he is expected to live. The district doctor Lvov is concerned in both cases and, obviously, he himself is not quite sound in his mind: he is an obsessive idealist.

The plot is based upon a *méprise;* but not, as in so many Scribean plays, upon an obvious misunderstanding. What is involved is a subtle question of interpretation which not even those most intimately concerned with it can settle. Ivanov married for love, but he cannot be certain it was not for money. The possibility that his marriage was motivated by mercenary considerations weighs constantly on his mind, and he fears that his disillusionment with Anya may well be related to the fact that he was, in a sense, cheated out of her dowry. None of this, perhaps, is actually true. Ivanov is very much the gentleman. His conscious motives are not questionable. But the unconscious is not a gentleman; and Ivanov cannot be sure that he is not, at bottom, precisely the sort of scoundrel that Lvov says he is.

His motives with regard to his second marriage are equally open to question. He believes his love for Sasha is sincere; but he is not emotionally stable; he hardly knows his mind, and the insinuation that he is once more marrying in order to save his estate is difficult to refute. It is, therefore, his own inner reproach of rascality that he finds unbearable, rather than the reproaches of others.

Dr. Lvov, on the other hand, is not only pathologically self-righteous, he is also incredibly stupid. For him Ivanov is "a Tartuffe, a pompous impostor." He does not understand him in the least, but he is sure he sees through him completely, and therefore feels it is his duty to exterminate him. Lvov is obviously a caricature of no great subtlety. He is the Ibsenist idealist reduced to the level of a meddlesome fool. Since this fool, however, represents and reinforces Ivanov's sense of guilt, he plays a crucial part in the action. Lvov is, necessarily, entirely soundproof. Nothing shakes his self-confidence:

> IVANOV: You're such a clever man. You think it's no great thing to understand what sort of chap I am. Right? I married Anya for her money, but I didn't get the money, I was tricked out of it, so now I'm killing her so I can marry another woman for her money . . . Right? How easy it all is! A man is such a simple, uncomplicated mechanism . . . No, Doctor. We all have too many wheels, gears, and valves to be judged by first impressions or through a few superficial traits. I don't understand you; you don't understand me; and also we don't understand ourselves. It's quite possible to be an excellent physician, and yet not to understand people in the least . . . [25]

This speech makes no impression whatever on Dr. Lvov, but it indicates clearly that Ivanov is more deeply troubled than anyone else regarding his motives. The others interpret his behavior in accordance with conventional hypotheses, or, at best, in line with their own natures. But Ivanov is an enigma to himself. He does not know why he does what he does, and he is too proud and too honest to rationalize his behavior or to justify it. He did not wish Anya to die, but it is certainly a relief to him when she dies. He does not really wish to marry Sasha, but it is true that when her dowry is suddenly reduced drastically, he has a sound mercenary reason for repenting of the match. If others suspect his motives, he himself is even more suspicious, and the thought that he has degenerated morally to the point where he is perhaps a scoundrel is the true reason for his suicide, and not the wish to save Sasha from a fate worse than death.

The characterization of Ivanov was evidently a matter of some difficulty for Chekhov. No one had attempted anything so complex before on the Russian stage. Chekhov's desire to see into the soul of a gentleman, to know him as Ivanov needed to know himself, was perhaps the basis of the anguished complaint he sent Suvorin while he was in the last throes of this undertaking:

> What gently born writers receive freely by right of birth, the lowly born buy at the price of their youth. Try then and write me the story of a young man, the son of a serf, a former shopkeeper, choir boy, high school and university student, trained to bow his back, to kiss the hands of priests, subjected to the ideas of others, grateful for each mouthful of bread, a thousand times whipped, running, miserably shod, to give a few lessons, a brawler, tormentor of animals, accepting gratefully the dinners of rich relatives, a hypocrite before God and man, without reason, simply out of the consciousness of his own insignificance. Then write how this young man squeezes the slave out of himself drop by drop, and how, rising one fine day, he realizes it is no longer the blood of a slave that flows in his veins, but the blood of a human being . . . [26]

In any event, there is no doubt that poor as the play might be, Chekhov had indeed created, as he wrote his brother, a character of literary significance. In setting up for the stage a psychological situation of such intricacy, he had, of course, found himself a little lost and lonely—he had not many forerunners in the field, and therefore turned for assistance to

Shakespeare, the only sure guide for the aspiring dramatist. Ivanov has a good deal about him that recalls Hamlet. He is, in line with Polevoy's interpretation, unashamedly melodramatic, over-articulate, theatrical; in addition, his relation to Platonov is painfully evident, and his amply documented suicide at the end of the play obviously takes the measure of the writer's inexperience as a dramatist at this point of his career. Nevertheless, the richness of the characterization is striking. Ivanov is the first of that remarkable gallery of portraits which Chekhov created, a face whose expression defies analysis, and on which our minds dwell with wonder. He is an exceptional character, lost, unfortunately, in a situation which gives him no opportunity to develop. But for Chekhov his significance was immeasurable, and the fact that his character was not quite realized at this time made it all the more likely that it would be reworked until it came completely to life. The play itself was soon forgotten, but the character remained a challenge, and, of course, the challenge was heeded. Two years later, Chekhov brought Ivanov vividly to life in *The Duel.*

Laevsky is developed far more completely than Ivanov, but his situation is less demanding. In *The Duel* the idealistic Dr. Lvov is elaborated into the biologist Von Koren, who is similarly obsessed with the need to redress what he considers a social evil. His hatred of Laevsky is rationalized along philosophic lines, but his reactions, as in the case of Dr. Lvov, are excessive—one is led to suspect that his rancor proceeds from something akin to jealousy. The conflict between the two men centers upon the unhappy Nadezhda, Laevsky's mistress, and the development of this conflict indicates how much further by this time the author had advanced as a novelist than as a playwright. *The Duel* is a great masterpiece. Its tone is by turns moody and comic. It has no melodrama and no theatricalism. There are no suicides in it and no dramatic speeches. On the contrary, in *The Duel* all is understated. The climaxes are quiet. The emotional current runs deep and still. Whatever sentimentality there is in it is touched with humor. *The Duel*, as a reworking of *Ivanov*, demonstrates clearly that Chekhov was at this time primarily a storyteller, accustomed to working in a free medium which he himself developed to a kind of perfection. He became a dramatist only when he gave up the technique of the stage. It was when, toward the end of his life, he quite abandoned the rules of playwrighting, and began to write for the theatre in his own natural medium, that he achieved greatness as a playwright. This process took time, ten years at least, and even then it was necessary for him to find a theatre capable of adapting itself to his technique. Nobody illustrates better than he the disintegration of the system which Ibsen inherited from Scribe, and Scribe from Corneille, and Corneille from Aristotle.

The Wood Demon

IN 1889 Chekhov once more girded up his loins to write something important. He had been reading Dostoevsky and Goncharov. He no longer felt their greatness. But Gogol aroused all his enthusiasm—"How direct and powerful Gogol is! And what an artist! . . . He is the greatest Russian writer."[1] The novel he had now taken in hand was presumably intended to develop, in the manner of Gogol, the adventures of a character similar to Chichikov in *Dead Souls*. But his interest in this project dwindled, and by the fall of 1889 he had abandoned it. He was living at this time in Yalta in the Crimea, the climate of which was said to be good for his lungs, and there about this time he began work on *A Dreary Story*. It was a reflection, he wrote the editor of *The Northern Herald*, of his depression of the preceding summer.

A Dreary Story was the most ambitious piece he had so far attempted, a story of the mental and physical degeneration of a great man. Nikolai Stepanovich is a professor of medicine at the University of Moscow. He finds himself, at the end of his life, loaded with honors, but mortally ill, desperately lonely, without hope, and without love. He is troubled because—like Chekhov—he has no definite world-view, nor any social viewpoint or unifying principle in his life; and partly because of this lack of a "general idea," he feels that his life has become meaningless, that his emotions have withered, and that he is powerless to do or say anything that can be of aid even to the people who are closest to him, when most they need him. At the end of a life devoted to science, he has become, in short, useless and impotent, an empty shell of a man, admired by all, loved by nobody, a living corpse.

This story, with its hopeless outcome, was compared unfavorably in the press with Tolstoy's celebrated *The Death of Ivan Ilyich* in which the hero, similarly afflicted at the end of his life, suddenly perceives the splendor of the inner light. But Chekhov, dedicated to the depiction of "life as it is," did not often write happy endings. The peripety at the end of *A Dreary Story* is not a turn upwards, but downwards, and demonstrates in a final way the spiritual emptiness of a great man's soul.

The suspicion is irresistible that there is a good deal of Chekhov in the old professor, and his loneliness, his lovelessness, his illness, and his curious psychic inability to come to grips with the troubles of others undoubtedly have some autobiographical basis. In any case, what Chekhov saw in the tragic life of the scientist and, later, in the tragic life of the bishop, in the story of that name, was the futility of wealth, the uselessness of talent, the emptiness and the loneliness of worldly honor, in short, the vanity of success. The bishop's fate, and his isolation, is not different from that of the great doctor; yet presumably the bishop has a "general idea": he has God. The "general idea," accordingly, does not seem to be the critical factor. Faith does not save the bishop any more than the scientist's skepticism damns him. Both are simply victims of life, persons displaced, through their own genius, from their normal environment. Both have striven mightily, and, in the end, both are worn out and cast aside, cut off from the soil from which they sprang, *déclassés* through their special talent and their ambition. What both stories most clearly illustrate is the isolation of the gifted man who, having risen from the lowest social level to the highest, finds himself at home nowhere. It is the tragedy of the outstanding individual.

Chekhov wrote very few stories in 1889: there were only nine in all. In this period he felt particularly attracted to the theatre. His one-act pieces, especially *The Bear* and *The Proposal*, were proving extremely profitable. He followed them up with *A Tragedian in Spite of Himself*, an adaptation of his story *One Out of Many;* and *The Wedding*, based largely on *A Wedding with a General*, which he had written five years before. In the summer of 1888, during a stay with the Suvorins at Feodosiya in the Crimea, he had discussed with Suvorin the possibility of collaborating on a play to be called *The Wood Demon*. Later that year Suvorin dutifully sent him a draft of the first act, whereupon Chekhov sent his collaborator a list of suggestions so overwhelming that Suvorin thankfully withdrew from the project, with the remark that the plot would make a better novel than a play. Chekhov continued work on *The Wood Demon* by himself. In May of the following year he wrote Suvorin that he expected to finish the play in about a month: "The play is terribly strange, and I am surprised that such queer things should come from my pen. I am afraid the censor will not pass it." [2]

The spring of 1889 was not a pleasant time for Chekhov. His mood flickered fitfully between euphoria and depression. He wrote Suvorin, to whom, during these years, he felt apparently he must confide every detail of his life, "Over the past two years, and for no earthly reason, I have grown sick of seeing my words in print; I have become indifferent to reviews, talks on literature, slanders, successes, failures, big fees —in fact, I've turned into an utter fool. There is a sort of stagnation in my soul . . ." [3] In this mood, he worked at *The Wood Demon* and, simultaneously, at *A Dreary Story*. Outwardly, however, he seemed to be in the best of spirits. His sister Masha described him at this time as full of joy; working, joking, and seeking company insatiably.

Through the spring and summer of 1889, his enthusiasm for the new play waxed and waned unpredictably. On May 14 he wrote Suvorin: "If the censor does not knock me on the head, you are going to feel such a thrill in the autumn as you never felt standing on the top of the Eiffel Tower looking down on Paris." Two weeks later he was in the dumps. The second act was finished, and the play was dull. He was bored to death, he wrote, and he could not go on.

The play, meanwhile, had been promised for Svobodin's benefit performance at the Alexandrinsky, and for Lensky's benefit night at the Moscow Maly, and it had already been announced in both capitals. In September Chekhov threw away the two acts he had completed and began afresh. This time the work went smoothly. In the first days of October the four acts were finished, and he sent a copy of the play to Svobodin and another to Lensky.

The result was unpleasant. The censor passed the play; but the Petersburg branch of the Dramatic and Literary Commission, of which Grigorovich was a member, rejected it for the Alexandrinsky for artistic reasons—the absence of action and the tediousness of the dialogue. A fortnight later, a letter of rejection came from Lensky in Moscow. It contained sound professional advice: "Write stories. You are too scornful of the stage and the dramatic form. You respect these things too little to write plays. This form is more difficult than prose fiction and—forgive me—you are far too spoiled by success to begin the study of the elements of dramatic form, so to speak, from scratch, and to learn to love it."

The principal objection to *The Wood Demon* seemed to be that it was not a play but a dramatized story. Nemirovich-Danchenko, to whom the play had also been sent for criticism, wrote Chekhov to the same effect: "Lensky is right. You ignore too many of the requirements of the stage, but I have not observed that you scorn them; simply, rather, that you don't know what they are." Chekhov took these criticisms in good part, and agreed cheerfully that as a dramatist he had no talent. But inwardly he felt he had been betrayed. He wrote to Pleshcheyev of *The Northern Herald:* ". . . Either I am a bad playwright, an idea to which I heartily subscribe, or all these gentlemen who love me as a son and implore me for the love of God to be myself in my plays, to avoid clichés, and to develop complex ideas, are hypocrites . . ." [4]

By this time *The Wood Demon*, and everything connected with it, inspired him with horror. He refused to let Suvorin see it, and he rejected all offers to print it. But by November he apparently felt better about the whole thing, and when the actor Solovtsov offered to do the play at the new Abramov Theatre in Moscow, Chekhov at once applied himself to a new revision, concentrating particularly on the fourth act, which he had never liked. *The Wood Demon* opened in Moscow on December 27. It was a failure. The critics were unanimous in their opinion: it was as if there had been a meeting to establish a consensus. The author, it was said, knew nothing of the rules of the stage and the necessary conditions of stage presentation. His idea of a play was a mechanical reproduction of the banalities of everyday life. His play was not a play.

One might imagine from such criticisms that in *The Wood Demon* Chekhov had actually attempted something original along naturalistic lines. Nothing could be further from the truth. The Moscow critics aped, in general, the pedagogic tone that characterized Sarcey's anti-naturalist criticisms in the Paris *XIXe Siècle*. *The Wood Demon*, however, had very little to do with French naturalism. The second act was magnificent; but on the whole the play was a perfectly conventional piece of dramatic rubbish, and it is difficult to say in what way it differed from the rest of the trash which encumbered the Moscow stage. By all odds it should have succeeded, and been highly praised.

The Wood Demon, like *A Dreary Story,* has to do with the troubles of an aged professor. "I have my knife out for professors," Chekhov had written Suvorin that fall, "although I realize they are excellent people. Like writers, they have no daring and much self-importance."[5] The professor in *The Wood Demon,* first called Blagosvetlov, and afterwards, Serebryakov, is not a scientist like Nikolai Stepanovich. He is a professor of art history, a classicist, a skeptic without religion, completely devoted to his work—"work, work, work, work, and the rest is all humbug and nonsense."

In the course of the various revisions to which he was subjected, this character suffered some denigration at the author's hands. To begin with he was projected as another aspect of Nikolai Stepanovich. He was, Chekhov wrote Suvorin, "a man without a single stain on his past. He suffers from gout, rheumatism, and ringing in the ears . . . He possesses a positive mind. He cannot stand mystics, dreamers, weak-minded religious maniacs, sentimentalists, and sanctimonious people . . ." This exemplary old gentleman ended badly. In the final version of *The Wood Demon,* he is seen as a crochety, egotistical, pretentious old man, full of complaints; moreover, he is said to be a fraud who has been lecturing for twenty-five years without understanding anything about his subject. He has married a young and beautiful woman whom he fills with disgust and loads with reproaches, and of whom he is justifiably jealous. No worse fate is imaginable.

The action is embarrassingly inept. There is something undeniably mealy-mouthed and moralistic about the play, but apart from the fact that some of the characters are shown the error of their ways, there is in it little or nothing to justify its qualification as Tolstoyan. *The Wood Demon* is certainly not conceived as a conflict of good and evil forces, nor is there any indication that, in the end, good triumphs over evil.

Nor is the ending truly happy. On the contrary, the evil relationship between the old professor and his young wife, which is central in the action, is perpetuated at the end, and there is no suggestion that this conflict is soluble.

It is possible to estimate the degree of Chekhov's development as a playwright from 1887 to 1889 by comparing the birthday party with which *The Wood Demon* begins with the birthday party in *Ivanov.* In that scene the people are grotesque puppets; and the party is a bore. The people in corresponding scenes of *The Wood Demon* are alive and interesting, witty and genial. They abuse each other freely, but their abuse demonstrates the closeness of their relationship. It is a group of dear friends who detest one another. In *The Wood Demon* these characters are introduced rather quickly, but all are efficiently described. Dyadin loves everyone and finds everything delightful. Voynitsky is a man of 47, witty and malicious, a cynical railer whose only interest in life is his brother-in-law's wife. His mother is a dedicated reader of pamphlets. His niece Sonya is a beautiful bluestocking, a spitfire. Khrushchov, the district doctor, is a moralist and a liberal, somewhat unbalanced on the subject of forest and soil-conservation. He is nicknamed the Wood Demon. There are, in addition, Zheltukhin, a rich landowner, and his very efficient young sister Julia; and, finally, a flamboyant bemedaled gentleman called Fyodor, a lieutenant in the Serbian army, who fancies himself as a Byronic figure of inescapable personal magnetism.

Voynitsky opens the play with a very bald exposition. He declares, in sum, that he detests Professor Serebryakov, his brother-in-law, and adores his wife. The belated entrance of Serebryakov and his wife Elena makes it clear how that is. The old man is insufferable. Elena is beautiful. Zheltukhin, to amuse himself, has already started a train of gossip by declaring positively that Elena is Voynitsky's mistress. But as soon as the two are left together, it is clear that Elena is nothing of the sort, but that, on the contrary, she is bored to distraction by Voynitsky's importunities. Almost with her first words, Elena announces the theme of the play:

> ... See how thoughtlessly you destroy the forests so that soon there will be nothing left on earth! In just the same heedless fashion you destroy human lives, and soon, thanks to you, loyalty, and purity, and self-sacrifice will have vanished along with the woods and forests. ... You spare neither forests, nor birds, nor women, nor one another ...[6]

The Wood Demon is a play about waste. In Russia, it is said, everything is wasted, forests, people, lives, intellect. The peasants waste the trees out of sheer thoughtlessness. The gentry waste each other out of sheer boredom. Voynitsky has wasted his life toiling on the farm to support Serebryakov, whom he once idolized. Serebryakov wasted the life of his first wife, Voynitsky's sister; now he is wasting Elena's youth and beauty. He wastes the timber of the estate in order to get himself a little ready money. He has wasted his own talent, senselessly hashing over other men's thoughts. Fyodor and Zheltukhin are wasting their inheritance through gambling and drink. All is waste, senseless and stupid.

The theme of waste was evidently obsessive with Chekhov. Brought up in poverty, he was a frugal soul, and he knew how difficult it is for a poor man to earn in the sweat of his brow what the rich toss away recklessly. The idea of waste, universal waste—since, obviously, nature is infinitely more wasteful than man—troubled Chekhov deeply. The theme is renewed in *The Sea Gull.* Its various aspects are developed further in *The Three Sisters,* and further still in *The Cherry Orchard.* All his drama, in some sense, involves this idea; for Chekhov, as for A. C. Bradley, the Shakespearean critic, the sense of waste is the prime source of the sense of tragedy.

The Wood Demon is, however, a comedy. The second act

takes place at night in the Serebryakov's dining-room, where the professor is sitting up late, sharing his arthritis with his family. We understand that he is, in reality, a pathetic old man who has worked too hard all his life; that he is cruelly bored in the country; and that he longs for fame and the admiration of his students, his only pleasures. He feels, rightly, that nobody loves him; and he takes the occasion to explain himself at length, thereby impeding the flow of the action. "Above all," Chekhov had instructed his brother Alexander in 1886, "avoid depicting the hero's state of mind; you ought to make it clear from the hero's actions . . ." [7] But, evidently, Chekhov himself had not yet digested this admirable precept. All the characters in *The Wood Demon* are at pains to depict in detail their states of mind. It was much later in his career that Chekhov learned how important it was for his characters to keep their counsel. In *The Three Sisters* all the characters, even the most voluble, are essentially reserved. In *The Wood Demon*, the characters elbow one another in their haste to uncover their inmost souls.

In the second act of *The Wood Demon* Chekhov really demonstrates his skill as a playwright; but not all of it is good. As soon as Serebryakov is borne off to bed, the action deteriorates. Dr. Khrushchov finds the occasion convenient to make love to Sonya, an unpleasant girl; and, in the course of the scene, he casts unnecessary aspersions on Elena, whose soul, he says, is black. The characterization of Khrushchov is archaic. He appears to be a very moralistic doctor, very rigid in his outlines, and quite without nuance. His surname, though it is by no means unusual, has a faintly comic color—Khrushchov makes one think of *khrushch*, one of the less ingratiating garden pests, a cockchafer. The rest of his name is, quite appropriately, Mikhail Lvovich: it is clear that he is not only descended from Dr. Lvov in *Ivanov*, but that he shares the less admirable traits of his idealistic ancestor. Evidently at this time Chekhov considered the Ibsenian idealist an indispensable member of his dramatic family. He was certainly slow to part with him.

In addition to being a soil-conservationist, Khrushchov is a liberal, and therefore somewhat out of his element in this aristocratic ambience. In the course of his love-scene, Sonya accuses him first of being a socialist, and then a fraud, and she ends by ordering him out of the house. The inexplicable brawls which punctuate this love-affair are undoubtedly vaudevillian in their intention, a reflection perhaps of the comic quarrels in *The Proposal*. But neither these scenes, nor the consequent characterization of Sonya, are successful. Sonya is depicted as a peppery girl with "suspicious eyes." Apparently it is her weakness to suspect everyone's motives: suspicion is her *faculté maîtresse*.

Elena, on the other hand, is the female counterpart of Ivanov. In the plan of the play Chekhov made Dr. Khrushchov her prime antagonist, thus carrying over the successful arrangement of the earlier play. Like Ivanov, Elena is handsome, but her character is at once pathetic and unpleasant. Although she has an irresistible fascination for the other sex, she is incapable of love; she is dreadfully bored by everything and everyone. She says of herself: "As for me, I am worthless, an empty and quite pathetic woman. I've always been worthless—in music, in love, in my husband's house . . . in fact, in everything. If I dare even for a moment to think about it, I realize—Ah, Sonya, I am really very, very unhappy. I can never be happy in this world. Never. What are you laughing at?" [8]

The intrigue which ruins Elena again recalls the plan of *Ivanov*. It is the clatter of evil tongues that makes Ivanov suspect his motives, and so drives him to suicide; in the same way the malicious gossip of the neighbors drives Elena to the verge of despair. It was obviously Chekhov's intention to suggest that it is in the nature of man—at least in Russia—to destroy whatever is beautiful, so that the presence of anything lovely and feminine would affect the Russian character as a red rag, a bull. The presence of a surpassingly beautiful young woman married to a cranky old man would doubtless be provocative in any environment. As it is, Elena is consistently on the defensive, and time has made her very bitter and sharp. Evidently she is also a bit priggish by nature, and considers herself a paragon of Russian womanhood. She feels that she owes it to the nation to be chaste; at least, so she says. At the same time, it must be conceded that the manner in which she is treated is far from subtle—the whole thing is rather in the tradition of bear-baiting than of the polite persiflage of the aristocratic salon.

The Wood Demon was no doubt intended as a comedy of manners. But in the absence of evidence, it is difficult to decide whether the author was not yet quite sure of how gentlefolk acted in these circumstances, or whether he intended to give a realistic picture of the brutal coarseness of upper class life in the provinces. Both are possible; but it is not unreasonable to suppose that the former was the case. Elena addresses the assembled company, in the third act, in words sufficiently melodramatic to embarrass even the most hardened translator:

> . . . Oh, to be free as a bird, to fly away from you all, your drowsy faces, and your stupid chatter, to forget that you ever existed! Oh, to forget myself and what I am! But I have no will of my own. I am a coward. I am frightened, and my conscience keeps telling me that if I betray my husband, all the other wives will do the same thing and leave their husbands also. And then God would punish me. If it were not for that, I'd show you what a free life I could lead! [9]

In the midst of these amenities, Sonya, who is full of happiness because of her love for Dr. Khrushchov, rudely hands Elena a *billet-doux* which she has picked up in the garden. It is addressed to Elena, and signed by Voynitsky, and, of course, Sonya has read it and is furious. She cannot keep up her usual courteous pretenses, she says, not now—her heart is too pure for deceit, and too full of love—and with this she flounces out. Immediately after this humiliation, Elena is forced to defend herself against the indomitable Fyodor, who makes a gallant effort to dominate her sexually. She boxes his ears.

The scene that follows is extremely well done, and Chekhov preserved it verbatim when he transformed *The Wood Demon* into *Uncle Vanya*. The legal basis of the situation is a little complicated, perhaps, for dramatic purposes, but not unintelligible. Since Serebryakov originally came into the estate through his first wife, he has only a life interest in it. The title reverts to his daughter Sonya at his death. Voynitsky, who originally waived his share of the inheritance so that his sister might have the farm for her dowry, has managed the farm in the professor's absence. By dint of hard work, he has succeeded in paying off the mortgage and in improving the property, while sending the surplus income faithfully to the professor in Petersburg. Serebryakov now calls a family meeting, which he addresses in his best lecture-room style. He informs the assembled relatives that he proposes to sell the estate, and to invest the capital in securities, which will pay a better return on the investment, so that he can live in the city. The result, of course, would be to throw Voynitsky and his mother out of their house, but this has not occurred to the professor as a possible objection to his plan. This proof of Serebryakov's ingratitude is too much for Voynitsky:

VOYNITSKY: A ruined life! I'm gifted, I'm intelligent, courageous... If I had led a normal life I might have been a Schopenhauer, a Dostoevsky! I'm talking rubbish! I'm going mad! Mother—I'm desperate! Mother...

MADAME VOYNITSKY: Do as Alexander tells you.[10]

What Voynitsky does is to run out of the room and shoot himself dead. There is a scene of general consternation. Elena, the innocent cause of the tragedy, cannot bear to stay in the house any longer, and she asks the impoverished neighbor Dyadin to take her away. The act ends on this effect.

The last act takes place at the nearby water-mill where Dyadin lives in hermit-like seclusion. Elena has been with the old man for two weeks, and now Dyadin tells her it is time to return to her husband. She is not a free sparrow, he points out, but a canary—she is meant for the cage. At this point, Khrushchov comes in, and after him the rest of the company. They have planned a picnic by the mill. Elena runs into the house unobserved. It turns out that Voynitsky's diary has been found, and that it clears Elena completely. Now it is Khrushchov's turn to be ashamed; and he bitterly repents his part in spreading the slander. Sonya has found a formula with which to salve her conscience. It was selfishness, she says, that caused the tragedy:

SONYA: There is no evil without some good in it. Our sorrow has taught us that we must forget our own happiness and think only of the happiness of others. Life should be a continual act of self-sacrifice.

KHRUSHCHOV: True . . . Madame Voynitsky's son shoots himself, but she keeps right on looking for contradictions in her old pamphlets. You've had a terrible experience, and what occurs to you is to console your vanity with thoughts of self-sacrifice. We are all heartless. You . . . And I . . . Everyone does the wrong thing, and everything is going to hell . . . [11]

It is in such passages that the beginnings of Chekhov's mature technique may be glimpsed. Sonya has nothing but clichés with which to mask her lack of feeling. The inanity of her speech indicates, but does not clarify, her train of thought. She has obviously no idea of devoting her life to the happiness of others, nor has she experienced anything like a Tolstoyan conversion. Her words are conventional cant with which she hopes to justify her intention of securing her own happiness by marrying Khrushchov as soon as she can. Khrushchov refuses to follow her in these hypocrisies. He unmasks her without delay, and she begins to cry.

In his later plays, Chekhov does not unmask his characters in this way. When they say something stupid, conventional, or insincere, he permits the speech to pass without comment, and leaves it to the audience to deduce the state of mind from which the utterance proceeds. This is what is meant by Chekhov's technique of indirect action. Through the stupid things people do to mask their true motives, and the drivel they speak in order to hide their true feelings, Chekhov is able to indicate what their motives and their feelings must be without stating them directly. Needless to say, this results in an extraordinarily realistic effect, for in life it is seldom that we announce our motives, even to ourselves, and it is, in general, our mistakes and our stupidities that most clearly represent us to the world.

The most obvious difference between life on the stage and life in reality is that stage speeches are ordinarily framed to reveal the true thoughts and feelings of the characters, while the function of speech in real life is more often than not to conceal the inner man from a hostile universe. It was in adapting his technique to accommodate this truism that Chekhov raised the level of modern realistic dialogue to the highest pitch it has ever attained.

It was certainly common enough in the theatre for villains and intriguers to conceal their nefarious motives behind dissembling words and, as a rule, this caused the spectator no confusion. But in the later plays of Chekhov, matters are more complex. Chekhov's characters, like real people, are normally on the defensive, and their words have an oblique relation to their thoughts. It is for the audience to surmise the nature of their truth. In these plays, for the first time, life in a stage drawing-room approximates life in a real drawing-room.

Not the least astonishing aspect of Chekhov is the speed with which he developed his genius for playwriting. Between the absurdities of *The Wood Demon* and the sublimity of *Uncle Vanya* there was an interval of no more than seven years, and perhaps, it has been argued, a good deal less.[12] Yet these few years span a gulf that seems at first glance impassable.

The Wood Demon ends in most unsatisfactory fashion. Khrushchov, who is never reticent throughout the play, reveals himself in the end as its *raisonneur*. He explains the title of the comedy, and, in some sense, defines the theme:

> ... We say that we're serving humanity, while all the time we are heartlessly destroying one another ... You call me a Wood Demon, but you are all Wood Demons, all of you. You are all lost in a dark wood, groping your way blindly like me. We all have just enough brains and just enough feeling to ruin our own lives and the lives of others ...[13]

At this point, Elena comes out of the house. She sits on a bench, still unobserved, while Khrushchov continues his homily:

> I considered myself an intellectual person, an understanding person, but all the time, I refused to forgive people the slightest mistake. I listened to idle gossip, and believed it, and gossiped like everyone else. When your wife offered me her friendship, I rejected it brutally, told her to leave me alone, said I despised her. That's the sort of man I am. There's a demon in me, all right, I'm narrow-minded, stupid, blind, it's true. And you, Professor, are no eagle either. And yet the whole neighborhood takes me for a hero, the women especially. I'm a great liberal, the man of the future! While you,

you're famous all over Russia! Now if people really think I'm a hero, and people like you are famous, then all I can say is we're in a terrible mess—there are no real heroes and no great men to lead us, and no one is going to repair the damage done by frauds like us. It means there are no eagles at all . . .

SEREBRYAKOV: I beg your pardon. I didn't come here to argue with you, or to defend my right to distinction.[14]

Elena now steps forward, to everyone's surprise, and offers to be reconciled. Her husband turns away reproachfully. Elena is bitter: "I see. So our problem is solved by not being solved. Very well. After all, it doesn't matter. I'm a bird of the cage, and entitled to the happiness of the cage, the happiness suitable to a woman. That means sitting at home for the rest of my life, eating, drinking, sleeping, and listening to your husband going on endlessly about his gout, his merits, and his rights. Why are you looking away? Does that embarrass you? Let's have a glass of wine. What difference does it make?" [15]

Apparently it makes none. The scene is suddenly interrupted by a far-off forest fire. Khrushchov rushes to put it out. The end is a scene out of operetta. When the Serebryakovs have gone home together, more or less peaceably, Khrushchov comes back and proposes to Sonya, who at once accepts him. Then the company hides behind a bush and watches the dashing Fyodor propose marriage to Julia, Zheltukhin's efficient sister. She accepts him gratefully. In the end, the stage is full of happy lovers, soon to be wed, and the curtain descends upon Dyadin's refrain: "Delightful! Simply delightful!"

Considering the theatrical rubbish with which he concluded *The Wood Demon*, Chekhov might well have wondered at the nature of the criticisms leveled against his play. He might have expected that such banal devices as the finding of the incriminating letter in the garden, the posthumous discovery of the exculpating diary, or the sudden unmotivated conversion of Fyodor, would have elicited some adverse comment on the part of the experts. Nothing of the sort happened. On the contrary, both Lensky and Nemirovich-Danchenko pronounced the play deficient with respect to the necessary conventions of the theatre, and the latter thought the plot too complex for an audience to follow. In truth, Chekhov demonstrated here not only his knowledge of the stage-conventions of the time, but also his profound respect for them. *The Wood Demon* in its final recension included every possible theatrical cliché.

What was specifically Chekhovian in this most conventional composition appears, however, to have escaped attention completely. Nobody commented on the bitterness with which the main theme was concluded, nor did anyone discuss the unresolved conflict which represented "life as it is." The impossible contrasts between the tragic and comedic aspects of the action, on the other hand, could scarcely have escaped observation. The suicide of Voynitsky and the sacrifice of Elena could hardly be reconciled technically with the festive mood of the various love-stories which are so mechanically resolved at the end, and it was doubtless these unplayable contrasts which were at the bottom of Lensky's unwillingness to put on the play. *The Wood Demon* raised also, for the first time, the question of Chekhov's idea of comedy, a matter which was to become increasingly embarrassing as time went on. But the production was not sufficiently important to evoke any divergence of opinion, nor any extended discussion of this matter. It was in connection with *The Sea Gull*, nine years later, that the problem became manifest.

The Wood Demon marked a low point in Chekhov's fortunes as a dramatist, but it contained some very good things, and Chekhov, for all his discomfort, was resolved to revise it. He asked Kumanin, the publisher of *The Artist*, a Moscow journal, not to publish the play, a copy of which was in his hands, until there was an opportunity to work on it a little. A month later he wrote Pleshcheyev that he would send him the play for *The Northern Herald* after it was revised. But by the time he sent it, in March 1889, Pleshcheyev's magazine had changed hands, and the manuscript was returned. Much later, he wrote his friend, the Moscow lawyer A. I. Urusov: "Please don't be angry with me. I cannot publish *The Wood Demon.* I hate this play and I am trying to forget it . . ." [16] But he did not forget it. When next it was seen, it had become *Uncle Vanya.*

In the meantime, Chekhov made a new departure in the theatre. He wrote *The Sea Gull.*

The Sea Gull

TOWARD the end of 1889, Chekhov began to feel the onset of the strange restlessness which was to send him across the continent to the penal colony at Sakhalin. The reasons for this seemingly irrational urge are not entirely clear. He had often been accused in the liberal press of not having a social outlook, and it is quite possible that the aged professor in *A Dreary Story* expresses something of Chekhov's feeling of inadequacy in this respect. Certainly the spiritual isolation of the great man who has worn out his bootstraps in elevating himself bore a significant relation to Chekhov's state of mind at various times in his life. He was mindful also of the fact that in the coming January he would be 30.[1] His youth was over.

The failure of *The Wood Demon*, and the harshness of the criticism which attended its production, had greatly depressed him. Suddenly he felt that he was spiritually bankrupt—he had no material to draw on, no background, and no knowledge. In the past year he had written little. Now he was sure he had written himself out. In December 1889 he wrote Suvorin that he passionately desired to hide for five years and do some really serious work. Nothing he had so far written was worth anything. As a writer, he said, he was a complete ignoramus: "I must teach myself, I must learn everything from the beginning."

Quite unexpectedly, he planned the journey to Sakhalin Island. Nobody understood why he needed to go so far and so hazardous a route. He wrote Leontiev-Shcheglov: "I am not going for observations or impressions, but simply to live for half a year as I have not lived before." [2] His journey had, ostensibly, a scientific purpose. He had set himself a task of sociological research, a study of the social conditions of the penal colony. He hoped in this manner to bring the iniquities of the prison system more sharply to the attention of the nation. It is conceivable that this useful undertaking was his answer to the reproach that as a writer he did nothing for his fellow countrymen save to amuse them.

Chekhov took his task seriously. He spent a number of months in laying out his problem and familiarizing himself with its details. Meanwhile, at the end of March 1890, his seventh volume of stories appeared. It contained two important pieces—*An Attack of Nerves* and *A Dreary Story*—both of which bore on the question of social responsibility. The following month he set off by himself across the vast expanse that separated Moscow from the penal island in the sea of Okhotsk.

He returned eight months later, laden with statistics, and heavy with a sense of the needless suffering that society inflicts upon itself. But for a time he was unable to work. He had not rid himself of his wanderlust. In March 1891 he set off with the Suvorins on a holiday trip to Austria, Italy, and France. Six weeks of holiday was all he could bear. In the spring he came back to Moscow. He was by now deeply in debt.

That summer he wrote *The Duel.* It developed further the dialogue which he had begun in *Ivanov,* and which he was to develop further still in *Ward No. 6.* He was rapidly acquiring a taste for the good things of life—comfort, fine furniture, and amusing company in pleasant surroundings. He wrote Suvorin in August: "I should now like carpets, an open fireplace, bronzes, and learned conversation. Alas! I shall never be a Tolstoyan! In women I love beauty above all; and, as regards mankind, culture expressed in carpets, carriages with springs, and keenness of wit."[3] All these things were costly. In consequence, he felt that he was chained to his desk, and the thought of the endless work that lay before him gave him much uneasiness. In *The Wood Demon* Professor Serebryakov is described as a writing-machine, and his constant admonitions to work, work, work are obviously directed ironically to Chekhov's inner tyrant as much as to anyone.

It was partly to escape the high cost of living in Moscow that Chekhov decided to buy a country place of his own where he could practice medicine a little, and at the same time devote himself to reading and serious writing, free of the necessity for turning out trash to pay the rent. Such, at least, was the rationalization. The truth, very likely, was that he had long nourished a secret desire to live like a gentleman on a manorial scale. By December 1891, the urge to buy an estate rose to fever-pitch, and after some disappointments, he engaged to purchase a run-down estate of 675 acres at Melikhovo, two and a half hours from Moscow by train. The house was not particularly convenient. It had no toilet. The farm was not good. But there was a fishpond near the house, and, nearer still, two mortgages, which he thought he could carry with ease. In March 1892 he took possession. He was now in high spirits, a country gentleman, the sort of person Turgenev had been, more or less.

The rest of the spring was given over to carpentry and husbandry. Chekhov plunged enthusiastically into the ways of landowners, planted trees by the hundreds, enlarged the cherry orchard, spent long hours digging in his garden, and stocked his pond lavishly with fish. He enjoyed himself so much that he began to feel frightened: "Looking at the spring,

I feel a dreadful longing for paradise in the other world. In fact, at moments I am so happy that I haul myself up surreptitiously and remind myself of my creditors." [4]

The following year Melikhovo was swamped with visitors. Chekhov invited everyone he knew, and kept his visitors as long as they desired to stay, or longer. He had brought a cart-load of medical supplies with him from Moscow. His house soon became a dispensary. Peasants came from far and wide to be treated and dosed, *sine pecunia*, by the new doctor. In July, Chekhov became seriously involved with the cholera epidemic which broke out in his district, and he agreed to take charge of local sanitation. It was back-breaking work. He wrote Suvorin toward the end of the month: "My soul is weary. I am bored to death. Not to belong to myself for a moment, to think only of diarrhea . . . to drive nags along unknown roads, to read about, and think about nothing but cholera, and at the same time to be utterly indifferent to illness and the people who have it—that, my dear sir, is something that might destroy anyone." [5]

By the summer of 1893 he was tired to death of his practice, and of everything that had to do with medicine: "It is terrible and dull and repulsive . . . pfui!" [6] He had by this time formed a rewarding connection with the liberal magazine *Russian Thought* in which he had formerly been taken to task for his lack of a social viewpoint. This was a truly high-brow publication, and he felt flattered to be among its contributors, but the connection involved him in serious difficulties with his patron. Suvorin's *New Times* was the stronghold of reaction, conservatism, and anti-semitism. It was always on the side of the government, and to its unswerving allegiance to the bureaucracy Suvorin owed much of his power and affluence. In connecting himself with *Russian Thought* as well as *New Times*, Chekhov found himself straddling the entire political spectrum. It was not a comfortable position, but it was the only position in which Chekhov felt at ease, and he held it almost to the end of his career. As his friendship for Suvorin was both deep and sincere, their differences were soon patched. They broke out again later in connection with the Dreyfus case; thenceforth Chekhov found himself more and more definitely committed to a liberal position and, though he maintained a neutral attitude on political issues as long as he lived, there was seldom any doubt as to where his sympathies lay.

He was a busy man in these years. From 1892 to 1893 he published twenty-one stories of varying length. In addition, he finished the *Island of Sakhalin*, the writing of which caused him much travail and much boredom. His finest and most successful story *Ward No. 6* was printed in *Russian Thought* in 1892. He had reached the peak of his maturity as a story-writer. He was 32.

Ward No. 6 carries on to something like a conclusion the dialectical conflict which Chekhov initiated in *Ivanov* and developed in *The Duel*. In this story, the good Dr. Ragin, discouraged in his first energetic attempts to reform the provincial hospital to which he has been assigned, has settled back comfortably into stoicism, lethargy, and boredom. He reads Marcus Aurelius and cultivates that indifference which, it is said, is the only reliable defense against the ills of existence. His system works very well until he discovers in the insane ward of his hospital an interesting madman called Ivan Dmitrich, whose exaggerated sense of the world's injustice has driven him into paranoia. This madman—the only intelligent person in the town—fascinates Ragin so much that he spends all his time conversing with him. Before long this unusual intimacy between doctor and patient arouses the interest of Ragin's ambitious assistant, who hastens to use this proof of eccentricity to have his chief declared insane and committed to the same ward as his patient.

It is evident that in the opposition of Ragin, who blames his passivity on the evils of the age, and Ivan Dmitrich, whose social fervor is matched only by his helplessness, Chekhov essentially recreated the conflict between Ivanov and Dr. Lvov, and Laevsky and Von Koren—that is to say, between the two poles of his own inner dialetic. Both Dr. Ragin and his mad friend are extremely witty and intelligent men; they are excellently balanced one against the other, and it is not as clear as it is in *The Duel* that the more aggressive personality has the better of the argument. Dr. Ragin is a stoic only in theory. In practice he is a cynic. But in either case, his rationalizations leave something to be desired, and it is impossible to escape the conclusion that his patient is neither more nor less mad than he. As Ivan Dmitrich very sensibly points out:

> "... dozens, hundreds of madmen are walking about in freedom because in your ignorance you are incapable of distinguishing them from the sane. Why then should I and these other wretches be forced to sit here as scapegoats for the rest? You, the assistant physician, the superintendent, and all your hospital staff are from a moral viewpoint immeasurably inferior to any of us; why, then, should we sit here and not you? Where's the logic in it?"

Dr. Ragin answers:

> "Morals and logic do not enter into it. Everything depends on chance. Whoever is locked up, sits there; and whoever is not, walks about freely; that's all there is to it. There is neither morality nor logic in the fact that I'm a doctor and you are a lunatic. It just turned out that way."
>
> "I don't understand this rubbish," Ivan Dmitrich said dully, and sat down upon his bed.[7]

As in *The Duel*, Chekhov does not presume to decide the issue, but he leaves us in no doubt as to how he feels about his characters. They delight him, both of them. They are both funny; they are both tragic; they are both a little disgusting. He loves them dearly. It was obviously not necessary for him to make up his mind with regard to their discussion. On the contrary, it was necessary for him to leave the issues open and the questions unresolved as long as he could. It was to such questions that he looked for his vitality as an artist, and he knew as well as anyone that a question that is answered no longer has any vitality; it is dead the moment it is answered.

The mood of indecision was Chekhov's prevailing mood. It was the area in which he functioned most truly as a writer, and in which, willynilly, he functioned best as a man. For Chekhov whatever was clear, decided, and certain was not in the province of art. Science dealt with such matters. But the artist dwelt in a world without outlines, a mysterious world in which all is open to question, in which a highlight on the neck of a bottle gives a sense of moonlight, and moonlight transforms the most banal landscape into a vision of eternity. It was the artist's function to sense the mystery of things, to capture, not the answer, but the feeling of the unanswerable in all its charm and urgency. Why? Why? Why?—this is the refrain that echoes through Chekhov's work, as it did throughout his life, and all his compositions are shaped so as to frame this question. Obviously, he was, at bottom, a romantic.

But in order to ask questions properly it was necessary to live; to work, to suffer, if need be, but, above all, to experience life. The philosophic apathy in which Dr. Ragin steeped himself was perhaps very much to Chekhov's taste; nevertheless, it was a luxury he could not afford, and whenever he came close to this alluring doctrine he thrust it from him violently. Wisdom counseled withdrawal and indifference; but there was something greater than wisdom that impelled one to action—life itself, the vital principle, which was not wise, nor even intelligent, but without which there could be no wisdom and no intelligence. It was in this tension, impossible to resolve, that Chekhov found the dynamic principle of his art.

Soon after his return from Sakhalin he had published *In Exile*, a very short story. Between this and *Ward No. 6* the difference in tone is marked. *Ward No. 6* is, in the main, an intelligent discussion. *In Exile* is set in Siberia and has to do with ignorant men, with convicts. The ferryman Semyon, nicknamed Canny, has found peace in his exile. He has found indifference, and is thus able to lecture his crew loftily on the foolishness of a wealthy gentleman of the neighborhood who is forever rushing about in futile efforts to cure his daughter's incurable disease. He goes on to speak complacently of the happiness he himself has been able to pluck out of his miserable existence:

> "Now you are young and foolish, the milk is hardly dry on your lips, and it seems to you in your foolishness that there is no one more wretched than you. But the time will surely come when you will say to yourself: 'No one can have a better life than mine.' You look at me: within a week the floods will be over, and we shall set up the ferry again. You will all go wandering off about Siberia while I stay here and start going back and forth from bank to bank. I've been going like that now for twenty-two years, day and night. The pike and the salmon are under the water, and I am on top of the water. That's the whole difference between us. And I thank God I want nothing more, nothing. May God give everyone such a life!" [8]

But the young Tatar who has been eating out his heart with loneliness in this exile has quite another view of the matter:

> The Tatar walked over to where Canny was sitting and, looking at him with hatred and disgust, shivering, and mixing Tatar words with his bad Russian, he said: "He is good . . . good! But you are bad! You are bad! The gentleman is a good soul, first-class, and you are an animal, bad! . . . The gentleman is alive, but what are you? A dead carcass . . . God created man to be alive,

> and to feel joy and also grief and sorrow. But you feel nothing, you want nothing; you are not alive, you are stone, clay! A stone wants nothing, and you want nothing! You are stone. God does not love you . . ." Everyone laughed.[9]

The dialogue between Ragin and Ivan Dmitrich is not on this level; the intellectual tone is certainly higher, and the joke also is better. The idea is the same. Dr. Ragin remarks that Ivan Dmitrich's presence in the madhouse is indispensable:

> "Once prisons and insane asylums are established, there must be found someone to sit in them. If not you, then I. If not I, then someone else. But wait a bit, one day in the distant future, prisons and insane asylums will no longer exist. Then there will no longer be barred windows and bathrobes. Sooner or later, of course, such a time will come."
>
> Ivan Dmitrich smiled derisively.
>
> "You're joking," he said, squinting. "What have men like you and your helper Nikita to do with the future? All the same, you may be sure, my dear sir, that better times will come. If I express myself in clichés, you may laugh, but the dawn of a new life is beginning to glow, truth will triumph—our turn will come to celebrate! I won't last that long, I know. I shall die long before, but somebody's great-grandsons will see it. I salute them with all my heart, and I am glad, glad for them! Forward! May God help you, my friends!"
>
> Ivan Dmitrich arose with shining eyes, and stretching his arms out toward the window, went on with emotion in his voice: "From behind these bars I bless you! Yes, long live the truth! I'm glad!" [10]

Dr. Ragin finds this gesture theatrical, but he likes it very much. Neither of these men doubts for a moment that the future of mankind will be glorious, though neither has the slightest idea of how this wonder is to come about, or when.

Chekhov, too, constantly affirmed his faith in the essential ingenuity of the human species, and its ability to shape in time a fine new world, but he was quite aware that this faith rested on rather uncertain grounds, or none at all. *Ward No. 6*, accordingly, ends in a question.

But while we ponder the question of the future, Chekhov intimates, there are urgent matters which have to do with the present, and which we would do well to settle at once. In *Ward No. 6*, the porter of the madhouse, Nikita, has no interest whatever in philosophy, but he has large fists, and he pounds his inmates unmercifully at the slightest show of resistance, without any regard for justice or other similar abstractions. The analogy is inescapable. The world, too, is perhaps a madhouse, and while humanity carries on its interminable discussion, it is observable that the wardens are brutal and unjust; the living quarters, squalid; the food, poor and scanty; and the inmates, systematically robbed and beaten into submission. There is certainly much room for discussion as to why this is so, and how things should be ideally, but while we are groping toward an ideal conclusion, it might be well to do something immediate to improve the living conditions. Such, at least, is the intimation in *Ward No. 6*.

This story made a sensation in literary circles. But Suvorin did not like it; he wrote Chekhov that it lacked alcohol. Chekhov did not defend himself. On the contrary, he conceded his lack of moral fervor and, like Laevsky in *The Duel*, he blamed his aimlessness on the times. He insisted, however, on his honesty—what he did not feel, he said, he would not counterfeit. His reply to Suvorin, often quoted, indicates how closely his story reflects his own inner conflict, and the sense of spiritual impotence which this conflict entailed:

> Tell me, in all conscience, which of my contemporaries—that is, people of 30 to 45—has given the world so much as a single drop of alcohol? Are Korolenko, Nadson, and

all the playwrights of today anything but sheer lemonade? Do Repin's paintings or Shishkin's make your brain whirl? Charming, talented, of course, you are delighted, but at the same time it occurs to you that you'd like a smoke. Science and technology are developing at a great rate, but for the arts the times are flabby, sour, and dull, and we ourselves are sour and dull . . . The causes for this are not to be found in our stupidity, our lack of talent, or our insolence, as Burenin thinks, but in a disease which for the artist is worse than syphilis or sexual impotence. We lack "something." That is true. What that means is that when you lift the skirt of your muse you discover there is nothing under it. Let me remind you that the writers we call great, or at least good, the ones who intoxicate us with their talent, have one essential trait in common, they are all headed somewhere, and they summon us to go along with them, and we feel, not only with the brain, but with the whole of our being, that they have something definite in mind, like the ghost of Hamlet's father, who did not come to disturb the imagination for nothing. According to their calibre, they have immediate aims—the abolition of serfdom, the liberation of their land, politics, beauty, or simply vodka, like Denis Davydov; others have more distant goals to seek—God, the life beyond the grave, the happiness of humanity, and so on. The best of them are realists and paint life as it is; but since their every line is saturated with consciousness of purpose, as if steeped in a juice, you feel, in addition to life as it is, life as it should be, and you are captivated. But we? We! We paint life as it is, but beyond that—nothing. Flog us—we can do no more. We have neither immediate nor distant goals, and our souls are soft and empty. We have no politics; we don't believe in any revolution; we have no God; ghosts do not frighten us; and, for myself, I fear neither death nor blindness. He who wants nothing, hopes for nothing, and fears nothing, cannot be an artist . . . You and Grigorovich think that I am clever. Well, I am clever

> enough at least not to conceal my illness from myself, nor to lie to myself, nor to cover up my nakedness with the rags of others, such as the ideas of the Sixties and so on. I won't throw myself down a flight of stairs like Garshin; but neither will I flatter myself with hopes of a better future. I am not to blame for my disease, and it is not for me to cure myself; for this disease, I must assume, has good purposes that are hidden from us, and is not visited upon us in vain.[11]

The *Island of Sakhalin* began to appear in monthly installments in *Russian Thought* at the end of 1893, but the censor held up its publication in book form for two years. The book, when finally published, was widely read; but its reception left something to be desired. It turned out to be a sober sociological work of 300 pages, more or less scientific in tone, and far from the impassioned document which Chekhov's public expected from his pen. Chekhov was proud of the book. In January 1894 he wrote Suvorin: "I am glad this rough convict's coat is hanging in my literary wardrobe. Let it hang there." [12] Meanwhile he had excellent stories in hand—*The Black Monk, Rothschild's Fiddle*—and besides, he had other things to occupy his mind, many clients and pensioners, and he was often ill.

It was now no longer possible to hide the nature of his illness, not even from himself. He had frequent premonitions of death, and he began to know a little what it is to be afraid.[13] His brother Nikolai had died of tuberculosis in 1889. He felt that his own life was slipping through his fingers, and that he had to make haste if he was to experience the fullness of it. He grew restive at Melikhovo. In March 1894 he went to Yalta to get rid of his "bronchitis." When he returned, he built himself a lodge behind his cherry orchard. It was meant to be a guest house; but his guests were everywhere, and in time the guest house became his refuge.

In these years it was observable that little by little his stories were taking on a more sombre tone. He was also becoming increasingly critical. He felt nothing but contempt for those writers who lived, like Sienkiewicz, by flattering the taste of the bourgeois: "The bourgeoisie admire the so-called 'positive' types, and novels with happy endings, which calm their minds so that they can accumulate capital, maintain their innocence, behave like animals, and be happy all at the same time." [14] He himself felt waspish. He had never avoided the seamy side of life, but the prankish humor which enlivened his early tales was giving way to irony. The joke was no longer entirely funny; often it struck too deep for comfort. He had begun as a humorist. He was fast becoming a social critic.

In the winter of 1894 he finished *Three Years*, his last attempt to write a novel. It was, in fact, a story of some length; but, as always, he was unable to develop it along novelistic lines. He had not the knack of contriving a conventional pattern, the sort of *intreccio* which was considered suitable for a prolonged narrative. *Three Years* is substantially a chronicle of merchant life in Moscow. Apart from the detail, the attention is concentrated on the relations of the hero, Laptev, a relatively passive man, and his virile friend Yartsev, who takes from him first his mistress, and then, it is intimated, his wife. What emerges as unforgettable is a series of portraits, and particularly the carefully detailed likeness of Laptev, the delicate heir of a race of strong, hard men, the sort of people in whom Ostrovsky specialized.

Three Years is not resolved, and has no proper ending. It is an excellent example of the story of "life as it is." On the other hand, *Anna on the Neck*, which Chekhov published in October of 1895, is perfectly, if somewhat unnecessarily, contrived, quite in the style of Maupassant, a cold and unfriendly tale which describes the rapid dehumanization of a beautiful girl who makes her way all too quickly in the bureaucratic society of the capital. Chekhov's best work of the year was *The Murder*. This story, were its taste not so bitter, might well be ascribed to Tolstoy. It describes the long circuitous path by which the Christian fanatic Yakov Ivanich comes through suffering at last to a revelation of truth. The story is superb, and especially interesting because of the narrator's style, a technique, relatively new with Chekhov, which for the first time presages his manner in the period of his greatest activity as a dramatist.

From the beginning almost to the end, the story of *The Murder* is related without the slightest expression, calmly, without sympathy or stress. The action itself is seldom directly described. Even the blow on the head which kills Yakov's brother is left to the imagination. In general, the narrator does little more than to hint at the action, though he dwells at length on its consequences. What is seemingly unimportant is described in detail. The important events are alluded to in passing. The story is a miracle of understatement. Until the end there is no trace of oratory. It is completely unemphatic.

The Murder is a long story, but it is resolved and pointed very quickly, as if by an afterthought, in the penal colony at Sakhalin on a bitter morning in the fall. A convict gang is sent out to the beach to load coals. It is dark and about to storm:

> Shivering with the autumn cold and the damp sea mist, wrapped up in his short, torn coat, Yakov Ivanich looked intently without blinking in the direction in which lay his home. Now that he was living in prison along with men brought here from the ends of the earth—Russians, Ukrainians, Tatars, Georgians, Chinese, Gypsies, Jews—listening to their talk and watching their sufferings, he had begun to turn once more to God, and it seemed to him at last that he had found the true faith for which all his family, from his grandmother Avdotya down, had so mightily thirsted, and had sought so long, and had not found. He had it all now, and he understood where God was, and how He was to be served, and the only

> thing he could not understand was why men's destinies were so diverse, why this simple faith which some men receive from God for nothing along with their lives, had cost him such a price that his arms and legs trembled like a drunkard's because of all the horror and agony which, so far as he could see, he must endure without surcease until the day of his death. He stared with straining eyes into the darkness, and it seemed to him that through a thousand miles of mist he could see his home, and his native province, his district, Progonaya, and all the darkness, the savagery, the heartlessness, and the dull, sour, animal indifference of those he had left there. His eyes dimmed with tears, but he continued to stare into the distance where the pale lights of the steamer gleamed faintly, his heart aching, and he longed to live, to go home, and tell them there of his new found faith, and to save from ruin if only one man; to live without suffering, if only one day.[15]

The technique of *The Murder* was not entirely new with Chekhov, though this story is rather unlike his other tales. Its manner closely recalls, on the other hand, the dramatic style which we remark for the first time in *Uncle Vanya*. The seeming simplicity of the narrative; the evident lack of plot and contrivance; the sharpening of the focus at the expense of the gross action, with the consequent brilliance of detail; the savagery of the climax, its immediate dissipation, and complete lack of emphasis; the impassive face of the narrator; and, finally, the irony of the conclusion—these are the elements of the peculiarly Chekhovian style which was now revealing itself almost in spite of the author, and which would firmly shape his destiny as a playwright.

For some time now Chekhov had been thinking of writing a play. Suvorin had recently added a theatre to his varied enterprises in Petersburg, and in response to his request for a play, in the spring of 1895, Chekhov said he might write him a comedy in the autumn. If he did, he wrote, it would be something strange.[16] In October he wrote: "Just imagine, I am writing a play, which I will probably not finish before the end of November. I am writing it with pleasure, though I sin terribly against the conventions of the stage. It is a comedy with three female parts, six male, a landscape (a view of a lake), much talk of literature, little action, and five *poods* of love." [17] He called the play *Chaika—The Sea Gull.*

A month later, he wrote Suvorin that it was finished: "I began it *forte* and finished it *pianissimo*—against all the rules of dramatic art. It has come out a novel. I am more dissatisfied than pleased with it and, having read through my newborn play, I am once again convinced that I am by no means a playwright. The acts are very short; there are four of them. Although it is still only the skeleton of a play, and will be changed a million times before next season, I've ordered two copies to be typewritten on a Remington (the machine writes two copies at once), and I'll send you one. Only don't let anyone else read it." [18]

The play he described in this letter corresponds only vaguely with the play that presently emerged from the Remington. The final version of *The Sea Gull* does not begin *forte* nor does it end *pianissimo;* quite the contrary, it begins softly, and ends—like all the plays which Chekhov had so far produced—with a pistol shot. The view of the lake is important. It imparts a curious fairy-tale quality to the action, which is in itself not especially romantic, and would be much less so if the lake were not there. In spite of Chekhov's disparaging remarks, *The Sea Gull* turned out to be a very workmanlike job, believable, coherent, beautifully characterized, and in every sense dramatic. For Chekhov it represented an enormous advance in his command of the medium. It was the first fine play he had written, and indeed it was one of the finest of his time. He insisted on calling this play a comedy.

The first draft of *The Sea Gull* did not please anyone.

Chekhov read it to several groups of friends, and encountered nothing but disapproval. The professionals objected, as always, that the play did not provide the theatrical "points" which they regarded as indispensable to a successful production. Moreover, it was said, the meaning was not clear. The characters were confusing; it was evident also that the play dealt closely, even indiscreetly, with well-known people and events. Chekhov was far from happy with this unfavorable reaction. He was not destined to be a playwright, he wrote bitterly—"When I write a play I feel uneasy, as if someone were peering over my shoulder." [19] And a few days later he added: "My play has been rejected without even being seen." [20]

In truth, *The Sea Gull* dealt quite transparently with matters that could hardly escape recognition in Moscow. The action was a complex tissue of interlaced stories, but the principal story involved the rivalry of two writers, one of them a young beginner, the other a successful professional, for the love of a stage-struck girl. The girl, infatuated with the older man, runs off with him, bears his child, which dies, and is eventually abandoned by him. The young man commits suicide. In this sequence it was impossible not to recognize the unhappy affair of Chekhov's friend Potapenko and the beautiful Lidiya Mizinova, Chekhov's flame of many years.

Chekhov was very fond of women. The list of his loves is long. What these loves amounted to, it is impossible to say. They seem at the most to have been prolonged flirtations. Chekhov was careful to avoid a serious involvement whenever anything of the sort threatened to disturb his peace. Until his very last years he staunchly resisted every temptation to marry. He liked women, but he could not abide any sort of domestic intimacy. His sister Masha devoted her life to looking after him. She kept his house, and this was the only domestic arrangement in which, apparently, he was comfortable for very long. In his thirties he had written Suvorin jokingly from Melikhovo that he would marry only on condition that his wife live separately in Moscow, where he could visit her from time to time: "I don't intend to get married. I should like to be a little, bald old man sitting at a big table in a fine study." [21] Indeed, when at last he made up his mind to marry, he chose the young actress Olga Knipper, whose career in Moscow effectively kept her away from him the greater part of the time. Meanwhile, like Shaw, he preferred to make love by mail. On paper he made a charming lover, witty, dashing, imaginative, and even importunate. It was when the word was made flesh that he became anxious.

The publication in 1947 of a posthumous memoir entitled *A. P. Chekhov in My Life* by the novelist Lidiya Avilova revealed what purported to be a long sentimental episode in Chekhov's life during the 1890's. The validity of this memoir has not been universally accepted, and it is possible that much, if not all of it, was the product of Avilova's imagination.[22] On the other hand, Chekhov's attachment to Lidiya Mizinova, whom he called Lika, is more than amply documented. Lika is said to have been a beautiful girl; her photographs indicate that she must have been handsome even by present standards. She was ten years younger than Chekhov, a close friend of the family, and a frequent visitor at his house. In addition she had a lovely voice, and dreamed of a career in the opera. Chekhov made love to her, in joking fashion, over a period of years, pretending fierce jealousy and undying passion, and courted her fiercely in letters signed with transparently assumed names—"I love you passionately, like a tiger, and offer you my hand!" [23]

The poor girl did not know whether to believe him or not. Her devotion was plain, but Chekhov evidently had no idea of marrying her; he played her, like the expert fisherman he was, until she was exhausted. In March 1892 he wrote her in a more serious vein: "Alas! I am already an aged youth, my love is not the sun, and it creates spring neither for me nor for the bird I love! Lika, it is not you I love so ardently.

I love in you my past sufferings, and my lost youth."[24] She wrote him desperately in 1893 to let her alone: "My strongest wish is to cure myself of the hopeless condition in which I find myself . . ."

In the autumn of 1893 she met the writer Potapenko, Chekhov's close friend, during a visit at Melikhovo. He was married and had two children. Lika attracted him. He courted her passionately. In October of that year she wrote Chekhov in something like panic that she must know if she was going to see him soon. Winter was approaching: ". . . only two or three months remain in which I can see you, and after that, perhaps never."[25] Chekhov apparently did not choose to see her. The following spring she met Potapenko in Paris. She was there ostensibly to pursue her vocal studies. By September Lika was with child in Switzerland, alone, and in despair. She wrote Chekhov, who was vacationing in Nice: "What was there for me to do, Daddy? You always managed to escape, you always pushed me on to someone else . . ." A few days later, she wrote, asking him to come to her: ". . . how these six months have overturned my whole life! However, I don't think you will wish to cast a stone at me. It seems to me you were always indifferent to people, their inadequacies, and their weaknesses."[26]

Chekhov did not act gallantly in this matter. He wrote his sister Masha that he was tired of traveling, and that Potapenko was a scoundrel. At the same time he wrote Lika a cold letter, saying that he could not visit her in Switzerland since he was with Suvorin, who wished to go to Paris. Lika had her baby by herself. Shortly after her return to Russia, it died, and Potapenko cannily moved to Petersburg with his family. When Chekhov saw him next in Moscow in December of that year, he had no difficulty in resuming their relations. His friendship with Lika languished; but after a time it too was resumed, though on a less feverish plane. Soon it was all as if nothing had happened.

But *The Sea Gull* shows clearly enough what happened. It throws some light also on the nature of Chekhov's art. Chekhov never revealed himself so plainly in anything else he wrote. *The Sea Gull* is in the nature of an expiatory offering, a sacrifice, and makes amends for what Chekhov must have felt to have been his sin toward Lika. Considering his long and intimate relationship with the girl, it is hardly conceivable that he felt nothing in the circumstances, neither pain, nor jealousy, nor regret; and her reproach evidently irked him, for he wrote to her in Switzerland in what appears to be the bitterness of his heart, "You ought not to have written of my indifference to people." [27] But his pain, if he felt any, was quickly dissipated. He was an artist, after all, and his feelings were soon transformed into something useful and literary. The reality was converted into fantasy; the people involved, himself included, became characters; and the entire affair, painful and squalid as it was, became a work of art, something in which one could take pride and pleasure.

"I've never liked myself," Trigorin says in *The Sea Gull.* "I don't like what I write. And, worst of all, I live in a kind of daze, and I often don't even understand what I'm writing . . ." [28] For the writer, Trigorin intimates, the process of creation is not only a way of life, it is a substitute for living. For such people, the line that divides fantasy from reality is never sharp. Everything is grist for the literary mill: "I take every word, every sentence I speak, and also every word you say, and stuff them at once into my literary warehouse—who knows? they may come in handy some day . . . I have no rest from myself. I feel as though I am devouring my whole life, and that for the sake of the honey I make for others, I pluck my finest flowers, tear them to shreds, and trample their roots." There is scarcely much doubt that here Trigorin is voicing Chekhov's inmost thoughts on the disadvantages of the writer's profession. It is true that in *The Sea Gull* Trigorin plays the role of the heartless Lothario and must therefore be identified, at least in this respect, with the seductive Potapenko. But it would be overly simple to identify Trigorin completely with Potapenko, and Chekhov with young Treplev. The creative process is a complex algebra; fantasy makes use of more abstruse spiritual equations than these identifications suggest.

Trigorin's speech, of course, recalls Flaubert's famous phrase, "*Nous sommes fait pour le dire et non pour l'avoir.*" Like Flaubert, Trigorin has found it necessary to nourish his art at the cost of his life, and, like Flaubert, he regrets the sacrifice. His soul is empty. In the play, he complains of its emptiness as bitterly as Chekhov does in his letters, and in much the same terms. The design of the play, certainly, inclines us to identify Chekhov with Treplev: but it is the young lover who is punished in *The Sea Gull*, and not the middle-aged seducer. Trigorin, having confessed his wretchedness, goes off whistling. He feels no more responsibility with regard to Nina than Chekhov felt, apparently, for Lika. But Treplev shoots himself. Obviously Chekhov is not Treplev; neither is he Trigorin: he is both, and also he is neither. These creatures of his fancy were framed to serve the writer's inner needs in a situation that touched him closely; therefore, in his imagination he played both the lover and the seducer, identifying now with the one, now with the other. It is the depth of his insight that truly measures the closeness of the identification in each case. As Trigorin, he is heartless, a living machine. As Treplev, he is bereft, and he needs to die.

Many odds and ends of experience were woven into *The Sea Gull*, among them, an incident involving the painter Levitan, one of Chekhov's closest friends. During a visit to Melikhovo in April 1892, Levitan took it into his head one day to go hunting, although he was no hunter, and he persuaded Chekhov to come with him. In the course of their walk the painter winged a woodcock. Chekhov picked up the bird. "It had a long beak, large dark eyes, and fine plumage. It was still alive, and looked at us with astonishment." The hunters were embarrassed, and Levitan, in considerable distress, begged Chekhov to finish it off. "I had to kill it for him," Chekhov wrote. "There was one beautiful creature of love less in the world, and two fools went home, and sat down to dinner . . ." [29]

Apart from the symbol of wanton destruction which this incident suggested, there is nothing in this oft repeated story that directly illuminates the play which Chekhov wrote three years later. In July 1895, however, there occurred an incident involving Levitan which may have had a more direct bearing on the design that was forming in Chekhov's mind. A lady called Turchaninova wrote Chekhov that Levitan had attempted suicide while staying at her house in the lake district of Novgorod, and she begged him to come at once to help the man out of his depression. Chekhov hurried to his friend's side. He found that Levitan had in fact shot himself, but had come off with only a slight scalp wound, and he spent five days cheering him up.

Other stories having to do with dead or dying birds in variously allusive situations have been circulated since the play appeared, but it seems likely that these anecdotes were inspired by the play itself, rather than by any actual event. What is certain is that the sea gull of the play belongs to that prolific genus of symbolic water-fowl of which the prototype is in *The Wild Duck* (1884). Ibsen's bird is sufficiently compendious as a symbol to include almost everyone and everything in *The Wild Duck*. So too Chekhov's sea gull symbolizes a good deal more than the wounded Nina or the wounded Treplev. It seems evident that as a metaphor it was intended to suggest the entire poetic content of the play.

The second draft of *The Sea Gull* was ready by the beginning of April 1896. Chekhov sent a copy at once to Potapenko. Potapenko evidently was not embarrassed by any possible resemblance between himself and Trigorin. Lika, on the other hand, when first she saw the play, exclaimed at once that it was her story that Chekhov had dramatized. The censor passed the play with little difficulty, and Chekhov was invited to stage it on October 17th at the Alexandrinsky Theatre in Petersburg for the benefit night of the comedienne Levkeyeva. The report of the Theatre and Literary Committee which approved the play for performance was not shown to Chekhov. Had he seen it, it might have given him pause. It was far from flattering.

Early in October, Chekhov began sitting hopefully through the rehearsals at the Alexandrinsky. He soon realized that he had cause for uneasiness. In spite of his frequent admonitions, the actors insisted on declaiming their parts as if they were acting a tragedy. Five days before the opening, the great Savina decided that the role of Nina did not suit her, and she resigned it to Vera Kommissarzhevskaya, at that time a novice. Chekhov began to feel real anxiety. For all his coaching, the actors gave no sign that they understood what was required of them. They tolerated no diminution of the pompous theatricality that was traditional on the Petersburg stage. Chekhov did his best to explain that his characters were simple people who must be played quietly and naturally as if they were human beings. The actors made nothing of this. The play bored them. It gave them no points to make, no grand entrances, no effective exits, no scenes of high climax. They felt they had nothing to do in the play, and they walked through their parts with the dignity of professionals who were bound to play whatever rubbish the administration assigned them, but who could not be forced to enjoy it.

The play was billed as a comedy. The actors could see nothing funny in it, and were at their wits' end for ways to make people laugh. They felt a momentary flush of excitement at the seventh rehearsal, when Kommissarzhevskaya's talent suddenly came to light, but it proved to be no more than a flash in the pan, and the company lapsed once more into its customary dejection. Chekhov's "bronchitis" suddenly took a turn for the worse. He began to cough up blood.

The Sea Gull opened before a full house. The audience had come to see the buxom Levkeyeva play one of her customary funny parts. She had cannily chosen a double bill for her benefit, first Chekhov's play, then a three-act comedy of traditional cut. When the curtain rose, the audience was puzzled, then it became impatient; soon it began to behave badly. A sharp laugh interrupted Nina's monologue in Treplev's play. A growing hum of conversation throughout the house drowned out the actor's voices. The audience had ceased to listen. The actors were terrified. The first act ended among boos and whistles and the stamping of feet. It was a disaster.

Chekhov took refuge in Levkeyeva's dressing room. When the play was mercifully over, he slunk out of the theatre alone, with his coat collar up to hide his face; but he did not altogether escape detection. For four hours he walked the streets. Meanwhile, his sister and his friends grew anxious, and sent emissaries out to find him. At last, at two in the morning, he turned up at the Suvorin's where he was staying, and went directly to bed. "If I live to be seven hundred," he told Suvorin, "I'll not give another play to the theatre. In this field I am a failure." Potapenko saw him off at the station the next morning. In order to avoid meeting Lika, who was there, Potapenko had deliberately avoided going to the theatre. A newsboy offered a paper. Chekhov waved him off brusquely. "I can't read," he said.

On the second night, the play was more thoughtfully received. But the press was almost unanimously vicious. Except for Suvorin and Avilova, none of the critics had a good word to say for *The Sea Gull*. After the third performance, which came off even better, Potapenko wired his congratulations, and wrote an enthusiastic review. It was too late. The damage was done.

The Sea Gull labored through five performances, then it closed. When Tolstoy read it, after its publication in the December issue of *Russian Thought*, he added his venerable voice to the chorus of critical opinion: "It is absolutely worthless. It reads like a play by Ibsen."

The Sea Gull does not, in fact, read like a play by Ibsen; but many thought it did. In its original report, the Theatre and Literary Committee had referred with distaste to "its symbolism or, more correctly, its Ibsenism . . . running through the whole play like a red thread." Ibsen, considered a nihilist, immoralist, and revolutionist, was hardly in favor in official literary circles at this time; moreover, in Russia he was generally thought to be ineffectual as a dramatist and incomprehensible as a thinker. Chekhov himself was not altogether consistent in his attitude toward him. He admired him, but he had often disparaged him. After seeing the Moscow Art Theatre's production of *Hedda Gabler* in April 1900, he remarked to Stanislavsky, perhaps in surprise, "See here, Ibsen is really not a dramatist at all!" [30] But by November 1903, evidently, his views on what made a dramatist had altered to some extent, and he wrote Vishnevsky at the Moscow Art begging him to set aside a seat for him for *Pillars of Society:* "I want to have a look at this amazing Norwegian play, and will even pay for the privilege. Ibsen is my favorite author, you know." [31]

As a matter of fact, Chekhov's debt to Ibsen was incalculable. The use of a pervasive symbol for the purpose of synthesizing the poetic content of a dramatic action was Ibsen's invention. With such plays as *Ghosts, The Wild Duck,* and *The Master Builder* Ibsen had demonstrated a type of lyric drama which was new to his time, and which was hardly understood even after Maeterlinck explained it in *Le Tragique quotidien.* Ibsen's special province was precisely that poetry of "life as it is" in which Chekhov also specialized, the poetry of ordinary happenings and ordinary people. And Ibsen was also an innovator in the use of a comic style for the development of a tragic theme, the technique which Chekhov tried all his life to perfect, and with which he caused as much confusion among his admirers as had Ibsen.

In the circumstances, one can only applaud the Theatre and Literary Committee's astuteness. It is only in Ibsenist terms that *The Sea Gull* can be understood as a comedy. *The Wild Duck* is certainly a comedy in spite of the fact that Hedvig kills herself in it. The joke is less apparent in *The Sea Gull.* It gives us less occasion for laughter, and even less reason for tears. Compared with *The Wild Duck,* it is a cold play. Its poignancy is not so much inherent in the action as in the poetic mood which the action evokes. Chekhov's theme is more uncertain, his meaning less clear; the lyrical mood is more evident; and there is much that strikes one as original and new—yet without Ibsen, Chekhov could hardly have written *The Sea Gull.*

Ibsen had never tried for the kind of objectivity which was Chekhov's professed goal as a writer. He dealt realistically with reality, but he did not consider himself a naturalist, and had no particular liking for the school of Zola. On the contrary, he thought of his plays as poems, and aimed chiefly at a poetic effect. But Ibsen feared the sentimental and the theatrical even more than Chekhov. He defended himself against melodrama by means of caricature, against sentimentality by means of ridicule, against oratory by emphasizing the absurd. These were precisely Chekhov's methods. Unlike Chekhov, however, Ibsen was an accomplished craftsman in the theatre. In adopting the realistic method, he taught himself, above all, to be thrifty. As a result, his plays, after *A Doll's House,* have a classic austerity and enormous reserves of energy, and, more than anyone else in his time, he demonstrated the possibility of controlling a vast amount of plot in a severely restricted action.

For Chekhov, Ibsen was inescapable. There was no other way, at the time, to avoid the empty ingenuity of the well-made play, or the inevitable tendency of the Russian stage to manufacture melodrama, than to follow the line which Ibsen had developed after the time of *Peer Gynt*. *The Sea Gull* was certainly Ibsenist, as the Theatre Committee had noted. It blended the pathetic with the comic in the manner of Ibsen; it kept the external action off the stage; it emphasized the characterization and understated the narrative. But the retrospective method which Ibsen had perfected demanded a different type of ingenuity than Chekhov had at his command in these years. The technique of *Rosmersholm*, in which an exposition is dramatized so that the past substantially materializes before one's eyes, was quite beyond Chekhov's capacity as a dramatist, and he very wisely did not attempt anything extensive along such lines. His manner was, in any case, much more spontaneous, simpler, and more direct than that of the great Norwegian.

To Chekhov, who could never quite manage a novel, Ibsen's method seemed novelistic; above all, it was too closely controlled for his taste. Besides, Chekhov had by no means escaped the current notions in the Russian theatre as to what was essential to a dramatic composition. In Ibsen, at his best, there were no "points," no theatrical effects, no heavy climaxes. He was deficient in the very things for the lack of which Chekhov had been criticized. It was natural, therefore, for Chekhov to consider Ibsen undramatic. Hauptmann, with his broader and more showy effects, and his wealth of detail, seemed to him much more to the purpose. Nevertheless, in *The Sea Gull*, the main action, the principal anecdote, is neither played nor reconstructed on the stage; it is reported in the baldest possible manner. Nothing less "dramatic" can be imagined, but this technique is not Ibsenian. While Ibsen followed the classical practice of beginning the play at the end of the story, Chekhov wrote his play on the margin of the narrative.

The plot of *The Sea Gull* is developed in the *entr'actes.* What is shown on the stage is the result, the effect upon the characters, of events which are related and alluded to, but not seen. What is actually staged is a secondary action, based upon and motivated by the primary material, but still entirely distinct from it, and by no means inevitable as its consequence. The plot, therefore, is an invisible skeleton, an indispensable armature which sustains and justifies, but is not in itself the action of the play. The result is an obliquity of construction which readily recalls the technique of Ibsen, without at all reflecting it.

Obviously, Chekhov had no idea of aping Ibsen. *The Sea Gull* is Chekhovian in a more ample sense than it is Ibsenian. The dialogue, absent-minded and inconsequential as it seems to be, parallels and reinforces the "indirect" technical approach of the author in a highly original fashion, and, up to a point, it is both ingenious and informative. In the new technique which Chekhov was developing, the thoughts and feelings of the characters are not directly adduced, as they are in *Ivanov* and *The Wood Demon.* They are deducible from what is said and done, but they are not completely amenable to deduction, so that the characters remain in some degree enigmatic. Treplev is still in some respects self-explanatory, like Ivanov. He remains a transitional figure. But Dr. Dorn, who anticipates and presages Chebutykin in *The Three Sisters,* keeps his counsel in true Chekhovian style.

Dorn is something of a *raisonneur,* but his commentary on the action is a series of seemingly inconsequential phrases, tags of poetry, snatches of song, grunts, and irrelevancies. He speaks articulately chiefly to Treplev. Yet Dorn is almost completely comprehensible. In spite of his indirection, he makes his points clearly. This technique was not new. Akim in Tolstoy's *The Power of Darkness* (1886) is even less articulate than Dorn. It is, nevertheless, he who interprets the action most clearly; and this trick of putting the truth of the play in the mouth of the least expressive character is extraordinarily effective. But in Chekhov's later plays, the technique of indirection went much beyond ingenuity. It became a test of intuition, and this, and the essential reticence of Chekhov's characters, made for a type of realism which so far had not been seen on the stage. In *The Three Sisters* all the characters are voluble, but it is only when the accumulated pressure of restrained emotion has become unbearable that the characters say what they really think. This rarely happens more than once with each of the principals; and in each case the speech has an explosive force which precisely measures the intensity of the emotion that is behind it.

The extraordinary vividness of *The Sea Gull* stems from the realism of the characterization, and this in turn depends on the fact that the play involves very ordinary situations in which nobody has any reason to act in a theatrical manner. Chekhov puts on the stage that part of life which we ordinarily see off the stage; but he shows it as an artist sees it. His plays exemplify to perfection that tendency toward the art of the unrelated which we associate with the second generation of impressionist painters. In life we see people; we do not see stories, and we do not hear thoughts. In the world, what is ordinarily played before our eyes is not a story, but a scene. The scenes that we see are in relation to other scenes, which in sequence perhaps suggest stories. These sequences are known only to those who have lived through them. What the ordinary spectator sees is merely people in various states of calm or excitement, quarreling, eating, yawning, weeping, laughing, chatting, sometimes one after the other, and sometimes all at once. The story, if there is a story, must be deduced from their expressions, their words, and their actions. It resides within the characters, and motivates their behavior;

but it is certainly not visible and, perhaps also, it is not there. Life tells us no stories. Every story is a surmise, a fantasy. In reality the art of observation depends upon the receptivity of the observer, his sensitivity to suggestion and implication, his powers of deduction and of intuition, above all, to his imagination. Accordingly, the effect that Chekhov attempted to re-create in the theatre was a state of heightened awareness on the part of the audience, an enhanced receptivity to impressions and intimations carefully arranged so as to elicit a reaction which is sometimes indicated, but seldom completely controlled. *The Sea Gull,* like most of Chekhov's plays, fairly bristles with suggestions; but there is no formulation, no definition, and therefore, in a sense, no story, or, at least, no clearly defined anecdote. In his plays, as in his tales, Chekhov never assumes the role of an omniscient being, creating and relating; nor is he ever a partisan, or a power sitting in judgment. He is modest, an observer with quiet eyes, listening calmly at the gates of the soul. This is the role also which, in Chekhov's theatre, is reserved to the spectator.

The Sea Gull is mainly about theatre people. Treplev's father began as a shopkeeper in Kiev, but ended as a well-known actor. Treplev's mother is an actress, a woman of forty-three who passes for thirty-five. The existence of a twenty-five-year old son is something of an embarrassment to her, therefore she keeps him hidden away discreetly in the country. Arkadina has her problems. She is striving with might and main to preserve her youth, her self-respect, her glamor, and, above all, her lover Trigorin. She stands close to the brink of the abyss toward which time drives all pretty women and, because she is greatly frightened, she is miserly and mean, for money is her only bulwark in a world that is not courteous to aged beauties. Since, in such a world, a grown-up son is a reproach and a danger, she is inclined to treat Treplev as if he were still a child, and his literary pretensions seem ridiculous to her, the more so as, like many young writers, he reacts violently against the established conventions.

As in most of Chekhov's later plays, the spectator's attention is not directed forcibly to any special point in the action. The play has not a rigid line. It concerns, nevertheless, mainly Treplev and Trigorin, and they are contrasted with respect to Arkadina and also Nina. Trigorin is younger than his mistress. He is a famous writer whose success has not brought him happiness. He accuses himself of spinelessness, has grave doubts as to the authenticity of his vocation, and occasionally wonders about the magnitude of his talent. For him, writing is a compulsion. He has no special aim in literature. It is mainly a means of support, and he much prefers to go fishing. His fame, he knows, will in any case be brief. When he is dead he will be thought of as a good writer, but not as good as Turgenev. Moreover, he is very conscious that he is hashing up his life in order to make literature, and that for him all that exists is without meaning save as a subject for fiction. The careful description of Trigorin thus comes quite close to Chekhov's idea of himself in his more depressed moments. We have no difficulty in piecing together Trigorin out of Chekhov's personal correspondence.

For this tortured professional, Arkadina serves the necessary function of an opiate. She is not only his mistress, she is the reassuring mother who looks after him in his hours of distress. But Trigorin has never loved as a man loves, and when Nina offers him an opportunity to try he accepts it eagerly. In fact, Nina gives herself completely and for always, but she is not at all suited to Trigorin's needs or to his possibilities. In love, she plays the young girl's part. She is the daughter, and what she requires is a lover who will play the father. This is the last thing Trigorin desires to be. He needs a woman who will support the weight of his spirit, and not at all an added burden upon it. Consequently, Nina soon ceases to exist for him, and he abandons her as naturally as one puts aside a glass of water when one's thirst is quenched. Then he goes back to Arkadina, whom he really needs, and for whose happiness he is necessary.

These psychic adjustments necessarily involve him unpleasantly with Treplev who, at the age of twenty-five, is already conscious of failure. Treplev is a young man of deep feeling. He is passionately attached to his beautiful mother, and he ardently desires to impress her as a man. He is deeply in love with Nina. But he serves no purpose in either of their lives, and is therefore of no particular interest to them or, in fact, to anyone who matters to him. For Trigorin, Treplev hardly exists—he is too much like himself to serve as the subject of a story. But Trigorin is Treplev's *bête-noire*. Casually, without thinking, and without prizing it in the least, Trigorin has appropriated everything that is most precious to Treplev—first, his mother, then Nina, finally that artistic success in which Treplev sees his only reason for living. The things that mean everything to Treplev mean nothing to Trigorin. The treasures that so persistently elude Treplev fall readily into Trigorin's hand, and he throws them away as carelessly as he acquires them. For Treplev, Trigorin drains life of its meaning. Yet, for all his jealousy, he cannot hate him. In the young man's eyes, Trigorin is a writing-machine which occasionally reveals human traits, but with which it is impossible for him to communicate on a human level.

Nina returns at the end of the play. She is somewhat troubled in mind, but strangely mature, and deeply interested in her profession. In spite of everything, she still adores Trigorin. Treplev realizes that, so far as she is concerned, he has no hope, and he feels a sudden and overwhelming sense of loss. At this moment his feeling of injustice is so deep, his sense of inadequacy so devastating, his fury so great, that he would destroy the world if he could. He does what he can. He destroys himself.

The situation is not precisely analogous to that of Hedda Gabler in Ibsen's play, but the similarities are striking. Like Treplev, Hedda is frustrated in the deepest core of her being. She too is ambitious, and life gives her no scope to express her spirit, neither in creation nor destruction. She can assert herself only in death. Treplev's death has perhaps less point than hers; he has not her wit. Obviously his death, like hers, is a gesture of protest. Yet it is so pointless a gesture, so ill-directed and ill-considered, that it can hardly affect anything. His death is simply a waste, the crowning stupidity of the sequence of absurdities which has been his life.

For Chekhov the idea that life is an absurdity was certainly not new, but he had never before stated it quite so clearly. Henceforth it was to play an increasingly important role in his thinking. In *The Sea Gull*, Treplev's death makes no sense whatever. It is absurd to suppose that he cannot live without Nina: he is an artist. He is not exhausted, like Ivanov, nor a hollow shell like Voynitsky. He is young, talented, and energetic, a youth with endless possibilities. Yet nobody needs him or understands him. He is entirely *de trop*. It is quite another aspect of the superfluous man than that presented by Rudin or Ivanov. It is not his fault that he is *de trop* in this world. It is the fault of the world.

It is true that Treplev, as he is depicted, has not the indispensable virtue of the artist, the capacity to endure rejection. His soul is fragile. Nina knows how important it is to have patience:

> I know now, Kostya, that what matters most for us, whether we are writers or actors, is not fame, or glory, or any of the things of which I used to dream. What matters most is the ability to endure, the ability to bear your cross with faith. I have faith now. My calling makes it possible for me to bear my suffering. I am not afraid of life.[32]

Treplev cannot say as much. He has neither faith nor calling. He has only a hopeless love, and he is afraid of life. He is still floating about, as he says, in a maze of dreams, without knowing what he is to do, and his death is a matter of importance to nobody, save Masha, who adores him in vain. His passage from this world is announced very quietly at the end of the play. It hardly interrupts the game of tombola.

This climax is completely non-theatrical. It is followed by a very quiet curtain. What is required here of the audience is neither tears, nor excitement, nor indignation—only its interest, and a contemplative silence. It is of no consequence to Chekhov that Arkadina has behaved badly, or that Trigorin has acted like a scoundrel. What is important for the success of the play is that for a moment we should catch a glimpse of these souls and understand their torment.

There is no particular need to sympathize, though we are free to do so. Chekhov's attitude is primarily objective and intellectual. His characters have a certain depth, which he illumines. The analysis, if there is to be any, is left to us. The dramatic experience in this sort of play is therefore based upon deductions and intuitions which the more heroic forms of drama exclude. It is to a certain extent an intellectual matter. Yet, beyond the analytical experience, the feeling of comprehension, and the compassion which flows from comprehension, there is an intimation of non-intellectual character in which resides the poetic value of the play, and it is in this somewhat rarified lyrical atmosphere that the most interesting part of the action takes place.

The design of *The Sea Gull* results from the struggle between the older and younger generations, a phenomenon of biologic character. The characters are marshaled in order of seniority. Sorin is at the end of life, Trigorin and Arkadina are passing its peak. Nina and Treplev are on its threshold. The conditions of existence being what they are, the young people and their immediate elders are ranged in competition with one another. On the one hand, there are the adults, desperately self-affirmative, and ruthless in their need to hold their ground; on the other, the sensitive, proud, and eager youth battering at the door of life. This is the fundamental conflict of the play. It is, therefore, not at all out of malice, but because of the imperative urge to defend themselves, that Arkadina and Trigorin trample these young lives. They do it without meaning any harm, and almost in spite of themselves, for they are, at bottom, pleasant and kindly people. Quite in the same way, without the slightest hint of malice, Nina would destroy Arkadina's life if she could, in order to supplant her as an artist and also as a woman. Treplev would destroy Trigorin in a similar fashion. The struggle is venerable, and cosmic in its scope; perhaps it is blessed. At any rate, there is nothing extraordinary about it. It happens all about us, everywhere, every day. It needs no emphasis. But this does not detract from the scale of the spectacle, or its inherent pathos.

The magnitude of the action which this play reveals, within the limits of its microcosm, is emphasized chiefly by the metaphor of the sea gull:

> NINA: What are you writing?
>
> TRIGORIN: Just making a note ... An idea for a story suddenly popped into my head. A young girl like you has lived in a house on the shore of a lake ever since she was a little girl. She loves the lake, and is as free and happy as a bird. Then a man comes along and sees her, and, having nothing better to do, he destroys her, like this sea gull here ...[33]

Nina is not, in fact, destroyed. Her parents renounce her; her lover abandons her; she is forced to a professional level that is not far above that of a prostitute. But she is also released in this manner for self-fulfillment as an artist. These are her growing pains. In the last act she tells Treplev not once, but several times, that she is the sea gull of Trigorin's story. The speech in which she assures Treplev, seemingly in distraction, that she is the very bird that was wantonly destroyed by the passerby would be intolerably melodramatic if it had only the obvious dimension. But it cannot be taken literally. The fact is, she is alive and active. She has had an intensely disagreeable experience. At 22 she has lost her youth, her child, her innocence, and her peace of mind; but she has discovered her vocation, and the joy of work, and therefore she is saved. But Treplev has not found the joy of work, nor, in fact, any joy. He is more fragile than she, more critical of himself, less gifted. The events that have freed her have shaken him beyond repair. And the truth is that, although he feels in himself a talent that dwarfs Trigorin, Trigorin writes better than he, and is able to succeed effortlessly where Treplev fails. The contrast between his own depth of feeling, which is futile, and the spiritual emptiness of Trigorin, which works infallibly, is intolerable for Treplev. He has a sense of injustice which a greater man than he might sublimate into a work of art, but which he himself is unable to control. The poignancy of Nina's speech becomes clear. While she dramatizes herself in heroic fashion, posturing effectively as the wounded sea gull, it is really Treplev who is destroyed. Nina feels desperately sorry for herself, but she lives and works, and will perhaps one day achieve the greatness she covets. Treplev, however, cannot go on. Her speech destroys him.

Levitan's woodcock was a lovely thing, we are told—"another beautiful creature of love." It was destroyed aimlessly by a pair of fools who had no wish to eat it, and nothing better to do. So these young lives have been ruined—Nina's, perhaps, and certainly Treplev's. It is no one's fault, and a matter of little importance; all the same, it is a waste, a pity. The symbol of *The Sea Gull* becomes clear. It is neither a question here of the girl, nor of the boy, but of the beauty of all living things—a wing against the sky, a girl's smile, a boy's pride—all the joy and beauty of life which are defaced at every moment by forces so blind and so careless that they cannot be called fate. In the wastefulness of nature there is no greatness, no tragedy, nor any trace of the heroic. What happens in the play is a very little thing. It is no more tragic than the plucking of a flower.

The difference between Chekhov's comedy and classical comedy measures the force of the wedge that romanticism drove between the antique patterns and those of our time. True comedy ridiculed the foolish for the amusement of the wise, but always with the admonition *de te fabula*. In general, classic comedy was objective and aggressive. It did not invite identification. Consequently none of the characters in comedy was truly sympathetic, and the author's attitude toward his *dramatis personae* was neutral and noncommittal.

In Chekhov's comedy also, the author preserves his neutrality; but all the characters are in some way sympathetic, and we may, if we wish, identify with all of them without doing violence to the play. The result is an undercurrent of compassion which is altogether lacking in the classic genre. It is evident that in spite of all efforts to retain his composure, Chekhov was forced by his essential romanticism into some degree of sentimentality, and the tone of his comedy is correspondingly warm and humane. What is residual of the comic spirit in a play like *The Sea Gull* is the predominantly intellectual viewpoint, and the fundamental absurdity of the situation.

Apparently Chekhov considered that, so far as he was concerned, comedy was a candid reflection of the lives of real people; not of any people, but of Russians. Viewed objectively, Russians were amusing, and by temper and training Chekhov was disposed to see their comic side first. They were also—like other people—both pathetic and grotesque; and he preferred to view the grotesque element from the side of the comic rather than the pathetic. Chekhov was careful about sentimentality. It is true that his plays are full of weeping women, and many of his men weep also, but these lachrymose natures are singularly volatile, and they laugh as readily as they weep. The upshot of this sort of presentation is a species of *tragédie-vaudeville*, its bitterness tempered by the lightness of its approach.

In this attitude toward his material, Chekhov was by no means unique. Gorky, for example, and Pisemsky, adopted similar postures. In the first book of his autobiography, after describing a sordid family quarrel, Gorky adds:

> As the meal dragged comfortably through its usual Sunday-and-holiday courses, I thought, can these be the same people who, a bare half hour ago, were screaming at one another, weeping, and sobbing, and preparing to tear each other to pieces? I could not believe it. I could not believe they were not shamming, that they were not still on the verge of tears. But these screams and shouts, these tumults they inflicted on one another, they flared up so often, and died down so quickly, that in time I got used to them, and no longer suffered palpitations or heartache when they started.
>
> In time I came to understand that out of the misery and darkness of their lives, the Russian people had learned to enjoy their grief, to play with it like a child's toy: seldom were they hesitant to exhibit their sorrow.
>
> And so, through their tedious weekdays, they make a carnival of grief; a fire is an entertainment, and on a vacant face a bruise is an adornment.[34]

Acted from this viewpoint, a play like *The Sea Gull* takes on values of somewhat greater complexity than those elicited by the usual production, which treats the play either as tragedy—which it definitely is not—or as a deeply pathetic *drame* —which in part it is. It is undeniable that the play has elements of real pathos, but what is specifically Chekhovian in it is the author's awareness of the absurdity of the situation he has created, the irrationality of the characters' behavior, the extravagance of the demands they make on one another, but most of all of the hopeless inconsistency of their lives. Treplev's last words express concern that the sight of Nina as she leaves may upset his mother. Immediately after this charitable thought, he blows his brains out, without bothering his head about whether this will upset his mother or not. This is perhaps funny, an effect suitable for vaudeville. And perhaps this term serves better than another to characterize the sort of thing *The Sea Gull* was meant to be. It is a bitter vaudeville.

That it does not work precisely as Chekhov intended is our fault as much as his. In an age such as ours, it is hard to assume the Olympian attitude which is indispensable for the enjoyment of such jokes as this. At the conclusion of this comedy one was probably expected to say "Lord, what fools these mortals be!" or something of the sort; but, as the final speeches show, not even Chekhov was sufficiently Puckish to manage the necessary grin at the end. In the theatre, at least, it is not altogether simple to make a carnival of grief.

The Sea Gull is a beautiful play, but far from perfect. In writing it, Chekhov made enormous strides as a dramatist, but he had not yet mastered his medium. The plot is poorly put together. The expositions in act one and act four are clumsy. The two-year interval between the first three acts and the fourth gives the last act a spurious autonomy, as if it were an epilogue, so that it is conceivable that, with very minor changes, it might be staged by itself, as a one-act play. Moreover, the return of Nina at the end is brought about in the most mechanical fashion, and the suicide of Treplev requires the services of a commentator, unless the role is played so that, from the very beginning, the character is seen to be unbalanced. But in that case the play becomes a study in abnormal psychology, and the theme loses its point.

One could do, also, with some *poods* less of love. Beyond a certain point, the A loves B loves C relationship, though indispensable to pastoral comedy, is not much to the purpose in *The Sea Gull.* Obviously the affair Treplev-Nina-Trigorin-Arkadina is necessary to the action, but it seems superfluous to involve the estimable Dr. Dorn with the jealous Polina, the farm-manager's wife, or to have Masha break her heart over Treplev only to marry the schoolmaster Medvedenko. These are needless complexities which serve mainly to obscure the narrative, and are doubtless vestiges of the method of interlacing plot-lines which is characteristic of the French well-made play. But whereas in the tradition of Scribe the subordinate plots are integrated with the main plot which they serve, and generally help to resolve, in *The Sea Gull* these adjuncts lead nowhere and resolve nothing. This may be due to Chekhov's objection to contrivance as much as to his lack of ingenuity, but it is hardly possible to understand the necessity for concentrating so many ill-assorted lovers in so small a community. Very likely Chekhov felt at this time that for purposes of dramatic unity it was best to tie all the characters together structurally like the springs of a sofa. If so, he did not repeat his error. In his next play, the love-interest is more sensibly managed, and the action makes a much neater effect.

The failure of *The Sea Gull* had a bad effect on Chekhov. He could not take criticism well, and this defeat disturbed him more deeply than any other. He had come to hate *The Wood Demon.* He detested *The Sea Gull;* and he felt the utmost reluctance to correct the proofs of a volume of his plays which Suvorin was bringing out. In December 1896 he wrote Suvorin of his deep sense of failure, and he added: "You will tell me again that this is unreasonable and stupid, that it is all due to my conceit, pride, etc., etc. I know. But what can I do? I would gladly rid myself of this stupid feeling, but I simply can't . . . On October 17th it was I, and not my play, that failed . . . I am quiet now, and in my usual mood, but I cannot forget what happened any more than I could forget a slap in the face."[35]

Possibly in order to escape the memory of his humiliation, Chekhov plunged now into a period of feverish activity. There was already talk of war with England. Chekhov spoke much of joining the army as a medical officer. Early in 1897, he was engaged in supervising the taking of the census in his district. He was also building a new school near Melikhovo, and helping to plan a People's Palace in Moscow. All through this period he was working assiduously on his long story *Peasants*. On March 21 he came to Moscow to attend a convention of theatre workers. That evening, while dining with Suvorin at the Hermitage he suffered a severe hemorrhage of the lungs and had to be taken to a clinic.

This time he came very close to death. His recovery was slow. Weary and convalescent, he left the hospital April 10, just in time to savor the excitement which attended the publication of *Peasants* in *Russian Thought*. The enormous success of this story, which for the first time treated realistically a subject usually sentimentalized into inanity, undoubtedly did much to hasten his recovery. But *Peasants* was not merely successful; it was also the subject of controversy. For some reason, it was considered revolutionary, and its publication occasioned Chekhov a little trouble. Meanwhile the constant stream of guests at Melikhovo continued to exhaust him. He was soon bored to death with his life in the country. At the end of August he set off for Biarritz, where his friend the editor Sobolevsky had a villa.

He spent a good part of the fall and winter of 1897 at the Pension Russe in Nice. "Culture here," he wrote, "oozes out of every shop window; every willow basket, every dog has the odor of civilization." He took walks in the sun, avoided exertion, studied French, and read a good deal of French literature. But he could not work in Nice, and his health did not improve. Toward the end of October he wrote Avilova that he was doing nothing, writing nothing, and had no desire to write anything.[36] A Russian author, he remarked, needed bad weather in order to work.

In November of that year he became deeply interested in the Dreyfus affair which now, after four years, was being re-opened. He followed with intense concentration the details of Zola's trial for libel, following the publication on January 13 of the letter headed "*J'accuse*" in the newspaper *L'Aurore*. The question of Dreyfus, which now divided Western Europe, brought Chekhov close to a break with Suvorin. Chekhov continued to incline more and more definitely toward a liberal position, and it troubled him greatly that Suvorin's *New Times* should adopt the militantly anti-Semitic position of the anti-Dreyfusards. His own viewpoint, however, was not militant, and he was firmly reconciled with Suvorin when they met early the following year in Paris.

In May 1898, when the weather turned warm, Chekhov returned once again to Moscow. At Melikhovo he began to work again. That summer, he wrote three fine stories—*The Man in a Case*, *Gooseberries*, and *About Love*, all of which are told by the same group of narrators. The first story shows the influence of foreign travel in its outspoken impatience with the stuffiness of Russian life. *Gooseberries* is almost violent in its appraisal of the selfishness of being happy in a world full of misery. *About Love* is a beautiful story that takes account of the social uncertainties that inhibit the elemental requirements of the heart. All three are desperately unhappy tales, and they speak eloquently of the sad and indignant mood in which Chekhov renewed his literary life after the long illness that followed the failure of *The Sea Gull*.

Immediately after his return, the wound left by that

wretched evening in Petersburg was opened once again. His old friend Vladimir Nemirovich-Danchenko had written to tell him of the new theatre he had organized, and to ask his permission to include *Ivanov* and *The Sea Gull* in its repertory.

There were at this time two dramatic schools in Moscow—the Imperial school headed by the actors Lensky, Pravdin, and Sadovsky, and the Philharmonic, over which Sumbatov-Yuzhin presided. Nemirovich, who was primarily a dramatist, had been for some time employed as a teacher of acting at the Philharmonic, but he was ambitious to direct a professional company of his own which would bring the new drama, especially the drama of Ibsen, to the Russian stage. The Imperial theatres had not been lucky with Ibsen. The Maly had produced *The Vikings at Helgoland* unsuccessfully. Korsh had had no better fortune with a version of *An Enemy of the People*. Duse had brought *A Doll's House* to Moscow, but she had used it, as always, as an acting vehicle, and there was not much left of Ibsen in her version of the play. The first real production of a play by Ibsen was actually put on by the pupils at the Philharmonic.

In 1897, the Griboyedov prize was awarded to Nemirovich-Danchenko for his play *The Value of Life*, which had been produced in Moscow and Petersburg during the very season which witnessed the debacle of *The Sea Gull*. At this time, Nemirovich was looking in vain for a theatre in which to produce plays acted by his students. It occurred to him that he might be able to organize an acting company with the help of the young amateur Konstantin Alexeyev, whose dramatic club had recently distinguished itself with several interesting productions in Moscow.

Alexeyev was a merchant, the director of a prosperous business house. He was at this time 33, prematurely gray, and a talented actor and director, ambitious, wealthy, and deeply devoted to the theatre. Under the name of Stanislavsky he had organized a highly disciplined group of amateurs which called itself the Society of Lovers of Art. The story of his meeting with Nemirovich at the Slavyansky Bazaar in Moscow on June 21, 1897, has been told often and in the greatest detail.[37] The upshot of their well-publicized conversation was the organization of an acting company composed of the pick of Stanislavsky's actors and the most proficient of Nemirovich's students. The new group, which included Moskvin, Meyerhold, and Olga Knipper, was first called The People's Theatre. It soon became known as The Moscow Art Theatre.

The Maly Theatre in Moscow at this time housed one of the best companies in the world. But it was an established theatre of long tradition, its style and its repertory were adapted to the exigencies of the group of distinguished performers who were at its head, and it was under strict bureaucratic control. The Art Theatre was dedicated to something other than the successful maintenance of a popular repertory. It was intended, like the *Théâtre Libre* which Antoine had organized ten years before in Paris, to produce works of art of the highest possible excellence quite free of official restriction or the pressures of popular taste. For this purpose, each production was to be the finished creation of a single artist, the regisseur. It would express his will, his taste, and his personality as completely as an orchestra expresses the personality of its conductor. From the first analysis of the play to the final touches before the opening, every facet of the production—the tone and movement of the actors, the tempo of the scenes, the design of the settings, the lighting plot, the costumes, and make-up—all the production down to the merest detail would follow the artistic conception of its director, so that the production would be his work of art, and his alone. Such total integration of the diverse talents and temperaments of the many individuals concerned in a theatrical production could be achieved, obviously, only under conditions of the most austere discipline and most devoted selflessness. The Meininger, whose work Stanislavsky had seen and greatly admired, were organized along semi-military lines; in consequence their mass-effects had something in them of the parade ground. The Art Theatre would not be set up like a regiment. It would be a school.

The idea was neither new nor revolutionary. Such methods had been current for some time in the ballet and the opera, both of which were dominated by their *maestri*, but they came into conflict inevitably with the star system. In the commercial theatres, where the audience came, in general, because of the actors and not the regisseur, it could hardly be otherwise. The reform in the theatre had to originate in the schools; thus the actors who were first subjected to the necessary discipline would be not stars, full of temperament and relatively unmanageable, but students involved professionally for the first time, and therefore quite open to new ideas and quite willing to take even the most rigorous direction. The methods of the acting-class would thus be extended to the commercial stage without encountering the usual obstacles to innovation.

At the Philharmonic, the instructor was customarily the director of the several productions which served as the final examinations in the various courses. In the newly organized Art Theatre, similarly, the pedagogue and the director would be one, and the pupil would be trained to subordinate his individuality completely to the interests of the ensemble and the exigencies of the role. Theoretically the director's word would be unquestioned; but the director would not command —he would advise, make suggestions, analyze problems, meet objections, and, in general, aid the actor in evoking the role out of his own inner life. The production would thus develop in the atmosphere of mutual respect and understanding that distinguishes an academic enterprise on the highest teaching level.

As for the audience, it was to be treated not as the patron, but as the guest of the production, a guest conditionally privileged to participate in an aesthetic rite which it might not perhaps completely comprehend, but to which it must give complete attention and respect. The theatre was not to be considered a place of amusement, but something in the nature of a place of worship. The public would be met courteously; but it must be made to submit, like everyone else, to the discipline necessary to the unity of a work of art. It must understand the role assigned to it as audience, and must play it well. Such, according to Nemirovich-Danchenko, were the aims of the new art theatre. If the difficulties were foreseeable, the conception, at least, was impressive.

The question of time was essential. The Maly, for all its brilliance, was too busy with its repertory to rehearse a play long enough to ensure a finished production. As a result, many of its productions were slipshod and accidental. The scenery, of course, was interchangeable as in all repertory theatres, and the same garden, hall, and living-room saw service in play after play, so that all plays seemed to inhabit the same theatrical environment. Stanislavsky, however, had been devising each of his amateur productions as separate and unique works of art. In his Circle, plays were first discussed thoroughly, then rehearsed slowly, progressing from scene to scene, with dozens of repetitions, and, since there was no rigid schedule, it was possible for him to postpone the presentation until he felt that the production was ready to be seen. This was the method adopted by the new acting company. Moreover, in the state theatres, costumes and make-up were left to the individual actor, and since dress-rehearsals were practically unknown until 1894, when Nemirovich introduced the practice accidentally in the production of his play *Gold*, the costumes, make-up, and settings constituted a surprise for everyone on the opening night. In the Moscow Art Theatre the principals rehearsed in costume and make-up on the set two months before the opening, and, eventually, there were five or more complete dress rehearsals before each première.

The Art Theatre came to life slowly and painfully. It had great need of money, and few sources of income. Eventually, with the help of the Grand Duchess Elizavetta Feodorovna, wife of the Governor-General of Moscow, and a group of wealthy merchants headed by the millionaire Saava Morozov, 28,000 rubles were subscribed to capitalize the new venture, and Nemirovich-Danchenko leased the Hermitage for the first season of the company. The plans were to produce Alexey Tolstoy's *Tsar Fyodor Ivanovich* first, and to follow with *The Merchant of Venice*, Hauptmann's *Hannele*, and a number of other plays. It was in this connection that Nemirovich had written to Chekhov in the spring of 1897 for permission to include his plays in the repertory.

Chekhov replied that he had neither the desire nor the strength to experience again the anguish of the theatre. He was no playwright, he said; there were better dramatists than he; in short, he wanted nothing to do with the new venture. Nemirovich, however, was not a man to be put off so easily. He praised Chekhov as the only contemporary dramatist in Russia whose work was significant for the theatre, and asked permission to visit him, so that, if he were given leave to do *The Sea Gull*, he might discuss the production with the author before going into rehearsal. Chekhov answered on May 16 that it would give him such pleasure to have Nemirovich visit Melikhovo that in exchange he would give him all his plays.[38]

The Sea Gull went into rehearsal that summer, at a *dacha* near Moscow, in an atmosphere of uncertainty. Stanislavsky made little of Chekhov as a playwright. He admitted frankly that he did not understand the play; but he was willing enough to design the production. The young actors who made up the cast were faced with the task of succeeding where the most experienced actors in the country had failed. They took up the challenge in great excitement. Most of them looked up to Chekhov; and they all believed wholeheartedly in this play, which for them represented a crucial test of the principles of the new company.

Chekhov attended several of the rehearsals. In general, he professed himself satisfied with the way in which things were proceeding, but he suggested that Stanislavsky play Trigorin instead of Dr. Dorn. The elaborate *mise en scène* which Stanislavsky had planned, he found excessive. He saw no reason for the off-stage croaking of frogs, the barking dogs, and the other effects with which Stanislavsky planned to embellish the production. What Chekhov obviously wanted was a production designed and acted in the best manner of the Maly company. Nemirovich-Danchenko remarks that in spite of Treplev's expressed desire for new forms in the theatre—"We need new forms, and if we don't get them, then we need nothing"—Chekhov himself had no special interest either in new forms or in the new theatre.[39] And he adds with some bitterness that a year after the Art Theatre's triumphant vindication of *The Sea Gull,* Chekhov demonstrated his gratitude by offering *Uncle Vanya* to the Maly.

Chekhov's interest in the kind of realism that Stanislavsky liked was, in fact, minimal. He had no special faith in the regisseur's spiritual midwifery, and apparently he considered that beyond a certain point the regisseur was intrusive. It is evident that Chekhov had no idea of revolutionizing the theatre. He did not regard *The Sea Gull* as a radical departure from established dramatic practice, but simply as an extension of this practice in conformity with his own temperament. *The Sea Gull* was intended to produce on the stage an effect that would be the dramatic equivalent of the kind of long story with which he had achieved success. A play, of course, would involve a degree of theatricality which in his stories he generally avoided; but it was after all a question of degree. The narrative, though dramatized, was intended to be simple and unaffected like the rest of his work, and he wished to have it played simply and sincerely. Russian acting style, even at best, tended toward extravagance. This was the principal ground for his dissatisfaction with the staging of his plays. In even the most restrained of the Russian actors of his day there was something of that Fenogenov whose stupendous performance in *Prince Serebryany* Chekhov had immortalized in *A Tragic Actor:*

> The performance was a grand success. The tragedian achieved wonders. When he carried off Elena, he held her in one hand above his head as he dashed across the stage. He shouted, he hissed, he stamped his feet, he tore his coat across his chest. When he refused to fight Morozov, he shook all over with such fear as no human being ever experienced, and in his terror he gasped as if he had a colic. The theatre rocked with applause. There were endless curtain calls. Fenogenov was presented with a silver cigarette case and a bouquet tied with long ribbons. The ladies waved their handkerchiefs . . . many shed tears . . . [40]

As an actor, Stanislavsky was at the other pole from this sort of artist, but it seemed to Chekhov that he compensated for the sobriety of his acting with the flamboyance of his production. At no time did he entirely trust Stanislavsky's instinct or taste. Stanislavsky, for his part, never quite understood what it was that Chekhov was driving at; and, according to Chekhov, he consistently misinterpreted his plays. It was in this spirit of profound mutual misunderstanding and mistrust that the magical productions of the Moscow Art Theatre proceeded.

The success of *Ivanov* had persuaded Chekhov that he had a native flair for writing well-made plays. *The Wood Demon* had amply demonstrated his mistake. In *The Sea Gull* he resorted to a technique he knew very well, the technique of the short story. Since this was the sort of thing on which his reputation as a writer was founded, his misfortune at the Alexandrinsky went deeper than a mere setback in the theatre—it called into question all his talent as a literary artist. But once the possibilities of *The Sea Gull* were demonstrated on the stage, Chekhov realized that he had stumbled on a technique of exceptional validity, and he hastened to develop this method in *Uncle Vanya* and *The Three Sisters*. In some measure, then, his extraordinary rise as a dramatist may be attributed to a happy accident. It depended on the fact that the conscious artlessness of his method coincided with the avant-garde reaction against the conventions of the Scribean system, the intricacies of which, fortunately, he had never been able to master. The effect he arrived at, more or less fortuitously, in *The Sea Gull* was precisely the effect at which the most progressive contemporary dramatists were aiming. Thus, in 1936, Nemirovich-Danchenko wrote with regard to his play *A New Project* (*Novoe delo*), performed at the Maly in Moscow in 1890:

> This was an important step in my work for the theatre ... The play had no hero, the main parts were intended for character actors. More hazardous still was the fact that the love-intrigue played a completely subordinate role; it hardly existed, even. Finally, there was not a single outward effect, no pistol shots, no swoons, no hysterics, no slap, no trick or, as it was then called, *deus ex machina* ... I wanted to elicit an interest in the scenic form itself, and to capture the secret of comedy by the simplest means.[41]

It was in the furtherance of these apirations that Nemirovich and Stanislavsky had organized the new acting company which, in imitation of the *Théâtre Libre*, was willing and able to work free of the conventions of "*le théâtre*." Chekhov fell in readily with these ideas, but at bottom he was too much the conservative to accept them entirely. The new style resulted in a vastly enhanced realism of which Chekhov did not wholly approve. It was not merely a question of eliminating the traditional rubbish of the actors' trade—the fat roles, strong exits, displays of temperament and passion, heroic postures, *bravura* passages, and pointed tirades, together with the usual opportunities for the display of professional virtuosity in projection and diction. The reaction to excessive displays of this sort went back a good many years, and Chekhov was in wholehearted concurrence. What was now involved was the elimination so far as possible of all the conventions which set the theatre apart from reality. The result was not only a lowering of the level of dramatic excitement to something that approximated the normal excitements of everyday life, but also the introduction of a new source of the *mirabile*, which centered in the production itself, and substituted the *bravura* of the director for that of the actor.

The goal of these endeavors was the achievement of an impression of overwhelming authenticity. In the case of *The Sea Gull* this was not an easy matter. Stanislavsky belonged to the merchant class. He had no intimate knowledge of the provincial gentry, or the country environment which furnished the background of most of Chekhov's plays. The petty quarrels, the atmosphere of indolence and boredom, the economic exigencies and social amenities of provincial life were alien to his experience, and had to be reconstructed imaginatively. The sense of the mystery of familiar things, the feeling of the supernatural in nature, all the wonder and poetry of the countryside to which Chekhov instinctively responded were quite foreign to his city-bred director. In the circumstances, Stanislavsky did his best. The mood which Chekhov desired him to create was not especially realistic. In some ways it recalled the evocative atmosphere of *L'Intruse* and

Intérieur, a type of lyricism to which Nemirovich responded, but which appears rather to have bemused his eminent collaborator.

In the summer of 1898, in addition to *The Sea Gull*, the Art Theatre rehearsed *Tsar Fyodor;* Pisemsky's *They Took The Law Into Their Own Hands; The Merchant of Venice;* and *Antigone*. Stanislavsky designed all the productions, and gave free reign to his fondness for exaggeration. Nemirovich writes that when there were high hats, Stanislavsky made them excessively high; long sleeves were made extraordinarily long. He had read somewhere that the boyars bowed thrice to the ground before the Tsar. In the rehearsals of *Tsar Fyodor*, he had his boyars touch their heads to the ground so often that they complained of pain in their backs. Everything had to be, in Stanislavsky's phrase, "curious." But Chekhov did not like things to be curious; and Stanislavsky's marvels seemed to him to be a useless intrusion upon the integrity of his play. In the ideal theatre, as he saw it, the marvellous would be primarily the absence of marvels.

For Stanislavsky as for Nemirovich, the significant difference between the new theatre and the old was in the dictatorship of the regisseur, an idea borrowed from the practice of Chronegk and the Meiningen company. They boasted proudly that "a single will reigns in our theatre." But for Chekhov this should have been the will not of the regisseur but of the author. That "true intuition" of the author's idea on which the regisseur prided himself did not always seem as perceptive to Chekhov as it did to Stanislavsky, and when Stanislavsky passed from the outer to the inner aspects of the *régie*, Chekhov often disagreed with the interpretation.[42]

In designing *The Sea Gull* Stanislavsky was mainly concerned with a rhetoric of external details. Although he did not, as Nemirovich-Danchenko reports, feel "the real Chekhovian lyricism," he devised fragments of reality with which to give mood and tone to the action—he illustrated colorfully the ennui and the irritability of the characters, and carefully documented the details of the autumn evening in the country. He liked to dramatize objects in the manneristic style of Antoine and Reinhardt—the flaming match and the glowing cigarette in the darkness—effects which at that time seemed new and marvellous in the theatre. Like Antoine, he pretended the fourth wall of his sets was made of glass, and his actors made a point of playing with their backs to the audience.

Chekhov had no desire to substitute a new set of tricks for the accepted conventions of the stage. Both Ibsen and Turgenev had worked within those conventions, and yet achieved a laudable mood of calm understatement. Chekhov preferred an even less obvious rhetoric than theirs. He sought a dramatic level that was barely elevated above the tone of ordinary life, and tried to create mood chiefly through the manipulation of silence. In 1900 he wrote to Olga Knipper, apparently apropos of *Uncle Vanya*, which was being rehearsed at this time: "I have written to Meyerhold and recommended to him not to exaggerate so much when representing a nervous person. Most people are nervous, many suffer, a very few feel sharp pain; but where, indoors or out, do you see people running about, hopping up and down, and holding their heads in their hands? Suffering must be shown as in life, that is, not with the feet and hands, but with the tone of the voice and the expression of the eyes . . . The conditions of the stage do not permit this, you say; but no conditions justify falsehood."[43]

But while Chekhov sought effects which looked real in the theatre, he had no idea of passing them off as reality. He aimed at nothing beyond an artistic truth, and saw no point in extending the production beyond the horizons of the play. Here he parted company with Stanislavsky, who desired to merge his play into the surrounding world so that it would be an experience indistinguishable from life. Chekhov was careful about the authenticity of detail, but he saw no advantage in the elaborate reproduction of offstage sounds in *The*

Sea Gull. Meyerhold, who later broke with Stanislavsky on the question of realism, recalls Chekhov's gibe at the regisseur's realistic pretensions: "There is a canvas by Kramskoy," he said, "in which he wonderfully depicts human faces. Suppose for the nose of one of those faces he substituted a real nose. The nose would be realistic, but the picture would be spoiled." [44]

The year after his production of *The Sea Gull,* Stanislavsky made his characters cover their heads against mosquitoes in the first act of *Uncle Vanya,* and the chirping of the crickets was intensified to the point where they quite obscured the dialogue. Chekhov's comment was: "In my next play I shall make the stipulation: the action takes place in a land which has neither mosquitoes, nor crickets, nor any other insects which hinder conversations between human beings!" In fact, Chekhov himself had dug these pitfalls for his director. He himself saw his characters as "inseparable from nature, from the weather, from the external world." [45] But Stanislavsky was an extremist; where Chekhov desired a small effect, Stanislavsky supplied a large one. In this he was ably seconded by his scenic artist Simov, who belonged to the realist school of painters with which Repin, Levitan, and Vasnetsov were associated. Chekhov, however, was not able to see the result of their labors at this time. He could only guess at the sort of production which the Art Theatre would give his play, and it is quite evident that he feared the worst.

Early in the fall of 1898 Chekhov began to feel ill, and in October he left for Yalta in order to escape the rigors of the northern climate. Some weeks later, he received news of his father's death. His domestic establishment was now in need of reorganization. His days at Melikhovo were in any case numbered. The estate was useless to him in the winter, and he was seldom there in the summer. He decided therefore to buy a piece of land in the suburb of Autka, some twenty-minutes walk from Yalta, and to take up permanent residence in this vicinity. What he bought was an old vineyard without shade, next to a Tatar cemetery, but it had a fine view of the sea and the surrounding mountains. A young architect was found to design the house. He planned, Chekhov wrote his mother persuasively, to have a kitchen with running water, and other American conveniences; there was to be a telephone, and electric bells to call the servants. His mother continued to have misgivings. She preferred to live near Moscow.

About this time, Maxim Gorky wrote from Nizhny Novgorod to express his admiration and offer his friendship, together with two volumes of his stories. A week later, he wrote again to say that he had seen a performance of *Uncle Vanya* at a provincial playhouse and was deeply impressed. In *Uncle Vanya* he saw "an entirely new kind of dramatic art," and he urged Chekhov to write more plays. Chekhov answered warmly, but he repeated his usual formula with regard to the drama: he had long ago lost touch with the theatre, and had no idea of writing plays.

The theatre was, however, very much in his mind at this time. The Moscow Art players had opened their season on October 14, a date selected by a gypsy woman as auguring well for their success. *Tsar Fyodor* was enthusiastically received. Moskvin became famous. But Nemirovich was not in a good mood. *Tsar Fyodor*, in spite of its success, was not making money. In *The Merchant of Venice*, for the sake of realism, Shylock had been made to talk with a Yiddish accent —it was a blunder, and the production was a complete failure. *Hannele* was forbidden by the Metropolitan of Moscow. As the final rehearsals of *The Sea Gull* began, the Art Theatre was on the verge of collapse.

The rehearsals, in fact, were going badly. There were last-minute cast changes. The actors were nervous. Chekhov's health had to be considered, in the event of another disaster, and his sister Masha pleaded hysterically with Stanislavsky to withdraw the play. It had been rehearsed twenty-six times.

It was impossible to withdraw it. The day before the opening, Stanislavsky insisted on the need for more rehearsals. Nemirovich refused, whereupon Stanislavsky asked that his name be removed from the playbills as regisseur. He did not as yet understand the play, and he had absolutely no faith in it.

Nevertheless, *The Sea Gull* opened on schedule on December 17. The house was far from full. The actors were frightened and, Stanislavsky later reported, the whole production smelled of Valerian drops, the usual sedative of the period. The curtain rose on a dark stage. All that could be seen was a moon, a lake, and, downstage, a long bench on which the actors were to sit, back to the audience, to watch Treplev's play. The audience was quiet. The play went forward smoothly. It was acted with the utmost simplicity, and in the greatest trepidation. No one could guess how the audience was taking it. When the curtain went down on the last act, there was complete silence. Olga Knipper was ill. She had played Arkadina in a high fever. The moment the curtain came down, she fainted. The other actors began to walk off the stage dejectedly, certain that the play had failed, and the theatre was doomed. Suddenly the house exploded in a frenzy of applause.

The stage manager hurriedly raised the curtain, catching the actors unawares. There followed one of those scenes which take place only in the theatre and even then only once in a hundred years. The audience shouted, roared, stamped, rose to its feet, surged forward. The actors embraced. Stanislavsky broke into a wild, spontaneous dance of joy. It was as if they were all suddenly possessed by Dionysos. The Art Theatre was saved. A new chapter began in the history of drama.

Chekhov did not believe the telegram in which Nemirovich informed him of his triumph. Soon he was deluged with telegrams. The illness of Olga Knipper caused the second performance to be postponed for some days, but when the run was resumed, the theatre was besieged by ticket-buyers, and it is said that people waited patiently in line night after night in the square outside the playhouse in order to have a chance to see the play. At last Chekhov was satisfied: "If I did not have to live in Yalta," he wrote Urusov at the beginning of February 1899, "this winter would be the happiest of my life." [46] But he could not leave Yalta. He had suffered still another hemorrhage. He was coughing badly. He had begun to reckon up his remaining years. It was clear there would not be many.

At this time, the publisher A. F. Marx offered to buy the rights to all his works, past and future, for a lump sum, plus certain payments for new material. After some haggling, the sum was fixed at 75,000 rubles, to be paid in large installments. Chekhov was to keep his theatrical royalties. It was not at all a shrewd bargain by ordinary standards. It enriched the publisher, and did little for Chekhov; but Chekhov was convinced that he had not much longer to live, and the prospect of a round sum in ready cash each year for the next five years seemed extremely attractive to him. To Suvorin, who disapproved of the deal, he wrote that his stories were of no financial importance; what was important was his theatrical royalties, and these he had retained.[47]

Early in April, Chekhov returned to Moscow. He was not well. Olga Knipper had by this time struck up a close friendship with his sister. She came of good family. Her mother was a celebrated singing teacher. Chekhov was much taken with her: it was not long before a serious romance developed. It grew more serious in the course of the summer, and was continued by mail when Olga began rehearsing in August for her second season with the Moscow Art company.

The Art Theatre's first season had ended well, though not profitably. The talk ran high, but the grosses were low; and the theatre ended its season with a deficit of 45,000 rubles.

Saava Morozov came to the rescue. The deficit was paid. For the new season Nemirovich announced Alexey Tolstoy's *Ivan the Terrible*, Hauptmann's *Lonely Lives*, and Ibsen's *An Enemy of the People*. In addition he planned to produce Chekhov's *Uncle Vanya*, which had recently been published, but had not yet been seen in either capital. But Chekhov wrote him that he had already promised Lensky the play for production at the Maly, and that it had been tentatively accepted.

They had reckoned, however, without the Imperial Theatre and Literary Committee, on which sat three university professors. This august body approved *Uncle Vanya* for the Maly on condition that the third act be re-written in a manner less offensive to Professor Serebryakov, who, as a member of the university, must be treated with respect. Chekhov immediately withdrew his play. Nevertheless, he was still unwilling to entrust it to the Moscow Art Theatre. He had never seen the company act. It was new and young and, in spite of its success with *The Sea Gull*, he had no idea of its ability. The Art Theatre was at this time closed; its lease had expired; its scenery was in storage; but Nemirovich was so eager to have *Uncle Vanya* that on May 1 he rented a theatre in Moscow, and gave an informal performance of *The Sea Gull*, without scenery, especially for Chekhov and a small group of friends.

Chekhov was not particularly impressed with the production. He disliked Roxanova in the part of Nina so much that he refused to have her play the part again. He thought Stanislavsky's interpretation of Trigorin too foppish. He should be played, in Chekhov's opinion, as a man utterly careless of his appearance. For the rest, he expressed no objection. He wrote more candidly to Gorky: "I cannot judge the play dispassionately because the Sea Gull played abominably and kept snivelling all the time, and Trigorin walked about and talked like a paralytic; his interpretation of the role was that of a man without any will of his own, and it sickened me to watch him. On the whole, however, the play was not bad, and it gripped me. In places, I could hardly believe it was I that had written it."[48] The production, at any rate, convinced him that the Art Theatre would play *Uncle Vanya* acceptably, and he gave Nemirovich the necessary permission.

Uncle Vanya was rehearsed all through the following summer, with Olga Knipper in the part of the beautiful Elena. Chekhov attended a number of the rehearsals. As usual he was not effective in dealing with actors. He was far from articulate in explaining the play to the regisseur, or the parts to the players. He interfered with the direction mainly to protest against obvious misconceptions, and, by way of guidance, contented himself with making cryptic statements over which people puzzled for years. He did better when he was back in Yalta in September; on paper, he was able to say quite clearly what he thought. It then turned out that he had quite definite ideas on the way in which his scenes were to be interpreted, but he had neglected to impart these ideas to Stanislavsky in the formative phases of the production, and, on the whole, the play ultimately presented the profile that Stanislavsky, rather than Chekhov, had imagined.

Uncle Vanya opened on October 26, 1899. The house was full and the audience receptive. The cast was tense and excited. There was much applause. But the play was less than a complete success. The reviewers in general praised the performance; they also found fault with it. Olga Knipper wrote that while the play had gone very well, she herself had acted badly and, as a result, had not slept all night, and could not stop crying. Chekhov consoled her. The play, he wrote, was not new. It was already dated and full of defects. If more than half the performers had not grasped the right line, obviously it was the fault of the author. He advised her not to worry over successes and failures, but to go on working steadily: "To write, or to act, and to feel all the time that one is not doing the thing right—that is so usual, and for a beginner so profitable!" [49] The company, he had written two days before, was spoiled with easy triumphs; it must settle down to a more reasonable level of expectation.[50] He himself was learning patience. After *Ivanov*, none of his plays had been well received at first, and he felt that he could do very well with a moderate success—the great triumphs embarrassed him.

As for *Uncle Vanya*, it was only after a good deal of repetition that the company was able to bring out what was unique in it. Even then, very likely, no one realized what it was that made it remarkable. Yet in time it became one of the mainstays of the company's repertory and, within a few decades, it was recognized everywhere as one of the masterpieces of the modern theatre.

Uncle Vanya

It is not possible to say with any confidence when *Uncle Vanya* (*Dyadya Vanya*) was written. Chekhov's correspondence supplies no clue as to the circumstances of its composition. It is clear that the failure of *The Wood Demon,* at the end of 1889, represented a real setback for the author. The wound took time to heal, and in the meantime Chekhov kept silent about it. Soon after his first difficulties with this play he had written to his friend Urusov, "I hate this play and I am trying to forget it . . . it would be a severe blow to me if it were dragged into the light of day and revived . . ." In 1896, Suvorin proposed to bring out a volume of Chekhov's plays which would include *The Sea Gull* and *Ivanov.* His editors, as usual, were dragging their feet and, on December 2, Chekhov wrote to complain that the proofs of his book were late: "Two long plays have still to be set up: *The Sea Gull,* which is known to you, and *Uncle Vanya,* which is not known to anyone in the world." This is the first mention of *Uncle Vanya* in Chekhov's correspondence. It is entirely possible that the play was completed sometime earlier that year. Evidence has been adduced to substantiate a much earlier date, perhaps the spring of 1890, but it is far from conclusive, and the similarities between the technique of *Uncle Vanya* and that of *The Sea*

Gull are such as to warrant the conclusion that the two plays were written at no great interval from one another.[1]

For reasons not hard to fathom, Chekhov insisted that *Uncle Vanya* was a completely new play. In some ways, doubtless, it was new; but only in its total effect. *Uncle Vanya* was built around acts two and three of *The Wood Demon*. Chekhov incorporated these acts almost word for word in the new version, together with some odds and ends of the original which might have been better omitted. The differences, however, are even more striking than the similarities. *The Wood Demon* is, by any standards, a piece of theatrical rubbish. *Uncle Vanya* is one of the great plays of our time. It is an interesting demonstration of how it is sometimes possible, with God's help, to make something out of nothing.

The Wood Demon has no special focus. It is appropriately subtitled *Scenes From Country Life*—a title which was duly transferred to *Uncle Vanya*—and it is impossible to say whether it was intended to emphasize principally the decay of the country landowners, the evils of slander, the theme of waste, or a moral lesson of Tolstoyan character. It has, moreover, three love stories: one involving an adulterous passion, which ends badly; and two leading to proposals of marriage, which presumably end well. *The Wood Demon* was now purged canonically of everything extraneous to the plot. The Voynitsky-Elena-Serebryakov situation provided the main action, with which the Sonya-Khrushchov love-story was closely interlaced. All the rest of *The Wood Demon* material was eliminated—the dashing Fyodor, Julia and her brother Zheltukhin, the elder Orlovsky, all the characters concerned in the chain of slander, as well as the slander itself, its consequences, the death of Voynitsky, the posthumous discovery of the diary, and the exculpation of Elena. The result was a tightly knit and sequential story concerning the wasted lives of a group of sympathetic country folk. In the original play the comedic intention is supported by a sudden and unexpected eruption of happy endings. In *Uncle Vanya* the ending is not happy. The mood at the end is elegiacal. The action is suspended rather than resolved. The play ends in an anacrusis; and here for the first time is sounded the genuine Chekhovian note.

The Sea Gull is a play principally about theatre people. *Uncle Vanya* has an academic background. Both deal with the intrusion of exciting urban elements upon the calm of country life. Uncle Vanya, his old mother Maria, his niece Sonya, and their impoverished permanent guest Telegin lead a quiet, idyllic existence on the Serebryakov estate, which Vanya and Sonya manage. The arrival of the owner, the retired professor of art Serebryakov, and his young wife Elena Andreyevna, sets the establishment by the ears. In the presence of the exquisite Elena, Uncle Vanya suddenly feels a great need for beauty welling up in his heart, and under its influence he becomes aware of passions and ambitions he had not known before. He also becomes aware of his age, his insignificance, his inadequacy, and his wasted life. The play is, therefore, from one viewpoint, a consideration of the critical period in a man's career; it describes the rites of passage from youth to age.

In the course of these ceremonies, the egotistical Serebryakov, highly inflated with self-importance, racked by his gout, his arthritis, and his sense of frustration, is the natural target of Vanya's aggression. Vanya blames all his ills upon him, and his mounting fury leads to the climax upon which the action turns.

Elena's beauty arouses other passions as well, but her effect upon the district doctor is not so devastating as her influence on Vanya. Vanya is soft and innocent. Astrov is made of sterner stuff. He is ten years younger than his friend, but his soul already has acquired a certain rigidity. He is a man of some experience, who has laid aside love in order to devote his time to more useful pursuits. Elena excites his interest and, in spite of herself, she is excited by him. Between Astrov and Vanya her situation rapidly becomes impossible, and, in order to extricate herself and her husband, she departs for the city, presumably never to return.

In the end, the scene is recomposed precisely as it was in the beginning. The storm has passed. Everything has been shaken: nothing has changed. The episode has no particular importance. It is only that this flash of summer lightning has suddenly revealed these lives in all their nakedness.

Elena occupies a central position in the action. She does very little, almost nothing; but her beauty is dynamic, and by her very presence she shocks the people around her into a desperate realization of their shortcomings, and the hopelessness of their situation. The action is, in fact, conceived in accordance with a design for which Chekhov was very likely indebted to Turgenev's *A Month in the Country*. Ibsen's *The Wild Duck* has a similar design: it is a useful dramatic formula. *Uncle Vanya* makes the impression of a vigorous chemical reaction. Into the seemingly stable lives of these country people, there is suddenly introduced a disturbing element, in the nature of a catalyst, and almost at once the whole little world begins to seethe and fume. Ultimately there is something like an explosion. With this display of energy, the disturbing elements are precipitated, the situation regains its equilibrium, and life once again presents its calm and limpid appearance, as if all its tensions were dissipated.

From the viewpoint of Elena, however, the action takes on another aspect. It is true that her beauty has something like a catalytic effect, but she herself is not inert. She participates actively in the situation she has inadvertently brought about, and she saves herself from its consequences only at the expense of her innermost desires. She shares, therefore, in the common destiny of the other characters; and her role becomes extremely complex and extremely interesting.

To bring into being this vastly enhanced Elena, Chekhov had to revise drastically the original conception of the role. In her new guise, Elena is not wronged. She suffers no public humiliation, and does not need to be exonerated. Her predicament is now completely psychological in nature. She is the victim, not so much of a despotic and unlikely husband, as of the tension between her irresistible beauty and her unyielding virtue. As these are, in the circumstances, incompatible, the result is an inner conflict of continuing nature, from which nothing can rescue her. Obviously, Chekhov did not choose Elena's name at random. He had in mind, doubtless, that other Helen whose beauty set the world by the ears and who, after much travail, returned in the end to a husband she despised. The difference is that Chekhov's Helen has no Paris, no Troy, no adventure, and no epic. At the most, she has a kind of comedy; but not a funny comedy.

The plight of the virtuous Elena whose loveliness is her principal misfortune has wider implications. Nobody was really happy, perhaps, on the Serebryakov farm before Elena's arrival, but everyone was seemingly content. For these country people—Sonya, who nourished a secret love for Astrov; Vanya, who had not realized he was no longer young; Astrov, whose work took up all his time and energy—life was not unpleasant, so long as they were not tortured by desire. The coming of Elena throws everything out of scale. Great beauty is very hard to bear. Even a glimpse of it is enough to dispel the illusions which make life tolerable.

As in Chekhov's story *The Beauties*, Elena's excessive loveliness brings to everyone an indefinable sense of loss, a feeling of unworthiness, the intimation of a happiness so far removed from earthly possibility as to beggar its values. It is not an easy thing to define this grief. Chekhov had several times attempted it. In the second episode of *The Beauties* it is the fat railway guard who suffers it:

> The guard was standing with his elbows on the railing, looking in the direction of the beautiful girl, and his battered, wrinkled, and unpleasantly beefy face, exhausted by sleepless nights and the jolting of the train, wore a look of tenderness and of the deepest sadness, as though in this girl he saw his lost happiness, his youth, sobriety, purity, wife, children; as though he were regretting in his whole substance that this girl was not his, and that for him, with his premature old age, his clumsiness, and his beefy face, the ordinary happiness of a man and a passenger were as far away as heaven.[2]

In his ability to formulate a sentimental situation of this sort without sentimentality, Chekhov demonstrates his unique quality as an artist. He was not an intellectual writer like Shaw or Strindberg, or even Ibsen. He had no theory of life to expound, no point to make, no thesis. It is quite unnecessary for the understanding of his drama to discuss his world-view. If he had anything of the sort, it was irrelevant to the subject of his art. His great talent lay in the sensitive depiction of the life around him, the physical and psychic landscape in which he lived. It was perhaps no great matter in the turbulence of those times to describe with precision the hopeless longing in the heart of an aging bachelor. Tolstoy, with his eyes fixed on far more important objects, thought this sort of work so much nonsense: it proved nothing, and advanced nobody. And yet to many in our day Chekhov appears to fulfill a higher artistic function than Tolstoy.

Tolstoy was a believer. Chekhov was not. In the absence of God, it becomes difficult to formulate the nature of being, and morality tends to take on a purely practical aspect; but the study of man as man remains a fundamental human preoccupation even in a world that has lost its meaning. Chekhov declined to speculate. He looked at the world with the innocent and penetrating eye of a child who, seeing it for the first time, finds it full of wonder and beauty, but not full of significance. Since he had no *parti pris*, he felt free to observe and to report what he observed without any need to formulate his perceptions in accordance with a preconception. And as he felt no obligation to explain life, but only to represent it truly, he was able to see and to exhibit what few dramatic writers before him had ever seen or exhibited.

It may be granted, if one pleases, that *Uncle Vanya*, like most of Chekhov's plays, has no special significance, and makes no point. But Chekhov, in his maturity, did not think a play need make a point. At the most, it might suggest one. Therefore he aimed at the evocation of a mood rather than the communication of an idea. It followed that, as he developed his dramatic method, his plays reached further and further into that part of the soul that is touched, in general, chiefly by those arts that speak without words, by painting and by music. It is perhaps not possible to explain why beauty makes one sad, or why life should give us a sense of waste; but it is possible to convey a mood of this sort in the theatre, and even to evoke it in all its complexity. It was to some such end, perhaps, that Chekhov directed his efforts in the revision of *The Wood Demon*. At any rate, in *Uncle Vanya* the tonal emphasis is completely altered, and in the lack of meaning of the action is suggested the deepest meaning of the play.

In *The Wood Demon*, as in *Ivanov*, Chekhov's intention was still frankly critical and didactic. As a result, the characters are incomprehensible, and none of them invites sympathy. But by the time of *Uncle Vanya* Chekhov had given up the traditionally pedagogical approach to the drama. He had stopped preaching, and reconciled himself to the more modest role of observer. His comic sense was not suspended; but in his effort to understand, and his enhanced understanding, the nature of the jest changed. The comedy deepened. He found room in it for compassion. All the characters in *Uncle Vanya* are sympathetic; a measure of sympathy is directed even to the thoroughly caricatured Professor Serebryakov.

In *The Wood Demon*, Sonya is a peppery bluestocking, of unstable character, whose outstanding trait is a suspicious nature. She is beautiful and rich; a desirable, but completely unsuitable match for the poor country doctor who loves her, and with whom she constantly quarrels. Chekhov revised her completely—in *Uncle Vanya* she becomes a plain girl with pretty hair, very forthright and sensible, without any of the nonsense that characterized the former Sonya. The new Sonya, it becomes evident, has been amalgamated with the practical Julia, and has acquired in the process the solid character of a human being. In this guise, she would probably make Astrov an ideal wife. But Astrov will not have her.

It would have been easy, and even natural, to contrive a happy ending for this affair. But by this time Chekhov was committed to the sober view of life which we associate with the French naturalists. Accordingly, Astrov does not experience the sudden revelation of Sonya's inner beauty which would be normal in sentimental comedy, and Sonya is doomed to a loveless life. Astrov is a fine man, but he has his limitations; he is, he admits, incapable of a love that is not physically motivated. In this he resembles Chekhov. Astrov, in fact, was one of Chekhov's favorite characters, and it is interesting that he is by no means depicted as the ideal human being. He is reckless, impulsive, contemptuous, and bitter; in some ways he is a cruel man; but even harder on himself than on others.

Vanya is more sympathetic than Astrov, and far more obvious as a character. Astrov works. He is vital and useful, and he has a brain. There is not much left of Vanya. He has a map of Africa on the wall of his room. With relation to this vast unexplored continent, his own life must seem absurdly small, but Vanya is no more able to leave his cage than is Elena. He is not, however, so much the prisoner of his environment, of which, like Astrov, he unceasingly complains, as of his passivity, the lack of vigor from which he has always suffered.

In Chekhov's world, to live is to suffer, and those suffer least who are least vital. His favorite characters are those in whom a sudden surge of desire reveals a tragic lack of energy. The lives of such people are normally small and wretched, but the possibility of a more intense experience is apparently more frightening for them than the continuation of the humdrum existence to which they are comfortably committed. Thus, Elena, who sees in Astrov the possibility of escaping, if only for a moment, from the monotony of her servitude, flies away from him as fast as she can lest something deep and vivid should trouble the calm surface of her boredom. So, too, in the story *About Love,* Alekhin finds himself powerless to consummate the love he has so long deferred even when all the obstacles to his happiness are removed, and he reflects sadly upon the vanity of the considerations by which men rationalize their psychic impotence:

> I confessed my love for her, and with a burning pain in my heart, I realized how unnecessary, how petty, and how deceptive everything was that had hindered us from having one another. I understood that when you love, you must reason from what in your estimation is supremely necessary, more necessary than happiness or unhappiness, or sin, or virtue, in their accepted meaning, or you had best not reason at all.[3]

Like Alekhin, Elena is virtuous and sensible. Her actions are those of a model citizen; but in rejecting, for whatever reason, her opportunity to live vividly in accordance with her desire, she demonstrates how thoroughly she has abdicated her humanity. She does what she considers to be her duty; but in the circumstances, the self-restraint which keeps her from committing what might be considered an imprudence is also the sign of her lack of vitality, her weakness, and her fear. For Chekhov what might be considered, in a more conventional setting, a triumph of virtue is indicative of the soul's disease of those who do not dare to live.

This is in the nature of a paradox. It is also an example of Chekhov's realism; and as such it indicates the fundamental romanticism of his viewpoint. For Chekhov, it was immoral above all to thwart nature, and worse than immoral to do so under the guise of moral obligation. But Elena's psychic predicament is not simple, and in describing it he must have thought more than once of the ambivalence which characterized his own state of mind—the constant urge to escape into the hurly-burly of action and adventure, balanced by the perennial attraction of home and regular meals, a settled income, and the serenity of sofa cushions and carriage springs. In his special case, of course, the normal polarity of impulse and inertia was disturbed by his bodily infirmity, which forcibly inhibited his periodic flights into a wider and more vital experience than the sedentary life of a writer could usually afford. None of the characters in *Uncle Vanya,* save the aged professor, has physical symptoms of any kind, but each of them is ill in his way, and all of them have wrapped themselves up more or less comfortably against the elemental blasts of life, which they dare not, and have never dared to brave.

The characters of *Uncle Vanya* are painfully aware of the existence of the outer world. The watchman's rattle speaks eloquently of the security which surrounds them, and also of the outlying universe; of the soul's prison, and the dangers beyond its wall. The wall is imaginary, of course, but it makes no difference. Nobody wishes to escape. From time to time the soul beats its wings. It dares not fly. Life passes, and that is all. The slackening tensions of the aging soul, not the blows of malevolent fortune, are the source of the tragic mood of *Uncle Vanya.* It is a mood as fragile and as sharp as the sense of despair which accompanies the sight of beauty which it is not our destiny to possess.

But while the undercurrent of tragedy in *Uncle Vanya* is unmistakable, the play is by no means tragic. As in the case of *The Sea Gull*, the action is trivial. The map of Africa throws the whole thing into scale. Besides, the play has comedic aspects which are quite incompatible with a tragic action. In the hopeless efforts of an aging Lothario to melt the heart of a cold woman with mawkish speeches there is something which no degree of pathos can dignify. Vanya stands in the shadow of the comic *senex*. The suggestion is not lost on Astrov, and Elena is quite aware of it. Evidently Vanya was not meant to be taken with complete seriousness. In classic times, he would have been entirely laughable; as it is, his demands on our sensibility are too insistent for us not to be aware of his comic implications. Chekhov did not label this character clearly. He is alive, therefore he is ambiguous. And for this reason, perhaps, of all Chekhov's characters he most warmly invites our interest.

The deepening tone of Chekhov's conception as he reworked *The Wood Demon* was clearly reflected in the changes he made in its detail. The names with which he had originally supplied his characters were meant to provoke a smile. Voynitsky's given name was Yegor. In *The Wood Demon*, in accordance with the affectations of his class, he is regularly called Georges. In the revision, he is rebaptized Ivan, an honest Russian name, and only his mother calls him Jean. He thus becomes *Dyadya* Vanya, acquiring an appellation entirely suitable for one whose destiny it is to be primarily an uncle.

The Wood Demon, Khrushchov, sheds his undignified entomological associations. In renaming him Astrov, a name which recalls the stars, Chekhov evidently meant to elevate his character significantly. Nevertheless, Astrov does not wholly sever his connection with Dr. Lvov, the idealistic busybody of *Ivanov:* he remains Mikhail Lvovich. The amiable Dyadin, now called Telegin, preserves his pock-marked complexion and his nickname of Waffles, together with his charm and simplicity of manner, but, in the interests of good showmanship, he acquires a guitar, and becomes primarily instrumental, a polka in human form.

The result of the rigorous simplification to which *The Wood Demon* was subjected was the swiftness and directness of *Uncle Vanya.* This play has movement. It begins incisively in its main line of development, and climbs very naturally to the strong climax brought about by the convergence of the two motives of the action—Vanya's hatred of Serebryakov and the frustration of his passion for Elena. It is significant that when Vanya finds Elena in Astrov's arms, his anger is not directed against his friend at all, but rather against his enemy, who then proceeds to detonate the situation by his outrageous proposal to sell the estate in his own interests. Structurally this development is admirable, and it is also completely valid psychologically; but the manner in which Chekhov explodes the resulting climax into something close to comedy is a marvel of dramatic ingenuity. When everything is prepared for him to play his great scene, Vanya misses his target—not once, but twice. In this climactic moment of his life, the habit of missing is evidently too strong for him to resist; his revenge proves as futile as everything else he does. The scene, which everything predisposes us to take seriously, thus collapses into something between the pathetic and the ridiculous, and the character, standing on the very threshold of the heroic, is suddenly diminished in a way that sounds a note of pathos deeper than tragedy itself.

This scene defines quite clearly what is meant by the Chekhovian effect. The external man is comically inept, but his ineptitude reveals the depth of his pain. The anti-climax is such that it is impossible not to smile; but this anti-climax is the very climax of the man's frustration, the snapping-point of his heartstrings: it is impossible to laugh. The difference is unmistakable between this sort of dramatic tension and the typically Ibsenist effect which comes closest to it. Ibsen's specialty is a tragic action played by comic characters, as in *The Wild Duck*. The tension in this case is between the nature of the action and the nature of the people involved in it. But in Chekhov's plays, it is the polarity within the soul itself that governs the action—or lack of action—and the joke is grim in proportion to the disparity between what is intended and what is done.

Unlike *The Sea Gull*, *Uncle Vanya* is a well-made play. It is, indeed, the first successful example of this technique in Chekhov's dramatic canon, and it indicates that after his various difficulties with *Ivanov* and *The Wood Demon*, Chekhov had finally achieved a certain proficiency in this exacting medium. The success of *The Sea Gull* very likely relieved him of the necessity for pursuing this technique further. At any rate, *Uncle Vanya* represents not only his first success but also his final effort in this style. *The Three Sisters* is not a well-made play. It is a chronicle in which may be discerned only the vestiges of a plot.

The first act of *Uncle Vanya* begins with a short expository scene in which the characters are duly introduced and described. Dr. Astrov has evidently been summoned to minister to the professor's gout, and the old nurse Marina is giving him a glass of tea in the garden. Astrov chats idly:

> ...see what a long moustache I have? A long, silly moustache. Yes, I am just as silly as all the others, nurse, just as trivial, but not quite as stupid, no...I have not yet grown stupid. My brain is not addled yet, thank God, though my feelings are dulled. There is nothing I want, nothing I need, there's no one I love except, perhaps, you. (*He kisses her hand*) When I was a little boy, I had a nurse just like you.

The exposition is continued by Vanya, who comes for his tea, yawning, still heavy from his midday nap. He is full of indignation against Serebryakov, and he describes him in detail. There is undeniably some awkwardness in this direct exposition, conventionally elicited through characters who have no reason to speak save the author's need to enlighten the audience with regard to the situation. The beginning of *The Three Sisters* is equally clumsy. Chekhov never mastered the difficult art of preparation, and it was not until he wrote *The Cherry Orchard* that he learned to manage the exposition with the grace necessary to a naturalistic style. The first act of *Uncle Vanya*, at any rate, covers the ground —all the characters are introduced or identified, and by the end of the act, the situation is defined and begins to unfold. The last speeches are taken almost literally from *The Wood Demon:*

> ELENA ANDREYEVNA: ...Do you know, Vanya, why you and I are such friends? I think it is because we are both lonely people, tiresome, and unsympathetic. (*Pause*) Yes, unsympathetic. (*Pause*) Don't look at me like that. I don't like it.
>
> VOYNITSKY: How else can I look at you, since I love you? You are my joy, my life, my youth. I know that my chances of being loved in return are infinitely small... no...not even that...nil, nonexistent; there is no chance of it at all. But I ask nothing of you. I don't want you to do anything. Just let me look at you. Let me listen to you speak...
>
> ELENA ANDREYEVNA: Be quiet! Someone may hear you.
>
> VOYNITSKY: Let me tell you of my love! Don't drive me off! I have no other happiness.
>
> ELENA ANDREYEVNA: Oh, this is torture!

With this, Elena goes into the house, with Vanya after her. On the stage, Telegin plucks a polka from his guitar. Marya makes a note on the margin of the pamphlet she is reading. The curtain comes down on a scene that is almost exactly duplicated in the last scene of the play.

Beyond this point the action follows the original plan of *The Wood Demon.* The second act opens in the drawing room in the middle of the night with Serebryakov ill and cranky in his armchair. There are the sounds of the gathering storm. When Serebryakov is helped off to bed, Vanya once again tries to make love to Elena. Nothing could be less opportune. Exhausted by her long vigil, she is not disposed to be gentle with him:

ELENA ANDREYEVNA: Let me go! (*She pulls her hand away*) Go away!

VOYNITSKY: The rain will soon be over; all nature will be refreshed . . . only I am not refreshed. I am haunted night and day by the thought that my life has been wasted and is lost forever. My past life is nothing. I frittered it away on trifles. My present is grotesque in its senselessness. What am I to do with my life and my love? What is to become of them? This glorious passion in my heart will be lost like a ray of sunlight in a dark chasm, and my life will be lost with it.

ELENA ANDREYEVNA: When you speak to me like that it is as if I had suddenly gone numb. I don't know what to answer. Forgive me. I have nothing to say to you. (*She turns to go*) Good night.

It develops that Vanya has been drinking with Astrov, and is not in complete command of himself. He becomes insistent. He falls on his knees. The scene really becomes grotesque. He is quite unaware that he is provoking Elena's cruelty. When at last he is left alone, he has an old-fashioned soliloquy in which he blames all his misery on Serebryakov, for whom he has sacrificed his life and his career, and whom he knows now to be a worthless fraud.

The revolt of Vanya, which presumably dates from the advent of Elena, follows traditional lines; but it is customary in this plot-formula for the worm, in turning, to develop considerable vigor. Chekhov's originality is seen in Vanya's failure to display the necessary degree of heroism. For the realistic Chekhov a worm that turns remains a worm.

A consequence of Chekhov's belief that, in general, people do not change, do not learn, and do not profit by their mistakes, is that in his later plays there is no peripeteia. A story like *A Living Chattel* shows how deftly Chekhov could manage a series of narrative twists when he had a mind to it; but *A Living Chattel* was intended to be funny. In the period during which he wrote *The Duel*, Chekhov still believed, perhaps, that people change—in that story, the sight of his mistress in the arms of another man is enough to cause Laevsky to revaluate his entire viewpoint, and his life. After *The Wood Demon*, Chekhov avoided such effects in the theatre. The pessimistic mood of his later drama is doubtless bound up with the idea that basic traits of character are not affected by external circumstances, so that the individual is irrevocably defined by his nature, which is a kind of destiny. It is to this deterministic attitude that the plays of Chekhov's maturity owe the uncomplicated linearity of their pattern. In the absence of an acceptable peripeteia, there can be little intricacy of plot. Chekhov's later plays, indeed, are presented as a chronicle of interlaced lives, with a minimum of intrigue, contrivance, or surprise, and a complete absence of narrative twists or reversals. In plays of this type, what is mainly felt as *mirabile* is their truth and the depth of the author's perception. This makes a very different effect from that of narrative ingenuity.

Vanya dramatizes himself extravagantly in the course of the play, but Chekhov does not flatter the character; he shows him "as he is." In this guise he invites sympathy, but not admiration. Vanya sees himself as an innocent idealist who has voluntarily sacrificed his life for the sake of those he loved. As he tells us, he had originally given up his share of the inheritance so that his beloved sister might bring the estate as a dowry to her husband, the rising young art historian.

When his sister died, Vanya took her daughter under his care so that the venerated professor, the pride of the family, might be free of the distractions of parenthood. Eventually Serebryakov was able to marry the beautiful Elena, whom Vanya had always admired; and now that he has retired, he has come to take possession of the estate which Vanya has tended for him. Obviously there is an entire novel behind the short action of *Uncle Vanya,* and it is only at the conclusion of the story that Vanya realizes the extent to which he has permitted himself to be exploited. The result is the explosion of act three, in which the pent-up energy of twenty years of unrealized resentment finds a sudden outlet.

The situation is not, of course, strictly analogous to that of *The Sea Gull;* but it has enough in common with it to warrant the assumption that the same mold served for both. Both plays depend ultimately on the contrast of youth and age. Vanya is much older than Treplev, but he acts like an adolescent, and, like Treplev, he is a country cousin. Serebryakov is older in proportion, evidently a later stage of Trigorin, a Trigorin in decay. In *The Sea Gull* young Treplev is despoiled and supplanted by the glamorous man from the city. In the same way, Serebryakov has pre-empted Vanya's place with his mother; he has taken the woman he loves; and he enjoys the fame and prosperity which Vanya has never had, but might have had, he thinks, if he had been permitted to develop his talents. Treplev's aggression, however, is directed principally against himself, and it kills him. Vanya's fury is turned against the offender. It is only when he demonstrates his ineptitude with the pistol that he thinks of turning his wrath upon himself. But he does not kill himself. Instead, he settles sadly and sensibly down to the business of living, and the play ends on a note that is infinitely more tender and truer than that of *The Sea Gull,* and certainly more powerful.

Although the two plays deal with the same theme, they could hardly be more dissimilar in effect. Both plays hinge on the question of waste; but the sudden destruction of Treplev is a very different matter from the slow process of attrition that consumes Vanya, Astrov, and Elena. It is not the disappointment of losing Elena that breaks Vanya's heart. He had little hope of winning her. What destroys him is the realization that in comparison with Astrov, he is contemptible in her eyes, and that he has come to the end of life, but has never lived.

This is, of course, the conscious aspect of his depression. The inner man, it is intimated, has a different story. From the psychic viewpoint, Vanya is depicted as a masochist who has taken every opportunity to deprive himself of the normal objects of man's desire, possibly because he prefers the pleasures of deprivation to those of satisfaction. But, as we know, a masochist generally has a threshold of suffering beyond which he experiences no delight, and if he is pushed beyond this point, he will react aggressively.[4] Vanya reaches this point quite suddenly in the third act.

Prior to Serebryakov's outrageous proposal to sell the estate, Vanya's courtship of Elena exhibits all the urgency of a neurotic drive. Very likely, his need to possess Elena reflects his mounting hostility toward her husband; but it would appear that her principal function in his life is to reinforce his conviction that nobody loves him. It is consistent with this assumption that he provokes Elena to humiliate him at every opportunity—he invites rejection whenever he can. It would doubtless be gratuitous to suggest, in the absence of any clear indication of the author's intention, that this beautiful woman has married a gouty old man mainly in order to be in a position to perform this sort of service for her admirers, but there is obviously something puzzling about Elena's obdurate virtue in the circumstances. One can hardly set it down to her sense of civic responsibility as she herself does in *The Wood Demon*. Indeed, she reacts normally to Astrov who is younger and a more desirable lover than Vanya. Astrov's advances seem crude. She finds him irresistible; yet in the end she will not have him; she takes only his pencil as a memento. As for Vanya, she takes nothing from him, save his manhood. Since this is precisely what he wishes to part with, his masochism is suitably gratified; but it is understandable that the man is depressed.

Love, then, plays a sad role in *Uncle Vanya*. The lovers are ill-matched, and all are more or less neurotically motivated in their passions. It is a discordant little world which Chekhov depicts—a group of pleasant people in idyllic surroundings, hopelessly at odds with themselves and with one another—and this world mirrors, it is suggested, the illness of the great world of which it forms part. Astrov has some therapeutic ideas with regard to this world. He proposes a program of reforestation, soil-conservation, and so on, but these are all physical measures. He has no idea of what is to be done about the soul-sickness which infects his world, and he is himself not immune to its attacks.

The pessimistic mood in which Chekhov often displayed the world around him represents, of course, a phase of nineteenth-century pessimism in Russia, in France, and elsewhere. The France depicted by the French naturalists was a jungle. The Russia revealed to us by the literature of the 1890's is a morass, and the writers of the succeeding period bring out with merciless realism the squalor of the cities, the poverty of the peasant villages, the corruption and stupidity of the bureaucracy, and the filth, brutality, drunkenness, and disease of the country in general, all the misery which the censorship sought in vain to conceal.

Chekhov's Russia, however, has nuances of its own. Astrov has an overwhelming consciousness of waste. His world is an organism suffering from the ravages of consumption, and Astrov's well-intended efforts to minister to its illness seem particularly pathetic in the light of the magnitude and the advanced stage of the disease. They are the earnest efforts of a physician, himself ill, to help a particularly intractable patient for whom he has no hope.

That Chekhov saw his Russia through the eyes of a dying man is a fact too obvious to require emphasis. It was inevitable after 1890 that he should see the world around him in terms of his own illness, and it was normal for him to project upon it his own symptoms. This world, his Russia, was a continent in decay. It was wasted by a disease that was perhaps curable, but there was no immediate prospect of a cure. The treatment would in any case be long, and the method was uncertain. In the meantime, the symptoms were unmistakable. The languor, the weariness, the hopelessness, the resignation of this Russia so clearly reflected his own exhaustion that the closeness of the correspondence was perhaps not entirely clear even to himself, for he was a man of buoyant spirits and naturally optimistic temper. But the world which he saw, and so vividly represented, was not quite the world that other people saw. It was the world of a man whose illness necessarily colored everything that was before his eyes, brightening some things and shadowing others in accordance with an inner principle of illumination that was specifically his own.

In France, the naturalistic dramatists were much concerned with the reaction against the corrupt democracy of the period. Their criticism was directed primarily against the hypocrisy and venality of the middle class, and its betrayal of the principles of the Great Revolution. Russia had not yet had a revolution. It had never known any sort of democracy, and the half-hearted reforms which Alexander II had instituted for local self-government were clearly not much to the purpose. It was altogether reasonable in these circumstances to take an optimistic view of the future. Chekhov's characters are generally agreed that though the present is hopeless, the world is poised on the threshold of paradise. In three or four hundred years, as Chekhov never tired of saying, life would be beautiful. The exact nature of the process that would bring about this change was not clear to Chekhov. It was clearer to Gorky; and perhaps under the influence of Gorky and others, Chekhov came, in the course of time, to believe in the efficacy of the coming storm which his characters occasionally predict. But Chekhov was at no time a Marxist. He was, at bottom, an admirer of the cultured landowning class, and aspired to belong to this class himself; at every opportunity he declared his candidacy and applied for membership. As we can see from *The Cherry Orchard*, the passing of this class gave him no pleasure—on the contrary, he identified its illness most closely with his own.

Chekhov was, at this time, if anything, a meliorist. Regardless of one's political convictions, there were things, clearly, that needed to be done within the existing social frame. There was great need for improved santitation, new schools, new libraries, new hospitals. Chekhov busied himself from time to time in organizing such institutions; but the artist saw further than the man, and the dialogue between the two madmen in *Ward No. 6*, the patient and the doctor, speaks as clearly as possible of the conflict in Chekhov's mind with regard to the future of the world. His attitude in the last decade of the century appears to be most faithfully reflected in the characterization of Astrov, the most complex and most comprehensive personage he had so far attempted to put on the stage.

Astrov is a man of great talent and vigor, a little beyond the flower of his manhood. He has a strong sense of vocation, and an almost equally strong feeling as to the hopelessness of his efforts. As a doctor, he feels it is his duty to minister to the sick; but the sick often persist in their determination to be sick. So it is, too, with the land, which he has also taken under his care, and which is equally recalcitrant. His resolute, but ineffective, efforts to nurse it back to health, his campaigns to get the peasants to burn peat instead of wasting the forests, to farm the soil sensibly, and rotate their crops rationally, bring out all the earnestness of his nature. But he knows that his life is wasted in this corner of Russia. Everything resists him, and he is weary. He is not a religious man. He does not believe in God. Yet the thought of God comforts him. He says to the nurse in act one: "I sit down and close my eyes—like this—and I think, will those who come after us two hundred years from now, those for whom we are breaking the way . . . will they remember us with gratitude? No, nurse. They will forget."

MARINA: Man forgets. But God remembers.
ASTROV: Thank you for that. You speak truly.

Astrov is spiritually ill. He feels, like the professor of medicine in *A Dreary Story*, that his soul is drying up. He himself is a waste land, and he is as powerless to avert his own emotional dessication as he is to alleviate the spiritual suffering of his friends. He realizes Sonya's misery and her love, but he is unable to help her. He can do nothing for Vanya in his hour of need, and it is his feeling of helplessness that makes him seem brusque and heartless. Just as Katya appeals in vain to Nikolai Stepanovich in *A Dreary Story*, and Masha to Dr. Dorn in *The Sea Gull*—just as Lika had appealed to Chekhov in reality—so Vanya turns to his friend in his agony:

VOYNITSKY: I can't bear it. What can I do? What can I do?
ASTROV: Nothing.
VOYNITSKY: Tell me! Tell me! Oh, God! I am only forty-seven. I may live to be sixty. I have thirteen years ahead of me . . . an eternity! How can I endure life all those years? What shall I do? How can I fill these years? Don't you see? (*He presses Astrov's hand convulsively*) Don't you see, if only I could live out the rest of my time in some new way! If I could only wake up one sunny morning and feel that life had begun again, that the past was forgotten and gone like smoke! (*He weeps*) Oh, to be able to begin life again! To start over! Tell me, tell me, how is it done?

ASTROV (*crossly*): Rubbish! What sort of new life can we —yes, both of us, you and I—what sort of new life can we expect? We have no hope at all.

VOYNITSKY: No hope?

ASTROV: None at all.

VOYNITSKY: But please—give me something to live for! (*He puts his hand to his heart*) I have such pain, such burning pain . . .

ASTROV (*shouts angrily*): Stop that! (*More moderately*) It may be that those who come after us, seeing our blindness and stupidity, will find some new way to happiness; but we—you and I, that is—have only one hope, and that is that we shall have pleasant dreams, perhaps, when we lie in our graves. (*He sighs*) Yes, my boy, in this entire district there were only two decent and intelligent men. You and me. But this miserable, trivial life of ours, this life we have lived the past ten years, has sucked us down and poisoned us, and now we are as contemptible, as petty, and as stupid as the rest . . .

When, at the end, Elena Andreyevna comes to say goodbye, Astrov parts from her without displaying emotion. He is aware of the unhealthiness of his interest in her, and of the futility of any possible relation they might establish. He knows also that, in this world, work is our lot, and that happiness is an unattainable mirage. Chekhov wrote Olga Knipper that this scene should be played without passion, in a quiet and casual mood: [5]

ASTROV (*pressing her hand*): Yes, you had better go. (*Thoughtfully*) You seem sincere and good, and yet there is something strangely restless about your whole personality. The moment you and your husband arrived here, all the people who up to that time had been busy doing useful things felt somehow obliged to give up whatever they were doing in order to concentrate their entire attention on you and your husband's gout. Between you and your husband you have infected us all with your idleness . . . I am quite sure that had you remained here much longer we should all have been overtaken by the most terrible misfortune. I, for one, would have died, and you . . . believe me, no good would have come to you, either. Go. Our little play is over—and it has had a happy ending. Go.

ELENA ANDREYEVNA (*snatches a pencil from Astrov's table*): I shall keep this pencil to remember you by.

The symbolic nature of this souvenir is perhaps too clear to require comment. It is noteworthy that without giving him any pleasure or comfort, Elena has effectively severed Astrov's relation with Sonya, and forced him to leave this house in which he had found peace, if not happiness. In a sense she has neutralized him sexually, at least for the time. In a very little while, Astrov leaves. Even before the sound of his carriage bell has died away in the distance, Vanya and Sonya are already working at their farm accounts. The scene recomposes itself as quickly as the sea in the wake of a passing ship. Marya makes a note on the margin of her pamphlet. Telegin plays a polka softly on his guitar. From the garden comes the sound of the watchman's rattle. The old nurse clicks away at her knitting. All is ready for the final aria:

VOYNITSKY (*to Sonya, stroking her hair*): My child, I feel so bad. You can't imagine how bad I feel!

SONYA: What can we do? We must go on living. (*Pause*) Yes, Uncle Vanya, we shall go on living. We shall live through the long succession of days, and the endless evenings; we shall bear with patience the trials that life brings us; we shall work for others, without rest, now and afterwards too, when we are old; and then, when our time comes, we shall die quietly, and in the world beyond the grave we shall say that in this world we wept and we suffered, and that our lot was bitter, and God will pity us, and you and I, uncle, dear uncle, shall see a life that is bright and beautiful and splendid; we shall rejoice and look back on our past life without bitterness, with a smile—and we shall rest. I believe it, uncle, I believe it with all my heart and soul... (*She kneels at his feet and lays her head on his hands, continuing in a weary voice*) We shall rest!

(*Telegin plays the guitar softly*)

We shall rest! We shall hear the angels, we shall see the heavens sparkling with jewels, we shall see all the ills of this life, all our pain, vanish in the flood of mercy which will fill the world, and our life will be quiet and gentle, and as sweet as a caress. I believe it, I believe it... (*She wipes away his tears with her handkerchief*) Poor, poor Uncle Vanya, you are crying. (*Through tears*) You have had no happiness in your life. But wait, Uncle Vanya, wait... We shall rest. (*She embraces him*) We shall rest... (*The Watchman taps on his board. Telegin strums quietly. Marya Vasilevna makes a note on the margin of her pamphlet. Marina knits her stocking*) We shall rest.

(*The curtain falls slowly.*) [6]

The speech is inexpressibly poignant, but all the more poignant if we consider that Sonya has so far given no evidence of a belief in life after death and that, in any case, the bright and beautiful life in the other world, with the angels and the rest of it, is evidently a child's dream, long ago relinquished, in which one finds comfort only because the need is so great, and there is no other comfort to be had in this life. Thus Sonya, whose own heart is breaking, plays the little mother for Vanya, and she consoles him with fairy tales in which neither of them believes, and yet they find them beautiful in their hour of agony.

Between Sonya's faith in a heavenly paradise with angels and, in *The Three Sisters*, Vershinin's faith in the earthly paradise of the future there is not much difference. What is principally significant in these expressions of faith, apart from their pathos, is the crying need for illusion, even the emptiest, in a world which fantasy alone can render tolerable.

Chekhov was now approaching 40. He was not rich. But he could at last indulge himself in the luxury of writing little and writing well. During 1899 he finished only two stories, and he began a third. These were among his finest—*The Lady with the Little Dog*, *In the Ravine*, and *The Bishop*, a wonderfully sombre piece of semi-autobiographical writing. In this period his thoughts were constantly of the theatre. Throughout the winter he wrote often to Nemirovich and Stanislavsky urging them to bring the company south in the spring. He was in a position to be persuasive. They were pressing him hard to finish a new play for the coming season in Moscow. He promised to discuss the matter with them at Easter when they came to Yalta. Nemirovich found it impossible to resist this bait and, after considerable shilly-shallying, it was agreed that the Moscow Art Theatre would visit Sevastopol and Yalta in April.

In the meantime news came, early in 1900, that Chekhov had been elected, along with Tolstoy and Korolenko, to honorary membership in the Academy of Science. It was an honor which elevated him to the rank of General in the Table of Comparative Precedence, and therefore entitled him to be called Excellency. Chekhov took this mark of distinction very much in his stride, remarking to Menshikov that he was pleased with the title, but would be even more pleased when he lost it, as in time he was sure to do.

In the first days of April, the Moscow Art company arrived in Sevastopol with a carload of scenery, and a trainload of friends and admirers. The tour became a festival. Some days after the appearance of the troupe, Chekhov arrived by steamer from Yalta. He was pale and ill, but somehow he managed to pull himself together, and he had the satisfaction of seeing *Uncle Vanya* for the first time in full production, with Stanislavsky in the role of Astrov. The performance was a triumph. He began to feel better. A week later, the company came to Yalta and repeated its success. When it left, after a wonderfully convivial visit, Stanislavsky took with him the definite assurance that Chekhov would have a new play for the coming season in Moscow. This new play was *The Three Sisters.*

The Three Sisters

THE *Three Sisters* (*Tri Sestry*) did not take form conveniently. In the fall of 1899, Chekhov wrote his friend the actor Vishnevsky—who was eventually to play Kulygin—that he was getting nowhere with the idea they had previously discussed in Moscow: "The play we were talking about does not exist, and I doubt very much that it will be written soon. Twice I began it, and twice gave it up—each time I got something other than I wanted." A month or so later he wrote Nemirovich that he could produce nothing that year: "The coming season will have to do without a play of mine—that's definite." At the beginning of December, in response to an urgent letter, he wrote that he realized how anxious the company was to have a new play for the coming season, and that he would do his best to write one, but "what if the play just does not come off?" And he added that he would discuss the whole thing with him at Easter.

Chekhov began working seriously on *The Three Sisters* in August 1900, after an idyllic month in Yalta with Olga Knipper. For the first time in his life he was in love. His mood was joyous. The play he had in mind was to be gay and funny.

Chekhov made, as always, extensive preparations for his new venture. He was in the habit of keeping a notebook in which, like Trigorin, he jotted down details from life, colorful notions, interesting turns of speech, and random observations which he considered useful in forming his characters. When he thought he had enough material to work with, he began to write. He composed his scenes, act by act, with a clear idea of the characters, but no very definite plan for the plot. The details of the narrative were expected to define themselves in his mind as he wrote. He disliked working within a rigid outline.

On August 5, 1900, Chekhov wrote Vishnevsky: "I have already written a good deal, but until I come to Moscow I shall not be able to evaluate it. Quite possibly what I am getting is not a play at all, but some Crimean nonsense. The title is—as you already know—*The Three Sisters*, and for you I am preparing the part of second master at a grammar school, the husband of one of the sisters. You will wear a schoolmaster's uniform with a decoration around your neck."

Some days later, he wrote to Olga: ". . . I am actually writing a play now—well, not exactly a play, maybe, but a sort of hash. A great many characters—very likely I shall soon get into a mess and give the whole thing up . . ." [1] August 18 he wrote her again: "The play is in my head; it is already coming out; it has somehow got itself into shape, and is clamoring to be put on paper; but no sooner do I sit down to write than the door opens and some ugly face pokes in. I don't know how it will be, but the beginning has turned out fairly well, pretty smooth, I daresay." [2]

Two days later, he was unhappy: "I have cooled off toward the beginning; it has all grown cheap in my eyes . . . and now I don't know what to do. A play ought to be written, you know, without taking breath, and this is the first morning that I have been alone . . . No matter." [3] Three days later matters were still going badly: "I'm afraid it will be dull. I shall write it, and, if I don't like it, I shall set it aside till next year or till I feel like working on it again . . ." He felt better about it, a week later: "Although it's rather tedious, I think it's all right; it's intellectual. I am writing slowly; that's something I didn't anticipate. If it doesn't come out as it should, I shall put it away till next year. Oh, how constantly I am interrupted! If you only knew! But I can't refuse to see people. I'm not equal to it."

By September 5, he had more complaints. "... I am not hurrying it, and it is even possible that I shall come to Moscow without finishing; there are a great many characters; it's crowded; I'm afraid it will come out indistinct or pale, and so it would be better to put it off till next season. *Ivanov*, by the way, was produced at Korsh's immediately after I wrote it, but all my other plays I kept by me a long time waiting for Nemirovich to ask for them, and so I had time to put in all sorts of corrections ..." [4] A few days later, he wrote his sister Masha: "I find it very difficult to write *The Three Sisters*, much more difficult than any of my other plays."

In the middle of September he felt ill and was unable to work for a time. He wrote a discouraging note to Vera Kommissarzhevskaya, who had asked for the play for her benefit night in Petersburg. Meanwhile his friends at the Moscow Art Theatre were pressing him for a copy of the script. He wrote to Olga that he was not yet ready. In any case, he wished to be present when the play went into rehearsal: "Let it lie on the table a bit ... Four important female parts, four young women of the upper class; I cannot leave that to Stanislavsky—with all due respect for his gifts and understanding. I must have at least a peep at the rehearsals." [5]

He was dejected at the beginning of October: "I have not worked at it for ten days or more. I've not been well, and I'm a little sick of it, so that I don't know what to tell you about it ... The play will be finished in any case, but, certainly not this season." [6]

He arrived in Moscow October 23 in excellent spirits. *The Three Sisters* was finished, and he settled down at the Dresden

Hotel to make a clean draft of the manuscript. From his correspondence with Kommissarzhevskaya, it seems clear that as late as the middle of September he was still of two minds as to whether to give the play to the Moscow Art Theatre or not. He still did not trust Stanislavsky. His lack of confidence grew even deeper after he attended the formal reading. Several times during the reading he was heard to exclaim: "But what I wrote was a vaudeville!" The actors were completely bewildered. They had no idea what it was Chekhov had in mind; whether it was to be taken seriously, as a *drame*, or treated lightly, as a comedy. After the reading, Chekhov heard them muttering the usual objections: "Not a play!" "No acting roles!" An actor began saying in a loud voice that, while in principle he did not agree with Chekhov . . .

Chekhov left the theatre without a word to anyone. Stanislavsky hurried after him to his hotel. He was afraid Chekhov had been taken ill. But Chekhov was not ill. He was in a cold fury. His play, he said, had been completely misunderstood. What he had written was a comedy. They were treating it as a tragedy. And now he was certain that the whole thing had been a mistake. Stanislavsky tried in vain to mollify him. But Chekhov was convinced that the play must be revised, and he began work on it at once.

He managed to get through two acts before the cold weather forced him to leave Moscow. On November 13 he wrote Kommissarzhevskaya that the play was definitely not for her. It had turned into a long, dreary, and gloomy drama; its mood, so he was told, was suicidal. On December 11 he set out for Nice, taking the last acts with him. The revision went quickly. The changes in act four, he wrote Olga, were drastic, startling; but act three was only lightly retouched. The revised script was in Stanislavsky's hands by December 23, and the play went into rehearsal at once with Olga in the role of Masha, and Kachalov as Vershinin. Chekhov was in Nice during the whole of the rehearsal period, and though

Nemirovich spent some days with him on the Riviera, he felt completely out of touch with the production. He complained to Olga: "Not a damned soul writes me a word about it!" [7]

In fact, from time to time, he did hear something about the progress of his play. What he heard was evidently not altogether to his liking. "In act three there is noise on the stage—why noise? There should be noise only in the distance, offstage, a confused hollow noise; on the stage everything is quiet, everyone is exhausted, almost asleep. If you spoil the third act, the play is done for, and I shall be hissed in my old age." [8] Stanislavsky had insisted on having Tusenbach's dead body carried across the set in the last act. It was an effect to which Chekhov had strong objections: "If the play is a failure, I shall go to Monte Carlo and lose till I cannot see straight." But he did not go so far as to interfere decisively with anything. He contented himself with grumbling inarticulately from a distance, like a threatening storm.

In matters of detail, Chekhov was even more fastidious than Stanislavsky. He was particularly anxious that the production should represent the detail of military life in *The Three Sisters* with all proper accuracy, and he had asked his friend Colonel Victor Petrov to consult with the director regarding the dress and the behavior of the officers. Petrov found fault with the young lieutenants and with Captain Solyony; he thought Colonel Vershinin's deportment in seducing a married woman extremely unprofessional; but he liked the play and the acting of the three sisters. Nevertheless Chekhov had dire premonitions. He continued to write often and anxiously for news of the rehearsals, but he moved about from place to place so rapidly during the crucial weeks that he was unable to receive any reports—one might imagine that he was actually avoiding the possibility of hearing anything about the fortunes of his play.

The play opened on January 31, 1901, while Chekhov was

in Rome on the way to Africa. A wire from Nemirovich reached him in Rome assuring him of the play's success. It was only when he reached Yalta some weeks later that he received Olga's telegram of congratulation, forwarded from Algiers. In the meantime Lavrov had published the text of *The Three Sisters* in the February issue of *Russian Thought* from proofs corrected by Nemirovich. Chekhov was furious at this unauthorized publication. It was actually not until the next year that his final version was published, in the seventh volume of his *Collected Works*. This version included a number of textual changes, and many new stage directions.

The truth is that *The Three Sisters* was no great success. It appealed strongly to people like Nemirovich, Stanislavsky, and Gorky, but it was a long time before the critics and the public accepted it. The play, indeed, is puzzling if one tries to fit it into the mold of the well-made genre, and the temptation to do this is all the greater since in form it is not so far from the accepted norms of drama as to suggest a wholly new departure.

The principal structural innovation is in the arrangement of the interlaced stories. The traditional design of Western comedy from the sixteenth century on involved the simultaneous management of two or more plots of climactic nature, subordinated according to the rank, age, or social condition of the participants, connected by common incidents which affect each plot line differently, the whole complicated by misunderstandings, deceits, mistaken identities, or disguises, and resolved by means of recognitions, discoveries, and peripeties. In *The Three Sisters* Chekhov made use of a novelistic technique in which several lines are unfolded simultaneously without any evident thematic dependence, no subordination, no surprises, and very little convergence of plot. The result is a story that seems relatively plotless.

Beyond the several actions which the play develops, there

is, however, the enclosing symbol which defines the whole and gives it unity and point—Moscow, the unattainable city toward which all the action tends, the dream which all the events of the play combine to thwart. The principal motif of the play is thus not so much an action as a tension, and what is emphasized is not what happens, but what does not happen. As the play is conceived, each of the principal characters has a story of his own. These stories are not of equal importance and they hardly bear on each other, but, developed in canon, they make an effect that is curiously polyphonic. The opening scenes, as is usual with Chekhov, are directly and efficiently informative. By the end of the first act, there are set on foot the stories of Vershinin and Masha; of Natasha and Andrey; of Irina, Tusenbach, Solyony, and Chebutykin; and lastly, the very uneventful story of Olga. These narrative strands, while dramatically independent, are interwoven so as to give the effect of texture. In consequence, the play, though it is crowded with incident, has very little forward impulse and gives the impression of stasis, a composition rather than a narrative.

The Three Sisters is a story of provincial life. In all likelihood, it reflects a mood which Chekhov experienced often in the years of his enforced absence from Moscow. Very little happens in the provincial town in which General Prosorov's brigade is quartered: people are born, live, die, and are forgotten. On the far horizon, Moscow glitters like a star, a beacon to steer by, an idea to sustain hope. It is more than a city. It is a paradise. The illusory quality of this dream is brought out clearly in the play, but evidently the dream is poignant. In his story *On Official Duty* Chekhov wrote of the young magistrate Lyzhin:

> The fatherland, the real Russia, was Moscow, Petersburg. But here he was in the provinces, the colonies. When one dreamed of playing a leading part, of becoming a public figure, for instance an examining magistrate

> in a particularly important case in a circuit court, of being a social lion, one always thought of Moscow. To live, one must be in Moscow. Here one cared for nothing, one grew easily resigned to one's insignificant position, and expected only one thing out of life—to get away from here quickly, quickly. And Lyzhin mentally moved about the Moscow streets, went into the familiar houses, met his relatives, his comrades, and there was a sweet pang in his heart at the thought that he was only twenty-six, and that if in five or ten years he could break away from here and get to Moscow, even then it would not be too late, and he would still have a whole lifetime before him . . .

Chekhov published this story in 1899. It must have been fresh in his mind at the time when he first discussed the theme of *The Three Sisters* with Vishnevsky in Moscow. In any case, the theme of the play is clearly foreshadowed here, and there is even some duplication of detail. When Lyzhin is comfortably ensconced in the fine house of the local squire Von Taunitz, and he meets the rich man's beautiful, cultivated daughters,

> . . . dreary thoughts prevented him from enjoying himself, and he kept thinking that there was no life here, but only bits of life, fragments, that everything here was accidental, that one could draw no conclusions from it, and he even felt sorry for these girls who were living their lives, and would end them, in the wilderness, in a province far away from the center of culture, where nothing is accidental, but everything moves in accordance with reason and law, where, for instance, every suicide is intelligible, so that one can explain why it has happened and what is its significance in the general scheme of things . . . [9]

The irony of this passage need hardly be pointed out. The young magistrate's reflections on the life of the cultural centres of Russia were certainly meant to elicit a smile from those who knew Moscow and Petersburg as they really were, and there was a long tradition of satirical comment on the subject from Griboyedov and Gogol to Goncharov and Saltykov-Shchedrin. In *The Three Sisters* the ironic implications of the girls' desperate longing to escape from the life they know to the life of their dreams are not so obvious. Life in Moscow would certainly be more amusing than life in Berdichev or Orel, and the longing of the daughters of General Prosorov for the brilliant life of the capital seems normal and justifiable. It is only because in their imagination the glamor of Moscow is exaggerated to such fantastic proportions that their longing takes on a comic nuance.

For these young women, Moscow is the solution to every problem, the answer to every prayer, the only possible hope of felicity on earth. Against the towering magnificence of Moscow everything that is at hand is diminished to triviality. Moscow reduces life to an absurdity. The result is a continual devaluation of present reality in favor of a mythical future state which it becomes increasingly apparent can never be realized. For the sisters, therefore, Moscow serves the same function as the ideal future for Vershinin. It is an opiate which reduces life to a dream, and transfers its immediacy to a fantasy which transcends any possible experience. It is only when the sisters at last despair of Moscow that they find some measure of maturity, and begin to work out their destiny in the world they really inhabit.

The connections between *On Official Duty* and *The Three Sisters* are probably too close to be accidental. The mystical intimation of an all-involving cosmic process, which Lyzhin suddenly experiences in the course of his meditations, colors a good deal of Chekhov's work, perhaps all of it, but it is especially clear in *The Three Sisters*. In the story, Lyzhin is thinking of Lesnitsky, whose suicide he has come to investigate, and of the old town constable plodding through the snow, the prototype, very possibly, of Ferapont in the play, and it occurs to him that:

> Some tie, unseen, but significant and essential, bound them together, and even bound them to Von Taunitz, and even bound all men together—all men. In this life, even in the remotest desert, nothing is accidental, everything is the result of a universal idea, everything has a soul, one soul, one aim, and to understand this, it is not enough to think, it is not enough to reason, one must have also, it would seem, a special gift of insight which is not bestowed upon all. So that the unhappy man who had broken down and killed himself . . . and the old peasant who spent every day of his life going from one man to another seemed to be accidents and unrelated fragments of life only to one who thought of his own life as an accidental fragment, but were seen to be parts of a single organism, marvellous and rational, by one who thought of his own life as part of that universal whole, and understood how closely everything was related. So Lyzhin thought, and it was a thought that had long lain hidden in his soul, and only now it was unfolded broadly and clearly to his consciousness.

This theme is emphasized particularly in a number of stories written in the period between 1888, the date of *A Nervous Breakdown*, and 1898, the date of *Gooseberries*. *On Official Duty* was written very soon after *Gooseberries*, and the coincidence of dates indicates that the idea was vivid in the author's mind immediately before his composition of *The Three Sisters*. The play is only lightly colored with the type of humanitarian thought we associate wtih Tolstoy, or with Herzen, but Vershinin, Tusenbach, and Irina recall the magistrate Lyzhin in more than one particular. In *On Official Duty* Lyzhin suddenly discovers, to his great surprise, that he has a social conscience:

> . . . And he felt that this suicide and this peasant's sufferings somehow lay upon his conscience. To accustom oneself to the idea that these submissive people must bear the burden of all that is hardest and heaviest in life—how terrible it was! To accept such sacrifices as one's due, to desire for oneself a life full of light and movement among happy and carefree people, to be continually dreaming of such a life, this simply meant to hope that there would be more suicides of men crushed by toil and anxiety, and more and more examples of weak outcasts of whom people would sometimes speak at supper in a mood of arrogance and mockery, without ever lifting a finger to help them . . .

It is evidently in some such sense that we must understand the final speeches of *The Three Sisters*. What has happened to Lyzhin in his exile from Moscow has happened also to the daughters of General Prosorov. The submissiveness of Ferapont does not weigh particularly on their conscience, but their misfortunes have taught them compassion, and opened a way for them to live in a world beyond that of their immediate desires and interests. They have lost, each of them in her own way, the possibility of gratifying their deepest wishes. In exchange they have gained such insight into the human condition as is not normally granted to fortunate people. They have learned, through suffering, that work, not happiness is the human lot, and thus they have become serviceable human beings, of value to society. The theme is familiar. The only complicating factor is Chekhov's skepticism.

The Three Sisters tells a very simple story, but since this is woven of three separate strands of narrative, the result is a tolerably complex dramatic texture. The play opens on the first anniversary of the death of General Prosorov. It is spring. The general's three daughters have remained in the town on which his brigade of artillery is quartered and, with their brother Andrey, they live in his house, which they have inherited. Olga, the eldest, is a schoolmistress. Masha has married a Latin teacher at the local high-school. Irina has a position in the telegraph office. The pride of the family is Andrey. He is expected to continue his studies at the university and to become a professor.

The general has given his daughters an excellent education. They are wonderfully accomplished girls, sensitive, and exquisitely brought up. Unhappily, in the small town in which they are stranded, there is nobody of their class but the officers of the garrison, and their hopes are centered on their brother, who will one day take them away with him to Moscow, where they can fulfill themselves in an environment better suited to their talents. But Andrey, like Ivanov in Chekhov's earlier play, is quickly drained of his youthful vigor and, perhaps to compensate for his lack of vitality, he has fallen in love with a town girl called Natasha. He marries this girl, has a child by her, and is soon neutralized as a human being. Natasha is stupid, but she is strong. The sisters, on the other hand, are too well-bred to defend themselves against her. As a result, she soon assumes a commanding position in the household.

In the meantime, a new lieutenant-colonel, Vershinin, arrives to take command of a battery. He is 45, a handsome man with a neurotic wife and two little daughters. He and Masha promptly fall in love, and for a little time they find happiness together. The story of Irina is more complicated. She is the youngest and most beautiful of the sisters. Two men woo her, Lieutenant Tusenbach and Captain Solyony. Solyony is a dangerous man, disagreeable and melancholy, a formidable duellist, with a touch of Satanism. He fancies himself a romantic figure in the style of Lermontov, whom he thinks he resembles. Tusenbach, on the other hand, is a likeable, but unimpressive young man with liberal ideas and a desire to make himself useful in the world, from which his aristocratic birth has alienated him.

Irina loves neither of these suitors, but of the two she much prefers Tusenbach. Solyony, however, has sworn that if he cannot have Irina nobody else shall have her. There is, moreover, another rival for Irina's affections. The regimental surgeon, Chebutykin, who once nourished a hopeless love for Irina's mother, finds the girl indispensable to his happiness. The relation between the two is that of father and daughter; but in Chebutykin's devotion there is something that is not altogether healthy.

These themes are developed in the course of the first two acts. In the third act, there is a fire which burns up half the town. The Prosorov's house is in the thick of the fire-fighting, and as the fire is brought under control, the house is overrun by excited and exhausted people. It is in this atmosphere that the threads of the play are at last drawn taut. Masha becomes Vershinin's mistress. Natasha finally asserts her supremacy as mistress of the house. Kulygin, Masha's husband, resigns himself to his sad fate as a cuckold; and Irina decides, in the absence of a better choice, to marry Tusenbach. As the situation thus takes on a definite shape, word comes that the brigade is soon to be transferred to a remote town in Poland, or perhaps to Siberia.

The last act takes place some months later. It is fall. The batteries are preparing to march. Other changes have taken place. Olga is established as headmistress of the school, and for her the dream of Moscow has faded completely. It has faded also for Masha. Her husband has been promoted and decorated; her lover is leaving forever. She too has struck roots in the town. Tusenbach, having resigned his commission, has accepted a job in a brickworks. Irina is about to marry him. But Tusenbach has been provoked into a duel with Solyony. Nobody acts to prevent the encounter. There is an exchange of shots offstage. Tusenbach is killed.

Against a background of martial music, the sisters embrace tearfully before they part. The brigade is marching out of the town, brave behind its trumpets and its singers. Chekhov had described the order of march in *The Kiss:*

> ... To right and to left, fields of young rye and buckwheat, with crows hopping about in them; if one looked ahead, one saw dust and the backs of men's heads; if one looked back, one saw dust and men's faces ... Foremost of all marched four men with sabres—this was the vanguard. Next came the singers, and behind them the mounted trumpeters. The vanguard and the singers, like torchbearers in a funeral procession, often forgot to keep the regulation distance and pushed a long way ahead ... [10]

The music fades off in the distance. There is nothing more.

The Three Sisters is Chekhov's masterpiece, the flower of impressionism in the drama. No play has ever conveyed more subtly the sense of the transitory nature of human life, the sadness and beauty of the passing moment. The action seems to be haphazard and amorphous, not because the play has no definite shape—it has a very definite shape—but because this shape seems to be constantly changing, like a cloud in the summer sky.

The story of Natasha principally gives the plot its outline. Her husband Andrey recalls the hag-ridden Platon Mikhailovich in Griboyedov's play, whose wife Natalya has reduced him to nothing. Chekhov's Natasha is a pretty woman of provincial cut. In the beginning, she is shy and awkward, and modest in her manner. It is obviously a great thing for one of her class to marry the son of the general of the garrison. Once she is safely ensconced, however, in the general's house, her true nature comes out. She becomes a despot. But with all the ridiculous show of importance which she assumes as her position improves, and all the social blatancy of the *arriviste*, she also demonstrates such strength of character as the well-bred sisters are incapable of developing. Her strength is graceless. She is brutal, coarse, and stupid; but she reaches out powerfully for what she wants, and it does not elude her. Thus the contrast is drawn vividly between the crude social climber who gains her point through her native shrewdness and the sharpness of her claws and the fragile, high-bred women who shrink from every indelicacy, and are therefore shouldered rudely aside by those who are not delicate.

There is no doubt as to how this process must end. The fine people are doomed. The cultivated classes, refined to the point where they can no longer endure the struggle for survival, cannot hold their own with the more vigorous social elements which desire to supplant them in the social heirarchy. As they do not deign to fight, and are therefore defenseless, they are certain to be overwhelmed by those whose skins are thick and elbows sharp. The meek are blessed, but they will not inherit the earth.

The prospect is not pleasant, but—such is the implication—it is in this manner that the race is periodically hauled up and invigorated. The refinements of culture filter down from above; its vitality wells up from below. The picture of social evolution in *The Three Sisters* is certainly not pretty, but it is far more optimistic in its implications, and far less brutal, than Strindberg's account of it in *Miss Julie*. Strindberg is emphatic, vociferous. Chekhov is quiet and calm. The two plays are at the poles of the rhetoric of the theatre, but with regard to the passing of the noble classes, Chekhov's point is not far removed from Strindberg's.

There is of course a vital difference. Strindberg's pessimism is thorough. Miss Julie destroys herself. The Prosorovs survive. They have no idea of what is happening to them; they know only their own wretchedness; but they are not wasted. *The Sea Gull* is heavy with the sense of waste. In *The Three Sisters* Chekhov suggests that the cosmic process is thrifty. It defaces the individual, but it does so in the interests of the race. The sisters will not have their desire; they will not go to Moscow; they will perhaps never know happiness. For this very reason, however, they will bring a little of Moscow with them into the wilderness. Olga will not marry, but something of her refinement will enter the minds and hearts of those she teaches. And so it will be with Irina, and with Masha, and even perhaps with Andrey, whose fate is the most pathetic and most comic of all. Because of these souls so rudely transplanted in alien soil, this wilderness in time will bloom; modestly perhaps, but surely. Vershinin says:

> ... Let's suppose that among the hundred thousand people who live in this town, there are just three people like you. Obviously you can't hope to prevail against the ignorance of the masses around you; in the course of your lives you'll have to give way little by little until at last you're merged in the hundred thousand. Life will swallow you up. But not entirely; you will have had some effect on those around you. After you're gone, there will be six more here like you, perhaps; then twelve, and so on, until ultimately most people will be like you ...[11]

Thus, little by little, the cultural frontiers are pushed forward. It is a military operation and results in casualties. The brigade of artillery was sent out into this wilderness for other than cultural purposes; nevertheless it brought its cultural baggage with it, and a little oasis of art and beauty was established where there had been nothing of the sort before. The general's family disliked the whole process intensely; it thought only of escape. But there was no escape, and willy-nilly these lives took root where they were planted. Thus the girls are forced to serve a purpose more useful than their own, and even the luckless Andrey, by marrying the indomitable Natasha, has served to blend the sensitiveness of his race with the vigor of hers. He has two sturdy children to prove his usefulness—at least one of which is his. The baby-carriage—and the wry implication—are both conspicuous in the final tableau of the play.

These incidents, in themselves trivial, are, in the aggregate, important in the human enterprise. It is a vast operation the purpose of which is not immediately apparent. Yet it appears to have a purpose, and even a directing agency; and if it has not, the result is the same. Whatever the rationalization may be, the batteries move forward to their next station. The story begins again.

In his oft-repeated expression of hope for the future, Vershinin sounds a good deal like a Spencerian evolutionist, but he is obviously not a systematic thinker. He is a man of faith. He himself is a victim of the evolutionary process. He knows himself to be expendable. It is his duty to man the outposts; and he moves forward with his brigade, and also with his daughters, who will perhaps live out once again the story of the daughters of General Prosorov.

With this play, the tendency to subordinate plot to portraiture which characterizes Russian drama from the time of Griboyedov comes to a kind of culmination. *The Three Sisters* marks the high point of the type of drama that has characterization for its object, and perhaps for that reason it indicates the need for a new departure in dramatic art. From the standpoint of realistic portraiture, this play may well be considered the crowning masterpiece, and also the end of a tradition.

The portrait of Natasha is the most vivid and also the least interesting. Chekhov had drawn her before, and in stronger colors, in the story called *In the Ravine* (1899). She is obviously a later version of that Aksinya who rises through sheer force of character from a level of servitude in the house of Tsybukin, whose deaf son she has married, to the point where she dominates the entire establishment, and even evicts her father-in-law.

So close is the similarity of the two characters that the description of Aksinya might guide one in casting the role of Natasha:

> Aksinya had gray, naïve eyes which rarely blinked, and a naïve smile constantly played on her lips. And in these unblinking eyes, in the little head on the long neck, in her shapeliness, there was something serpent-like. Dressed in green, with a yellow bosom, and a flickering smile, she looked about her as a little snake looks, stretching and raising its head, peering curiously at the passerby from a field of young rye in the spring.[12]

Like Natasha, Aksinya is determined to make her way in life. She clears every obstacle from her path, she is capable of every sort of crime and baseness; and, in this manner, she rises to the very top of her world, and even higher. In the end, "when she drives to her factory in the morning with a naïve smile, beautiful, happy, and, afterwards, when she gives orders in the factory, a great power can be felt in her." [13] So it is also with Natasha. She is strong and shrewd. She is stupid and ruthless; and people who are none of these things are quite at her mercy. She is quite hateful, but a great power can be felt in her. From the viewpoint of dramatic design it is clear why Chekhov would wish to contrast this forceful woman with the relatively nerveless characters who people his world. Like Lopakhin in *The Cherry Orchard*, she embodies the principal source of tension in the play, and thus provides a vivid accent in what might otherwise be a dramatic monotone.

Chebutykin is an extraordinary character, an apt illustration of how with a few touches of genius a stereotype can be transformed into a masterpiece of portraiture. Chebutykin, like Solyony, is at bottom a caricature, a vestige of the romantic drama. He is a little man, who complains often of his insignificance. At 60, or thereabouts, he is still playing the part of the broken-hearted lover, a tragic pose which suits him admirably, and gives him greater pleasure, doubtless, than he could possibly have expected from that love which was so long ago denied him. The portrait is superbly ironic. Chebutykin, like Solyony, has patterned his life after a picture he found in a book, a romantic stereotype. When he was a young man, the girl he wished to marry, Irina's mother, rejected him in favor of a more interesting suitor. But Chebutykin would not take no for an answer. He installed himself in Prosorov's domestic circle, and lived, in an avuncular capacity, in close proximity to his beloved all the years of her life. Irina is the living image of the woman he loved so long and so hopelessly. He has treated her as his daughter ever since she was a child, and it is in token of his love that on her twentieth birthday he presents her with the silver samovar which is the traditional present of husband to wife on the twenty-fifth anniversary of their marriage. The gift embarrasses everyone, but Chebutykin is not embarrassed:

> CHEBUTYKIN: My children, my sweet ones, I have no one in the world but you. You are dearer to me than anything. I am nearly sixty, I am an old man, a lonely, insignificant old man. The only thing in me that's worth anything at all is my love for you, and if it were not for you, really, I should have died long ago. (*To Irina*) My child, my darling, I've known you ever since you were born—I used to carry you in my arms—I loved your mother.[14]

As he says, Irina is indispensable to him; after his retirement, he intends to live out the rest of his days with her. For him, presumably, Tusenbach and Solyony are equally dangerous. It is not to his interest that Irina should marry either of them and, in fact, it would be preferable that she should not marry at all. His determination to have Irina for himself is therefore one of the elements in the final outcome of the action, but Chekhov forbore to emphasize it. So subtly is this motive worked out that the inference is perfectly reasonable that Chebutykin himself is not aware of the selfishness of his actions. But behind the cloak of good-humored apathy with which he protects himself from the world, Chebutykin feels strong emotions; occasionally these emotions flash out violently. When Irina remarks in the third act that she too is leaving the town, presumably for Moscow, Chebutykin smashes the porcelain clock which they have treasured because it was her mother's. The scene is evidently intended to be critical:

VERSHININ: . . . They were saying yesterday that our brigade may be transferred somewhere a long way off. Some said Poland; others somewhere near Chita.

TUSENBACH: I heard that also. And then what? The town will really be empty.

IRINA: We're leaving too!

CHEBUTYKIN (*drops the clock and breaks it*): Smashed to bits!

(*A pause. They all look upset and embarrassed*)

KULYGIN (*picking up the pieces*): Imagine breaking a valuable object like this! Ah, Ivan Romanich, Ivan Romanich! Take a demerit for conduct.

IRINA: That was mother's clock.

CHEBUTYKIN: Maybe so. Well, if it was your mother's, it was your mother's. And maybe I didn't smash it; maybe you just think I smashed it. Maybe we only think we exist, and we don't really exist at all. I don't know anything, and you don't know anything either! (*He stops at the door*) What are you looking at? Natasha is having a romance with Protopopov, and you don't see it! You sit around, and you don't know anything, and you don't see anything! Natasha is having a romance with Protopopov. (*He sings*) "Won't you please accept this date?" [15]

The symbol of the smashed clock is, as is usual with Chekhov's symbols, both ample and ambiguous. Chebutykin is drunk. It is impossible to say in this context whether Chebutykin means that his life was long ago smashed to bits, or that Irina is now smashing his life by leaving him. But the uncertainty of the impression is precisely what is necessary to the desired effect. It is not necessary that anyone should understand just why he has smashed the clock. It is only in books that such things are explained fully. In real life we are usually left to wonder at the things people do, and this sense of uncertainty is obviously the effect the scene was intended to produce.

In the last act, Chebutykin does not raise a finger to prevent his friends from killing one another. Solyony is murderous; but the duel is actually over a trifle. In the circumstances it would be normal for a third party to intervene, just as the doctor intervenes in *The Duel*. In *The Three Sisters*, Chebutykin might perhaps have stopped the proceedings simply by telling Irina of the danger that threatens her fiancé. As it is, he puts off her question with the brusque phrase, "*Nichevo. Takaya istoria!*"—"Nothing at all. What a business!" He is brusque and uncommunicative all the rest of the act, muttering into his newspaper, and humming a foolish ditty over and over to himself:

Ta-ra-ra-boom dya
Sizhu na tumbe ya.

That is, literally, and without benefit of rhyme:

Ta-ra-ra-boom de-ay,
I'm sitting on a bar stool.

If this song is intended to symbolize his feelings, it is about as informative as the symbol of the broken clock. The suggestion is that Chebutykin is not involved in the absurdities of his environment. He is sitting in his imaginary tavern, getting drunk as a sensible man must in a world that is too stupid to be taken seriously. His detachment, he suggests, is complete. But he is obviously lying—even to himself. He is deeply interested in the outcome of the duel. If Tusenbach is killed—and this is likely in view of Solyony's fame as a marksman—Irina will be left alone, and she will be his, perhaps forever. The consciousness that he is not completely guiltless in this affair makes him rude and cranky. He does not admit his satisfaction. If he did, it would be his duty, as a man of honor, to interfere.

All this is left to inference. Chebutykin does not explain himself, and the author does not explain him. But the intimation is that something quite intricate has been going on in his mind, and that the solution to his problem does not entirely please him. Masha comes upon him in the garden, reading:

MASHA: You look comfortable.
CHEBUTYKIN: Well, why not? Anything doing?
MASHA (*she sits next to him*): No. Nothing. (*A pause*) Tell me something. Were you in love with my mother?
CHEBUTYKIN: Yes. Very much in love.
MASHA: Did she love you?
CHEBUTYKIN (*after a pause*): I don't remember any more.

It is an interesting passage, especially when we consider that Chebutykin has made something of a career of his love for Masha's mother, and that everyone knows it. A few minutes later, Andrey mentions Solyony's provocation of Tusenbach, and Chebutykin tells them exactly what happened the day before. They all take a curiously detached view of the matter, as if Tusenbach were merely a casual acquaintance, and not one of their closest friends:

MASHA: What about the Baron?
CHEBUTYKIN: Well, what about him? (*There is a pause*)
MASHA: I don't know. Anyhow, you shouldn't let them fight. He might wound the Baron, or even kill him.

CHEBUTYKIN: The Baron is a fine man; but what's it matter, really, if there's a baron more or less in the world? What difference does it make?

Nobody seems to think it makes any difference. It is as if they felt the same sort of abstract interest in the possible death of their friend as Ranyevskaya in *The Cherry Orchard* feels with regard to the probable loss of her estate. When Solyony comes to fetch him, Chebutykin is visibly annoyed. Once more the couplet from Krylov's fable is tossed about:

He'd hardly time to catch his breath;
The bear was hugging him to death.

The phrase seems to express Solyony's sense of the swiftness of reprisal. He uses it first when Masha brings him up short in the first act:

SOLYONY: When a man philosophizes, you get philosophy ... or, at least, sophistry. But if a woman or two start philosophizing, you might as well give up.
MASHA: What do you mean by that, you horrible man?
SOLYONY: Nothing.

"He'd hardly time to catch his breath;
The bear was hugging him to death."

In the last act, the couplet comes up again while Solyony is walking off with the doctor to fight with Tusenbach. Chebutykin sighs disgustedly. Evidently he would rather not witness the duel.

SOLYONY: What are you grumbling about, old man?
CHEBUTYKIN: Oh, nothing.
SOLYONY: How do you feel?
CHEBUTYKIN (*sarcastically*): Wonderful!
SOLYONY: No need to feel upset, old boy. I won't go too far. I'll just wing him, like a snipe. (*He takes out a perfume bottle and perfumes his hands*) Used up a whole

bottle today, but still my hands smell—of death. (*Pause*) Remember those verses of Lermontov?

"And he, the rebel seeks the storm
As if in storms alone he can find peace..."

CHEBUTYKIN: Yes.

"He'd hardly time to catch his breath;
The bear was hugging him to death."

In a little while there is a shot in the distance and some minutes later, Chebutykin comes and whispers to Olga that Tusenbach is dead. His mood has changed:

OLGA (*shocked*): Oh no!

CHEBUTYKIN: Yes—it's a shame. I'm tired. I'm done in. I don't want to discuss it. (*With annoyance*) Anyway—what's the difference?

MASHA: What's happened?

OLGA (*puts her arm around Irina*): What a horrible day! I don't know how to tell you, darling...

IRINA: What? Tell me quickly. What is it? For heaven's sake, tell me! (*She begins to cry*)

CHEBUTYKIN: The Baron has just been killed in a duel.

IRINA (*crying quietly*): I knew it! I knew it!

CHEBUTYKIN (*he goes to the table and sits down*): I'm done in. (*He takes a newspaper from his pocket*) They want to cry; let them cry. (*He sings quietly to himself*)

Ta-ra-ra-boom de ay!
I'm getting tight today!

...What's the difference?

It is impossible to say precisely what Chekhov intended us to understand by this episode. Evidently he had in mind in this, and in the preceding scene with Masha and Andrey, to suggest the helplessness of people to change the course of events, but it is likely also that he was suggesting the reasons for their impotence in this crisis. At this time, it was not customary to interfere in matters of honor among the military. Besides, these people have other things to think about. Masha is losing her lover. Overwhelmed as she is with her own misfortune, she is not much concerned about Irina's troubles. Andrey is too deeply absorbed in his own unhappiness to care what happens to Tusenbach. He is, in any case, a useless man, and contents himself with the pedantic statement that it is downright immoral to fight duels or even to witness them. Chebutykin, even if he had no personal interest in the duel, would be too much the military man to intervene in the affairs of brother officers. In the absence of any precise indication, one is at liberty to adduce all or any of these reasons for the fact that the duel is permitted to take place.

It is this imprecision, this unstudied reluctance to assign precise motives for the actions of his characters, that characterizes Chekhov's style as a dramatist. As an impressionist he was chiefly concerned with the surface, and he made no obvious inference as to what, if anything, lay beneath it. His plays represent behavior in meticulous detail, the thing done, and the thing said; the rest is left to the spectator. The dramatist's easy assumption that he knows his characters to the bottom of their souls is a type of literary pretentiousness to which not even professional Freudians can lend themselves with dignity. It was a result of Chekhov's impressionistic attitude that he forbore the usual analysis of motive; it was also a mark of his extraordinary probity as a writer.

The result of this resolute objectivity is an immense gain in the vitality of the characterization. Modern drama, with its rigorously analytic method, often gives the impression of an autopsy, an examination of the walking dead. But Chekhov's characters spring to life readily, in all their dimension, intact and self-contained the moment they are contemplated. They are neither analyzed nor dissected; their inner life is their own. They remain mysterious, and their mystery interests us particularly because the author does not suggest that he understands it; and if he understands it, he makes no move to betray it. Thus, while in general the characters of drama make the impression on the stage of characters in a play, Chekhov's characters give the impression of living people.

The advantages of this method are too clear to require emphasis. Its chief disadvantage is that the play exercises very little control over the actors; and this Chekhov discovered to his cost in his various disagreements with the Moscow Art Theatre. It is possible to rationalize Chebutykin's behavior, but at best he is and remains a puzzle. Nevertheless, he must be played; and the actor who plays him will not play the part properly unless he has some idea of what he is doing. Upon his analysis and his conclusions, obviously, the success of the characterization will depend. It is understandable that all this puts an unusually heavy burden upon the actor, and one can only sympathize with Stanislavsky in his effort to secure a maximum identification of actor and character through a projection of the actor's inner experience upon the data furnished by the author. When the character is presented by the author as an enigma, the answer can be sought only in the inner life of the actor, and that only when he is completely alive in the part. Since something creative along these lines can be looked for only in actors of extraordinary intuition, it is to be expected that characters of this sort will commonly be presented in accordance with the usual stereotypes of the theatre, and, indeed, this is what generally happens.

If Chebutykin is difficult to define, Vershinin is more difficult still. One sees on the stage, from time to time, at least three versions of this character, each one a desperate attempt to fit him into a suitable cliché. Vershinin is presented as a fine man, devoted, brave, well-read, and very likely handsome. Masha finds him captivating from the first. But we cannot accept Vershinin at Masha's valuation. She finds the good Kulygin, her husband, very hard to bear, and she is romantically preoccupied with the image of the green oak with the golden chain around it. She is an unusually passionate girl, brusque in her manner, high-spirited, and ripe for love, and in her eyes the philosophical soldier appears in some degree of magnification. Chekhov, on the other hand, presents Vershinin sympathetically, but on a very realistic level.

Vershinin is certainly no Lochinvar. Though quiet, he is full of passion; he has a history of unhappy loves: he has been something of a lady's man. He is "not a thinker, not a philosopher, but simply a dilettante," who has found a refuge from despair in his faith in the future, a faith which he airs compulsively, like a devoted believer, and for analogous reasons. For that faith in God which, as an educated man he has had to relinquish, Vershinin has substituted an equivalent faith in man, at least in future man; and this faith serves him as the fancied resemblance to Lermontov serves Solyony, and the ever-present newspaper serves Chebutykin. Evidently Chekhov wished to point the contrast between the romantic posture of each of these characters and the much less glamorous reality which they represent. At any rate, he did not hesitate to make Vershinin look a bit of an ass, like the others, and this was an extraordinary dramatic departure with respect to a character who must carry the chief romantic interest of the play.

Vershinin's habit of speculating discursively at every opportunity, and always in the same way, makes it difficult to take him with complete seriousness; but it would be in the last degree inappropriate to suppose that the other characters find him a bore. On the contrary, it is necessary to the economy of the play that he be held in high respect and, in fact, he acquits himself very well. He is, as Tusenbach remarks in the first act, no idiot; but life has dealt him a buffet or two, and he is not unscathed. His often repeated formula is evidently an incantation to ward off pain, a bit of magic which makes the present endurable because it is unimportant. His creed is the only religion possible to a man who has lost his faith, but not his need of faith.

He is deeply aware of the flux of being:

> VERSHININ: Yes. We shall be forgotten. Such is our fate and there's nothing to be done about it. And what seems so very important to us now will also be forgotten in time, and it won't seem to matter a bit. (*A pause*) It is strange to think that we cannot possibly tell today what will be considered great and important tomorrow, and what will be thought to be trivial and foolish. Take the great discoveries of Copernicus, or Columbus, didn't they seem useless and insignificant at first? While some empty rubbish written by a crank was regarded as a tremendous revelation of truth. It may well be that some day the life we are now living will be considered primitive and ugly and brutal, and perhaps even wicked . . . [16]

In giving speeches of this sort to a character who is overly talkative, Chekhov detracts in some measure from their gravity. Vershinin, like all the other characters of this play, has his comic aspects; but insofar as he plays the role of *raisonneur*, the things he says are precisely those which Chekhov himself had said quite seriously and quite often; there are unmistakable traces of Vershinin all through Chekhov's correspondence. At the time Vershinin was conceived as a character, Chekhov could look forward with confidence to not more than a half-dozen years of life. The present must have begun to take on the provisional look of an ephemeral experience.[17] In any case, his world-view was, as we have seen, never clearly defined. He was, at times, not far from Chebutykin's negativism; but Vershinin, like Astrov, represents the positive side of his character.

Chebutykin and Vershinin are never directly confronted in *The Three Sisters*. Though they are often together on the stage, they have little to say to one another. But Vershinin and Tusenbach are sufficiently close to warrant a debate, and their discussion in act two puts one in mind of Dr. Ragin and Ivan Dmitrich in *Ward No. 6.* The scene is quite complex, for Masha is an interested participant, and the effect upon her of Vershinin's words gives dimension to the dialogue. It is an interesting example of Chekhov's dramatic style at this period of his career:

VERSHININ: Well, if we're not going to get any tea, we might as well talk.

TUSENBACH: Fine. What about?

VERSHININ: What about? Let's try and think, for example . . . what life will be like after we're dead, in two hundred years, say—or three . . .

TUSENBACH: Where's the problem? After we're dead, people will no doubt fly about in balloons, coats will be different, a sixth sense will be discovered and developed, perhaps, but life itself will be the same; it will still be as mysterious, and as difficult, and as full of happiness as it is now. In a thousand years people will still be sighing and groaning, "Ah, what a life!"—and yet they'll be just as much afraid of death as we are, and just as reluctant to die.

VERSHININ (*after thinking a moment*): How shall I put it? To me it seems that little by little everything on earth is bound to change; in fact, it's changing now, before our very eyes. In two hundred years, three hundred, or even a thousand—the exact time doesn't matter—there will come a new life, a happy life. Of course, in that life we shall have no part, but that is what we are living for now, that's what we're working for, yes, and suffering for—we are creating the future; and that gives our life all its meaning, and, you might say, its only happiness.

At this point in his discourse, Masha laughs quietly. It is evident that she sees nearer possibilities for happiness. Tusenbach does not understand.

TUSENBACH: What's that for?

MASHA: I don't know. I've been laughing all day.

Nor is Vershinin aware as yet of the cause of her gayety. His mind is too firmly fixed at the moment on the wonders of the future for him to admit the possibility of any present happiness. Like his prototype in *Gooseberries*, he cannot accept the idea of happiness in the world as it is. The idea seems sinful. But as he speaks, there is a subtle change in the turn of his thoughts. He continues to address himself to Tusenbach, but it is clear that his words are directed more and more to Masha:

> VERSHININ: I went to the same school as you, but I didn't get to the Academy. I've read a good deal; but I'm not much at choosing my books, very likely I've been reading the wrong things; all the same, the longer I live, the more I want to know. My hair is turning gray now, I'm getting old, and I know so little, ah, so very little! But the main point, I daresay, I can grasp, and I grasp it firmly. And how I wish that I could make you see also that happiness in this life is not for us; it's not right that we should have it; and we shall not have it. For us, what is needful is work, and work! Happiness is for those who come after us. (*A pause*) Not for me; perhaps for my children's children!

In this speech it is not difficult to catch the plaintive note, the hidden longing, the veiled challenge to Masha. It is a speech full of delicate overtones, a very roundabout form of love-making. Masha understands him very well and, as if to emphasize the point, the two young lieutenants enter quietly with a guitar and begin to sing softly. These subtleties are lost on Tusenbach:

> TUSENBACH: According to you, then, we shouldn't even dream of happiness! But suppose I am happy now?
>
> VERSHININ: No.
>
> TUSENBACH (*throwing up his hands and laughing*): Obviously we don't understand one another. Now how can you be convinced?
>
> (*Masha laughs quietly*)

Tusenbach continues:

TUSENBACH: . . . life won't be any different, no, not in your two or three hundred years, not even in a million years. It will be just the same as ever. Life doesn't change, it's always the same, it follows its own laws, which have nothing to do with us, and which anyhow we'll never understand. Take the birds that fly south in the autumn, the cranes, for example. They just fly; it makes no difference whether they have ideas, big ideas or little ideas in their heads, they fly just the same, without knowing why or even where. They fly and will go on flying no matter how many thinkers they may have flying along with them; let them think as much as they like, so long as they keep flying . . .

MASHA: And what sense does it make?

TUSENBACH: Sense . . . Look, it's snowing. What sense does it make? (*A pause*)

MASHA: It seems to me a person should believe in something or, at least, look for something to believe in, otherwise his life is empty, empty . . . How can you live without knowing why the cranes fly, why children are born, why there are stars in the sky? You must know what life is for, or else it's all rubbish and a waste of time . . .

VERSHININ: Still, it's a pity that youth passes . . .

The conversation dwindles into banality. Chebutykin chimes in:

CHEBUTYKIN (*reading from his newspaper*): Balzac was married in Berdichev.

(*Irina, who is playing solitaire, hums softly*)

CHEBUTYKIN: That I must really put down in my little book. (*He makes a note*) Balzac was married in Berdichev. (*He resumes his reading*)

IRINA (*laying down a card thoughtfully*): Balzac was married in Berdichev.[18]

As a philosophic discussion, perhaps, this leaves something to be desired, but from a dramatic viewpoint it is superb.

Vershinin talks as if he were an active socialist, one of those army officers of advanced views whom Kropotkin describes in his memoirs; but in fact there is nothing to indicate that the work he speaks of is other than imaginary. Tusenbach, on the other hand, professes no faith in the future of mankind, but he has already resigned his commission, and proposes, in Tolstoyan fashion, to work in a brickyard as a laborer, quite in the manner of the hero of Chekhov's story, *My Life*. The total disintegration of the discussion is punctuated by Chebutykin's comment on Balzac's marriage. Balzac was indeed married to Madame Hanska in Berdichev in 1850. This interesting fact is completely alien to the topic under discussion, but it has a certain interest for Irina—the intimation is that distinguished people have been married in places far less glamorous than Moscow, and if a man like Balzac was content to be married in a little town in the Ukraine, Irina has no occasion for despair. The association in her mind is clear, at least, to Tusenbach, and he begins speaking at once of his own future.

This passage illustrates quite well the manner in which Chekhov motivated his dialogue. The speeches are seemingly inconsequential; but their sequence reveals the underlying train of thought in each of the characters, and it is seldom that the associative links are completely lacking. It is entirely probable that the seemingly disjunctive nature of Chekhov's dialogue reflects his own habit of mind. His friends have commented on his way of interpolating a complete irrelevancy into a conversation in such a way as to indicate that he had been carrying on a train of thought quite apart from the subject under discussion. Of this idiosyncrasy, Chekhov made ample use in characterization, and the resulting technique, traces of which may be found in *Uncle Vanya* and in *The Sea Gull*, was brought to its perfection in *The Three Sisters* and, later, in *The Cherry Orchard*. It resulted in a dialectic texture of extraordinary richness, the beauty of which is immediately apparent, although its intricacy can be judged only if one takes the trouble to follow the course of the individual strands of thought as they weave below the surface, and then are brought up to mesh in the design. The brilliance of Chekhov's scenes, all the more remarkable since they are normally not at all eventful, is due in great measure to the fact that Chekhov very skillfully managed in this way to keep all his characters alive all the time they are before our eyes. Their silence is quite as expressive as their words, and the subtle play of associations keeps us continually aware of the hidden currents of thought and feeling which work below the surface of the visible action, and give it another dimension, the nature of which is intimated but the full extent of which can only be surmised.

The feeling of depth produced by the artful inconsequentiality of the dialogue is enhanced by the shrewd inconsistency of Chekhov's characterizations. Chekhov's personages do not trouble to be consistent like characters in a play. They voice their moods like people in real life, and are frequently involved in contradictions. In the second act, Tusenbach professes to have no faith in the future, and it is Vershinin who is the apostle of work. But in the first act, we find Tusenbach on the windward tack, and it is his words which have the proper prophetic ring. Irina has been talking about work:

TUSENBACH: ... They protected me from work. But I doubt that their protection will prove completely successful ... I doubt it! The time has come, a terrible storm is bearing down upon us, an enormous tempest is at hand, it's almost here. It will sweep away all the laziness, indifference, and boredom, all the scorn for work that is ruining our society. I'm going to work, and in twenty-five or thirty years, everyone will be working! Everyone!

CHEBUTYKIN: I won't be working.

TUSENBACH: You don't count.

SOLYONY: In twenty-five years, thank God, you won't be around at all. In two or three years, you'll be dead of a stroke, or else I'll lose my temper and put a bullet through your head, my angel. (*He takes a scent bottle from his pocket and sprinkles his chest and hands.*) [19]

There is, accordingly, a touch of irony in Tusenbach's disillusioned mood in the second act, for by this time he has actually resigned his commission and is ready to go to work, and the future which in the first act seemed to him so bright and certain now presents itself somewhat more realistically to his eyes. Irina, too, begins with a laudable zest for work, but she finds it difficult in the long run to sustain her enthusiasm:

IRINA (*trying to control herself*): Oh, I'm so miserable... I can't work, I won't work any more. I've had enough, enough! First I worked at the post office, and now I'm secretary to the town council, and I loathe and detest every bit of it, all of it! I'm nearly twenty-four, and all I've ever done is work. My brain is drying up. I'm getting thin. I'm getting old and ugly, and I have absolutely nothing, nothing to look forward to, no pleasure in life at all, and time flies past, and I feel I'm moving further and further away from any hope of a life that is really important and beautiful, and coming closer and closer to the brink of the abyss. I'm desperate, and why I go on living, why I don't kill myself, I can't imagine... [20]

These torments mark the transitional phase in the life of Irina. So long as she persists in her efforts to frame her life in accordance with a romantic preconception, she is wretched, but when at last she relinquishes her hope of Moscow and romance, life once again becomes meaningful, and she is able to feel its joy and its zest. She does not love Tusenbach, but he offers her an acceptable compromise, a decent and useful life with a pleasant man. She accepts this solution, but even this sensible decision is thwarted by Solyony.

In the end, Irina is left alone. She has no alternative but to find a position somewhere as a school teacher, to devote her life to "the people who need it." Her prospects are not bright; but she has found strength at last: "It's autumn now, soon it will be winter, and everything will be covered with snow . . . and I shall work, I shall work. . ." [21] The story of Irina thus ends less happily than the story of Nina in *The Sea Gull*, which in some ways it recalls. Nina too has lost her happiness, but she has found her vocation, and though life has dealt her a blow, she has something definite to hope for. Irina's vocation is less well defined than Nina's and her future is far from clear. Yet her story ends on a note of hope. In Chekhov's world, as in ours, there is much to be done; and fortunately there is work even for those who have no vocation.

But, as Chekhov conceived the play, the question of what is to happen to Irina seems in the end quite unimportant. Chekhov avoids conclusions. He traces Irina's life through an episode which ends with the death of Tuşenbach, but he leaves the question of Irina unresolved. Her life, presumably, continues beyond the play, and is lost to view among the many lives which pass across the stage, much as the brigade of artillery moves into and out of the area of the action.

The life which we glimpse in *The Three Sisters* is a continuum in which a few events are seen to make a vortex, a shape which is swallowed up in the flux as quickly as it was formed. In the story of *The Three Sisters* nothing is presented as other than ephemeral, and no event bears any special emphasis. The play simply marks a moment in eternity. In the impressionist view of things, of course, eternity is essentially a matter of moments. But Chekhov is by no means simply an impressionist. To understand him, it is important to add to the sense of episode, the sense of process, and, after that, the all-enveloping doubt.

The Three Sisters concentrates attention momentarily on what may be considered a trivial aspect of the evolutionary pattern, namely, the plight of the individual in the cosmic scheme. Evolution makes nothing of individuals. But within its outlines, insofar as they are intelligible, the drama of the individual may be magnified, if one has a mind to it, to something like universal proportions. In respect to the universal, the human drama is necessarily a microscopic art, and it is important for the dramatist to preserve his sense of scale. But once it is conceded that a particular destiny can have in itself no more than minimal importance, one is free to generalize its significance in terms as vast as the heavens; there is no limit to the artist's fancy. A drop of water can reflect a world.

The theme of *The Three Sisters* is so elusive as to be almost indefinable. The play involves considerable discussion of current problems; there is talk of work and happiness, of the necessity for preparing the future through education, of hope for an earthly paradise to come, and of the present need for self-sacrifice and social service. The action illustrates a familiar aspect of the social process, and this process appears to be evolutionary in its workings, but it is not at all certain what its goal may be, or of how it is to be reached. On the far shore of these troubled lives, Moscow flashes like a beacon. But it is a useless mark, a source of aspiration, but even more a source of frustration and unhappiness; and it is eventually relinquished in favor of other landmarks, less bright and less alluring, but more certain.

The situation in *The Three Sisters* is treated with austere realism. Life has its little satisfactions, but on the whole it is not a pleasant experience. The recurrent question is: why? Vershinin ventures one sort of answer; Tusenbach another; Chebutykin wastes no words. Apart from Vershinin and, in the end, Olga, none of these characters has any special awareness of the current which propels their lives. Individuals think of themselves as discrete entities, each with his own destiny. It is implied that they might better think of themselves in the aggregate as a wave, sharing a common impetus, and that their insistence on maintaining their individuality at any cost is a chief source of their discontent. Vershinin alone touches upon this point, but quite superficially, in the way of small talk in a drawing-room. His words are sufficiently impressive to induce Masha to stay to lunch, and Irina remarks that what he says should really be written down: this is their total effect. The implication is humorous.[22]

Olga echoes Vershinin's thought quite solemnly at the very last, it is true, but what she says is rather musical than meaningful. Her speech is less elegiacal and more energetic than Sonya's speech at the end of *Uncle Vanya*, and is therefore supported, not by a polka played on a guitar, but by drums and trumpets. Yet the net effect is not altogether different. The music, in fact, tells us as much as the speech:

> OLGA (*puts her arms around both her sisters*): The music sounds so gay, so brave, that I want to live! Oh my God! The years will pass, and we shall die and be gone forever, we shall be forgotten, forgotten—our faces, our voices, they will even forget how many of us there were; but our sufferings will bring happiness to those who come after us; peace and joy will reign on earth, and there will be kind words and blessings for us and for our times. Oh my dear sisters, our lives are not yet over. We shall live! The music is playing so joyously, so happily, and it seems to me that, very soon now, we shall know why we are living, and why we are suffering . . . If only we knew! If only we knew!
>
> (*The music grows fainter. Kulygin, smiling cheerfully, comes in with Masha's cloak and her hat. Andrey pushes in the baby carriage with Bobik in it.*)

CHEBUTYKIN (*sings quietly*):

Ta-ra-ra-boom de ay!
I'm getting tight today!

(*He looks into his newspaper*)

It's all one. All one.

OLGA: If only we knew! If only we knew! [23]

It is on this antiphony that *The Three Sisters* ends, not on a positive note, but on two levels of uncertainty. There is a distinct expression of faith in the future; but, obviously, it puts a severe strain on the imagination to discount present sorrow in the expectation of better times to come in some hundreds of years. To substitute the dream of the earthly paradise for the dream of Moscow is perhaps sensible in the circumstances, and even useful, but chiefly as a device for sustaining the flagging spirits of those whom life has cheated. *Uncle Vanya* is, on the whole, pessimistic. The strain of idealism is strong in *The Three Sisters*, but whether the note of irony on which it ends is as sharp as its counterpart in *Uncle Vanya* is a matter of opinion. In any case, it hardly matters. From an artistic viewpoint the result is the same.

In *The Three Sisters*, Vershinin evidently speaks for Chekhov, and his views are clear. But Chebutykin also speaks for Chekhov, and his views are equally clear. The old skeptic believes in nothing, and expects nothing. He is cynical, spent, a little wicked, yet in his way quite as sympathetic as Vershinin, and for him it is all nonsense, the past, the future, and the present—it all adds up to nothing, and the play virtually closes with his words: *Vse ravno! Vse ravno!*—"It's all one! It's all one!"

The indeterminate area between faith and skepticism measures the extent of Chekhov's spiritual discomfort. Vershinin speaks for his faith; Chebutykin, for his doubt. Chekhov's soul was capacious. There was room in it for the one and for the other, and he saw no way to reconcile the two. We cannot doubt that this continual inner altercation was of major importance in his life as a dramatist. Possibly it represented in conscious terms the dynamic principle of his art, the polarity which gave it movement. His mind was calm, but his soul was not placid and, more clearly than any other of his plays, *The Three Sisters* reflects his spiritual tension.

The Three Sisters marks an important stage in the evolution of the type of drama which depends for its magnitude on the association of its characters with a cosmic process external to themselves. This is the tradition, essentially Hegelian, which we associate with Hebbel and Ibsen. The difference between *The Three Sisters* and a play like *Rosmersholm*, however, is that while Ibsen is often ironic at the expense of his characters, he is completely serious with respect to the order of change in which they are involved, while Chekhov takes nothing for granted. Chekhov concedes the possibility of the social process which Vershinin expounds, but he cannot accept the idea wholeheartedly, and the suggestion is inescapable that perhaps all these hopes, these dreams, and these efforts are in the end equally meaningless and equally absurd.

By the time of *Uncle Vanya*, Maeterlinck, Ibsen, and Hauptmann had amply demonstrated the uses of symbolism in the theatre, and their works were being played in Russia. Chekhov came very readily under the spell of Maeterlinck. In *The Three Sisters* as much is conveyed symbolically as is expressed in words, and in the interplay of expression and suggestion Chekhov developed a more complex counterpoint than anyone had so far attempted in the theatre. Apart from such solid stuff as the silver samovar, the baby carriage, Natasha's candle, and the lamps she is constantly extinguishing, there is the tissue of memories, and all the wealth of literary reminiscence against which the action is played—the image of the green oak and the golden chain from Pushkin's *Ruslan and Lyudmila*, the couplet from Krylov's fable, the scraps of verse, popular tunes, and odds and ends of rhyme and proverb that form the warp through which the narrative weaves its texture. But beyond this, the play itself is symbolic of a greater drama, the cosmic drama which it suggests, and with which it corresponds. The nature of this correspondence is broadly hinted at by Vershinin in several passages, but very subtly and delicately by Tusenbach in the scene at the end of the play:

> TUSENBACH: Strange how trifles, stupidities, sometimes become so important in our lives, suddenly, without rhyme or reason! You laugh at them, the same as always, you see that they're nonsense, yet all at once you find that you are being swept away by them, and have no power to stop. Oh, let's not talk about that! I am full of joy. It's as if I am seeing these pines and maples and birches for the first time, and they all seem to be looking at me, waiting. What beautiful trees! And, now I think of it, how beautiful life must be when there are trees like these! (*Shouts offstage*: "Hey! Hurry up!") I must go now . . . Look at that tree; it's dead, but it still sways in the wind with the others. Yes, when I am dead, I think, I too shall continue to have a share in life in one way or another. Good bye, my darling . . . [24]

The lyrical quality of a play conceived along these lines is achieved, necessarily, at the expense of more usual dramatic values. A fine play in the Scribean manner is a marvel of ingenuity, in which every line serves either to advance the action, or to characterize the speaker, or both. In such plays, no words are wasted; whatever does not serve to propel the plot is judged to be extraneous and dispensable; and the characters work their way forward with all their might, each intent on his desire. This kind of drama conveys, accordingly, a sense of urgency which in real life we feel only in our more hysterical moments, and also an enhanced awareness of the play of motives, the interchange of pressures, and the clash of wills. The design is primarily mechanical in principle, and the result is a piece of dramatic engineering, a machine.

Chekhov's plays are of another stamp. In general, his characters feel no urgency and transmit none; they create no suspense. In comparison with the characters of well-made plays, they seem languid and bored. Aside from the comic characters of such vaudevilles as *The Bear* and *The Proposal*, the personages who convey a sense of energy in Chekhov's plays are exceptional, and seem to belong to another world than the rest of the cast. The usual Chekhovian character is a half-hearted participant in an action that barely excites his interest. His desires, when they are manifested, seem to run against the grain of the action. The bustle which characterizes Scribean drama is nowhere evident in Chekhov's theatre. There is a certain tension; but nobody is in a hurry, and even when, like Elena in *The Wood Demon*, a character desperately wishes to escape, there is nowhere to go. This very lack of direction is a source of uneasiness.

It is possible that in these incongruities Chekhov saw something comic. All of his later plays may be considered examples of *comédie rosse*. They are not, of course, written in the style of Jean Jullien or Henri Becque; between the Russian spirit and the French there is half of a world of difference. But it is not altogether unlikely that Chekhov had something in mind when he wrote *The Three Sisters* and *The Cherry Orchard* which is analogous to the bitter comedy of Becque.

The type of vaudeville which Chekhov was accustomed to write would develop readily into hard comedy. Probably, plays like *La Sérénade* or *La Parisienne* came quite close to Chekhov's idea of *comédie-vaudeville;* indeed, it is by no means certain that it was not through the vaudeville that Becque arrived at the comic genre which he evolved. From the comic point of view, at any rate, the inappropriate efforts of Chekhov's characters to compensate for their shortcomings are perhaps laughable. In *The Three Sisters*, Chebutykin makes up for his ignorance by a compulsive addiction to the fillers in his newspaper. Vershinin compensates for an unhappy life by fixing his mind on the future happiness of the race. Solyony tries in vain to sweeten his sourness by sprinkling his chest and hands with scent. There is certainly something funny about Irina's periodic Tolstoyan impulse toward a life of social service, just as there is something both touching and ridiculous in Vershinin's love-making, and something both tragic and clownish in Chebutykin's nihilism. In the days of Molière, it would probably have been easy to laugh at these characters, to smile at Masha, or to chuckle over the infinitely pathetic Kulygin. In our day, however, after some centuries of sensibility, it is hardly possible to play these roles comically, and it was perhaps unreasonable of Chekhov to insist that they should be given a comic interpretation.

Even if we concede that all its characters lend themselves to irony, it is impossible to give a comic bias to *The Three Sisters*. In order to treat characters comedically it is necessary, at the very least, to view their behavior with the detachment proper to a predominantly intellectual experience. Sympathy is not conducive to merriment, and the more intense our emotion, the further we move from comedy. The principal characters in Chekhov's later plays are all conceived in such a way as to invite a very high degree of identification on the part of the spectator; one can laugh at them only by laughing at oneself.

It may be, of course, that Chekhov was capable of maintaining his artistic objectivity to a degree beyond the ordinary. Kind and generous as he was as a man, he was sometimes accused by those closest to him of something like inhumanity in his lack of emotional identification. If this is true, he certainly went to extraordinary lengths in his plays to compensate for his lack of warmth. Almost every scene in *The Three Sisters* makes a demand on the emotions. It is true, on the other hand, that Chekhov's characters have an amusing tendency to dramatize themselves and that, in their efforts to give tragic magnificence to their lives, they occasionally invite a smile. Certainly the final tableau of *The Three Sisters*—the girls grouped in the center, as if sitting for their portrait, Chebutykin on one side buried in his newspaper, and Andrey on the other with his baby carriage—makes an effect, at least visually, that is much closer to comedy than to tragedy. But *The Three Sisters* strikes far too deep for laughter. It would be inhuman to chuckle through Olga's final speech; and it is unlikely that anyone ever will.

After *Ivanov*, Chekhov's mistrust of melodrama, and his fear of overstatement, were such that he rarely permitted his climaxes to rise much above the level of the preparatory action. In *Uncle Vanya* the climax is deflated by Vanya's ineptitude; in *The Sea Gull*, it is sabotaged by Nina's determination to play a tragic scene; in *The Three Sisters*, the climaxes are so unobtrusive that one is hardly aware of them. Evidently Chekhov did not see life in terms of climaxes and *scènes à faire*, that is to say, in terms of theatre. None of his later plays is theatrical; and the indefinable sense of paradox that his works evoke is very likely the result of the application of a dramatic system designed to arouse passion to a subject-matter which stubbornly resists any such treatment.

This curious incongruity was the consequence of Chekhov's naturalistic bias. In his opinion, a dramatist who desires to depict life honestly must put on the stage the experiences of ordinary people, and deal with the laughter and tears inherent in ordinary happenings. In real life what is visible is generally trivial and commonplace. But for centuries playwrights had been in the habit of associating drama with moments of high excitement, great gestures, and impressive utterances, precisely those things which are lacking in our ordinary experience. The result was the impassable gulf which has always divided reality from the fantasies of the theatre.

It was Chekhov's ambition to bridge this gulf. As he said:

> After all, in real life, people don't spend every moment in shooting one another, hanging themselves, or making declarations of love. They do not spend all their time saying clever things. They are more occupied with eating, drinking, flirting, and saying stupidities, and these are the things which ought to be shown on the stage... People eat their dinner, just eat their dinner, and all the time their happiness is taking form, or their lives are being destroyed.[25]

There was nothing especially new in this idea. But while both Zola and Maeterlinck had quite recently described the drama of everyday life, nobody had so far attempted actually to write such a play. It was very difficult in the theatre to relinquish the extraordinary. The novelty of Chekhov's technique lay not in his theory, but in his practice. He was the first dramatist to write realistically for the stage.

Because he was primarily a realist, one looks in vain to Chekhov for that quality of neatness which was so highly prized by the dramatists of the Second Empire. Chekhov's plots are not neat. "Plays should be written badly, insolently," he told his brother Alexander. In his later plays, when the action ends, the narrative is not concluded; it is merely suspended. *The Three Sisters* ends with a tableau. The audience is invited to contemplate for a moment those who have departed, and those who remain. For a moment the play is at rest. But in fact, nothing is at rest—the tableau holds together only for that moment. Like the final tableau in *The Revizor*, the scene is charged with energy and ready to fly apart the moment the author relinquishes his control.

Here, as elsewhere, Chekhov succeeds in giving his characters an extension of vitality that goes beyond their dramatic utility. They have a dimension that is peculiarly theirs, in which they are free to live. As characters, they are enlisted to serve the plot; but they have an autonomy of their own. Certain characters—Chebutykin, for example—appear at a certain point to secede from the ensemble, as if they refused to take any further part in the action. In general, Chekhov's personages preserve the imprecise outlines and the enigmatic quality of people. They exhibit a normal reluctance to engage themselves, and the author makes no effort to penetrate their reserve. The consequence is not only the strange relation of character to narrative that is peculiar to Chekhov's plays, but also a derogation of plot which presages a different order of drama from anything that properly belongs to the nineteenth century.

The Cherry Orchard

In May 1901, after much backing and filling, Chekhov at last made up his mind to marry Olga Knipper. He had been recently examined by a Moscow lung specialist. Serious lesions had been found in both his lungs, and he was ordered off to the province of Ufa to take the kumyss cure. The problem of what to do about his mother and, more particularly, about his sister Masha, troubled him more than his illness. After all these years of close attachment, they were certain to take his marriage badly. His hitherto untroubled domestic life began to look stormy. Bunin noted in his diary: " . . . Yes, this is really suicide. Worse than Sakhalin."

Nevertheless, Chekhov arranged an impressive banquet at which he assembled a host of relatives and friends and, while the wedding party waited vainly for their appearance, he and Olga were married quietly in a Moscow church, and made off for the sanatorium at Aksenovo. There they spent a month together. By the end of this honeymoon, Chekhov had had his fill of Ufa and its kumyss, and he returned to Yalta with his bride. He was not very well.

The friction between Olga and Chekhov's mother and sister developed very rapidly, quite as had been predicted. Toward the end of August, Olga left for Moscow. Chekhov joined her within the month. He was assiduous in attending the rehearsals of *The Three Sisters*, now in its second season, and he tried Stanislavsky's patience by insisting on restaging personally the scene of the fire in the third act. The play opened on September 21. The reviews were gratifyingly enthusiastic, and Chekhov was happy. As he strengthened his position more and more securely in the theatre, he became increasingly critical of Ibsen. He wrote his friend Sredin in Yalta in a complacent mood: "*The Wild Duck* did not do well on the stage of the Art Theatre. It was sluggish, uninteresting, and weak. However, *The Three Sisters* went off magnificently, brilliantly, a great deal better than the writing deserves. I did a little staging, and made some suggestions, and they say the play comes off better than it did last season." [1]

By the end of October he felt ill, and had to return to Yalta. That winter both Gorky and Tolstoy came to the Crimea. For a time Chekhov was happily absorbed in their company. Nevertheless, he missed Olga. He wrote to her almost daily, almost always in an amorous vein. "My sweet angel, my dog, my darling, I beg you to believe me, I love you, I love you deeply; don't forget me, write . . . My bed seems so lonely, as if I were a miserly bachelor, ill-natured and cold." [2] But Olga was wedded primarily to her career, and his constant expressions of loneliness ended by wearying her. She was having a gay and exciting time in Moscow. As the wife of the famous playwright, she was invited everywhere and treated with lavish consideration. The contrast between her ample life and her husband's meagre existence became increasingly evident. Chekhov showed no signs of jealousy. Early in the spring, after a brief passionate visit to Yalta, Olga won an immense personal success in Petersburg. Chekhov was delighted, and wrote her a warm letter of congratulation; but he was human —he could not forbear adding: "My darling, there is nothing better in the world than to sit on a green bank and fish, or to stroll about the fields." [3]

At the end of March, Olga suffered an unexpected miscarriage, and came to Yalta to recuperate. Two months later, in Moscow, she suffered a sudden and severe attack of peritonitis. Chekhov nursed her through it patiently. Her recovery was slow. She spent all of July convalescing at the Stanislavsky estate near Moscow. Chekhov spent the time fishing, and planned his next play. He wrote Stanislavsky, who was spending the summer abroad with his wife: "Only one thing is bad. I feel lazy, and I am not working. I have still not begun the play; I am only thinking about it. I shall probably not start writing until the end of August." [4] But at the end of August he was back in Yalta with his mother and sister, and he was involved in a bitter quarrel with his wife.

Seven years before, he had told Suvorin that he would make a splendid husband provided he found a wife who would not, like the moon, appear in his sky every night. He had been with Olga almost constantly during her illness. With the exception of a short vacation at Morozov's estate in the Urals, he had spent five months in her company. It was apparently more than he could bear; and the true reason for his long procrastination in marrying her, his remarkable lack of jealousy with regard to her admirers, and his willingness to let her pursue her career far away from him became increasingly clear. He liked women very much, but, save for his sister Masha, he could not endure the company of any one woman for very long, and the thought of having Olga constantly about him gave him no pleasure. It was while Olga was away that he found her most attractive. He made a charming epistolary lover; and it is tolerably clear that what he liked best of all was a passionate renewal of love in circumstances that did not entail any prolonged exposure to the rigors of domesticity.

Chekhov suffered from periodic attacks of ennui, and soon tired of whatever situation he found himself in. From time to time, he had an irresistible compulsion to change his environment, to see new faces. Little of this was lost upon Olga. In the course of their short, but sharp exchange of letters on this subject, she analyzed their relationship with remarkable insight: "I feel that you need me only as an agreeable woman; as a human being I am lonely, and I am a stranger to you... You, indeed, are a remarkably fidgety person; you are always bored. It seems to me that if I were with you all the time, you would either grow indifferent to me, or you would take me for granted, like a table or a chair. Am I right? We are both somehow incomplete people."[5] It was, doubtless, true, as it must be true of all artists, that as people they left something to be desired. It was also true, and Olga pointed it out to him with a total absence of tact, that in this marriage it was she who played the masculine role: "You know, Antonka, I am really the husband, and you are the wife. I work; I come to pay visits to my wife; I watch out for her welfare—really, are you not my wife?"[6]

The fact was that Olga's insights were deep, but not deep enough; she was cruel. Chekhov was 42, and already a great man, but in many ways he was still the little Yegorushka of *The Steppe*, a bright child, full of astonishment, and a little frightened by the great world into which he had been thrust. Olga wished him to play the father; but the father had been too imposing a figure in his own childhood for him to usurp that place now, or ever. Olga localized his aspirations, and gave him something definite to long for, but she was far more valuable to him psychically than physically, and it is clear that intellectually he found her something of a bore. He had a neurotic need to know precisely where she was, and what she was thinking. Her presence, he needed only occasionally. In the flesh, she could be a hardship. He was tactful about this:

> You keep writing, my own, that your conscience stings you because you are in Moscow and not living with me

> here in Yalta. But, my dear, what can we do? Think of it sensibly: if you lived with me in Yalta all winter, your career would be ruined, and I should feel the pricks of conscience, which would hardly be an improvement in my condition. I knew I was marrying an actress; when I married you, I fully realized that you would spend the winters in Moscow. I don't regard myself as injured or cheated one millionth part of a bit; on the contrary, it seems to me that all is going well, or, at least, as well as can be; therefore, my darling, don't bother me with your pricks of conscience...
>
> Now that I am working, most likely I shall not write you every day; you must forgive me.
>
> Let us go abroad, do let us go! [7]

The quarrel, such as it was, was quickly made up. Olga continued to write him every day, and almost every day she exhorted him to take his castor oil, and to get on with his play. The Art Theatre was moving into a new house, planned in the latest fashion of theatre architecture, with the most advanced fittings, including a revolving stage, and Stanislavsky was especially eager to have a new play of Chekhov's with which to open his season. Chekhov had been nourishing an idea for a comedy through the fall of 1901, and had gone so far as to discuss his idea with Stanislavsky early in 1902. Olga's unremitting efforts to spur him on with his project proved to be a source of annoyance rather than of inspiration. In the spring of 1902 he wrote her an affectionate note, signed "Your hen-pecked husband A—," in which he petulantly disclaimed any intention of going on with his play. "I am well, I am coughing less, and I am in fairly good spirits. I am not writing my play, and I don't want to write it; there are entirely too many playwrights nowadays, and playwriting is becoming a boring, commonplace business..." [8]

He was becoming increasingly critical of his work. As time went on, he worked more and more slowly, and at greater cost. The composition of *The Three Sisters* had caused him much anguish. *The Cherry Orchard* (*Vishnevy sad*) caused him even more; he found it a long and fatiguing piece of work. He had already taken it in hand twice, and twice given it up, when at the end of August, he wrote Olga: "Nemirovich is asking for the play, but I'm not writing it this year, although the subject, by the way, is splendid." [9]

Instead of going on with the play, he turned his attention to a short comic piece he had originally published in 1886, *On the Harmfulness of Tobacco*. He revised this drastically with the intention of having it printed in Volume VII of Marx's edition of his works. The effect of the revision was to change what was originally intended as a joke into a piece that is incredibly sad. That year also he finished *The Bishop*, one of his finest stories. It was obviously a deeply felt piece, essentially autobiographical, and in part it recalls the mood of *A Dreary Story*. In the touching relationship of the distinguished prelate and his mother, a simple peasant woman who is so completely overawed by the magnificence of her son that she can hardly talk to him, and in the bishop's nostalgia for the carefree days of his boyhood, we may sense the mood of Chekhov's later years, when he felt the loneliness of the eminent man among those who are not eminent, and his boredom among those who are. The story invites comparison with Pirandello's play, *Quando si è qualcuno*, and the difference in treatment is an interesting measure of the difference between these two storytellers who in their later years achieved greatness on the stage.

In December news came to Yalta of the brilliant success of Gorky's *The Lower Depths* at the Art Theatre and, shortly thereafter, of the magnificent reception of *The Sea Gull* at the Alexandrinsky in Petersburg, where six years before it had failed so miserably. Success and honors were piling up everywhere, but Chekhov hardly savored them. He had aged a great deal in the last two years. At 42 he was an old man, thin, gray, and incapable of exertion. His work absorbed all his energy. He worked painstakingly, turning out at the most a story a year. Yet these years were, from an artistic viewpoint, the best of his life, the most precious, the very flower of his career.

They were not happy years. He knew now that he was dying, and this knowledge absorbed more and more of his attention. He wrote Olga plaintively: "Oh, what a mass of projects I have in my head! And how I long to write! But I feel that something is missing, either in my surroundings or in my health . . . I ought not to live in Yalta, and that's a fact!" [10] A month later, he declared himself heartily sick of his profession. He was writing *The Betrothed*, slowly, painfully. It was to be his last story.

The Betrothed is a story of some twenty pages. It took him five months to write, and four months to correct the three sets of proofs he required: "I write six or seven lines a day; I couldn't do more even if my life depended on it. Every day I have diarrhea . . ." [11] He was dainty now with his revisions. He feared the vital spring was running dry, and he was reluctant to part with what he had written until he was sure it was perfect. He even asked his friends, Gorky among them, to read his proofs.

The heroine of *The Betrothed*, Nadya, looks confidently to the world of the future, just as Vershinin does in *The Three Sisters*. Under the influence of her tubercular friend Sasha, she rejects the respectable and unexciting marriage which is planned for her, and runs off to the university by herself to seek a new life. It is not altogether easy for Nadya to break with the past. The old life, obviously, has its points—it is leisurely and gracious, the women are pretty, the men are handsome and well-dressed, and their manners are elegant. Her grandmother's house is beautiful. It is true that the servants sleep on the floor in the kitchen amid filth and roaches, but Nadya had not noticed such details, not until Sasha brought them to her attention:

> You must think, you must realize, how unclean, how immoral this idle life of yours is . . . Do you understand that if, for example, you and your grandfather do nothing, it means that someone else has to work for you, that you are eating up someone else's life—and is that clean? Isn't that dirty?

Once her social conscience is awakened, Nadya realizes that the old life is no longer possible for her. Her awakening, however, is not sudden. She realizes very well how improbable Sasha's dreams are, how impractical, but his childishness does not blind her to the essential truth of his words or to the beauty of his vision:

> Only enlightened and holy people are interesting. It is they only who are needed, and the more such people there are, the sooner the kingdom of God will come on earth. Of your town, then, not one stone will remain. Everything will be blown from the foundations, everything will be transformed as if by magic. There will be immense magnificent houses here, wonderful gardens, marvellous fountains, extraordinary people . . . but that is not what matters most. What matters most is that the masses, as we know them, as they exist now, will not exist then, because every man will have faith, and every man will know what he is living for, and no one will seek moral support in the crowd . . .

Yet when she goes to see Sasha in Petersburg, having already made her decision, she realizes that Sasha too is not altogether sanitary. His home is filthy; he is a slovenly man, and he is ill. Almost at once, she outgrows both him and his ideas. She becomes aware that his words, his thoughts, and even the intelligentsia to which he belongs, are already "something out of date, old-fashioned, long ago finished and done with and perhaps already dead and buried. Something else was needed, something more practical and more immediate." When she revisits her home the summer after her first semester at the university,

> ... it seemed to her that everything in the town had grown old, was out of date, and was waiting for the end; or else for the beginning of something young and fresh. Oh, if only that bright new life would come more quickly, that life in which one would be able to face one's fate boldly and squarely, and know that one was right, and be lighthearted and free! Sooner or later, that life would come. The time would come when Granny's house, where things were arranged so that the four servants must live in one room only, in filth, in the cellar, the time would come when not a trace of that house would remain, and it would be forgotten, and no one would remember it.

News comes presently that Sasha has died of consumption:

> ... Nadya went on walking about the rooms and thinking. She recognized clearly that her life had been turned upside down as Sasha wished; that here she was, alien, isolated, useless, and that everything here was useless to her; that all the past had been torn away from her, and had vanished as though it was burnt and the ashes had scattered in the wind. She went into Sasha's room and stood there for a little while. "Good bye, dear Sasha," she thought ... [12]

It is clear that in *The Betrothed* the theme of *The Cherry Orchard* is already stirring. The old life, beautiful and gracious as it seemed, was founded upon the labor of slaves, upon the degradation of the servants and peasants, and the misery of the factory hands, so that it was impossible for an honest man to live this life once his eyes were opened to the facts. Granny's beautiful house must go, and Granny with it, and all the fine, gentle, cultured people of the past generation. Their passing was a cause for regret, but their beauty was not a healthy thing. It was the result of a social disease; therefore that beauty and that way of life were doomed, and must be buried and forgotten.

The theme was certainly not new. It had been touched on long ago, even before Turgenev and, since his time, it had become something of a commonplace. Sasha is certainly no Bazarov; but it is not difficult to see the resemblance between the two characters. Bazarov is brusque and energetic; Sasha is languid and talkative; but in the quality of their nihilism, and in the ironic manner in which they are presented, they are unmistakably similar.

It was by giving Sasha a tinge of the absurd and the grotesque that Chekhov rescued him from banality. Nadya is made fully aware of these aspects of her emancipator, and she respects him in spite of his shortcomings. In *The Cherry Orchard* the student Trofimov inherits Sasha's role, and in his case, the comic nuance borders upon slapstick. It is unlikely that Chekhov intended Anya to be as fully aware as Nadya of her friend's absurdity; but it is not impossible that she was meant to have some intimation of it, just as one may suppose that Vershinin's innocence is not wholly lost upon Masha in *The Three Sisters*. It is, in fact, in the highest degree likely that in the story and the two plays, the conception of the radical idealist is essentially the same. These characters, all three of them, are lovable, believable, and a little ridiculous, and none of them is altogether healthy.

Toward the middle of March 1903, Chekhov had *The Cherry Orchard* well under way. He wrote Olga that he had high hopes for it and that, in the interests of an intimate production, he was limiting the number of characters as much as he could. The following month he wrote that he could make no further progress with the play in Yalta. There were too many distractions. He would finish it in Moscow.

In Moscow, he found that the new apartment which Masha and Olga had rented was up three flights of stairs. It took Chekhov a good half-hour to climb to it, and once he was there, he was reluctant to descend. He wrote his friends to come to see him. Before long he was as deeply involved with visitors as he had been in Yalta.

On the advice of his doctor, the eminent specialist Ostroumov, he canceled the European trip he had planned, and decided instead to spend the summer in the vicinity of Moscow. Yalta, he was now told, was unhealthy for him at any season. He was advised not to return there. At this time, as he began to feel financially pressed once more, he accepted the literary editorship of *Russian Thought*, a post which entailed the reading and correction of innumerable manuscripts. Meanwhile, he was making no progress whatever with his play. Suddenly, in July, in complete defiance of his doctor's orders, he left for Yalta.

He settled down at once to write *The Cherry Orchard*, with Stanislavsky, Nemirovich, and Olga circling him like hawks. Stanislavsky, at least, felt some remorse at the pressure they were putting on the sick man, but above all he was worried lest something happen to Chekhov before the play was finished. In July, he wrote Olga, who was then with her husband: "Do not think badly of us. We grieve for Anton Pavlovich and those around him, we think of the play only in those moments when we are worried about the fate of our theatre. However you look at it, our theatre is Chekhov's, and without him it will go ill with us." Olga answered reassuringly: "He now works every day; however, yesterday and today he was ill and did not write... if his health permitted, he would work more. Don't worry—he just sat down this minute to work."

The second act caused him much travail, but by the beginning of September a good part of the play was finished. "I call the play a comedy," he wrote Nemirovich, and he added that the part of Ranyevskaya was intended for Olga. Two weeks later, after another spell of illness, he wrote Stanislavsky's wife that he hoped to send along four acts very soon. He was worried now about Nemirovich, who evidently expected him to write something serious. "What has emerged from me is not a *drame* but a comedy; in certain places, even a farce." On September 20, he wrote Olga in despair: ". . . I am beginning to lose courage. It seems to me I have already outlived my day as a writer, and every sentence I write strikes me as good for nothing, and of no use at all . . ." [13] The next day he felt better about the whole thing: "I no longer look wrathfully at my manuscript. I am already writing and, as soon as I finish, I will wire you. The last act will be merry, and indeed the whole play will be gay and giddy. Sanin won't like it; he will say I have grown shallow." [14]

The first draft of *The Cherry Orchard* was finished September 26, 1903. Chekhov was elated. He wrote Olga: "I fancy there is something new in my play, however dull it may be. There is not a single pistol-shot in the whole thing, by the way . . ." [15] But at the beginning of October the four acts had still not arrived in Moscow, and the Art Theatre was in panic. Olga wrote, complaining bitterly of his laziness. His answer was such as to tear the heartstrings: "Don't be cross with me about the play, my darling. I am copying it slowly because I cannot write any faster. Some passages I don't like at all. I am re-writing them and re-copying them. But soon, pony, I shall finish it, and send it off . . . Darling, forgive me about the play! Forgive me! On my honor, I have finished it and I am copying it." [16]

A few days later he wrote that he was still copying the script: "I tell you the holy truth, darling, if my play is not a success you can put the blame entirely on my intestines. It is all so revoltingly nasty! It is ages since I had a normal bowel movement, I don't even remember when." But at last, on October 12, he wrote: "The play is finished, finished at last ... If changes are needed, they will, I fancy, be very slight. The worst thing about the play is that I wrote it not at one sitting, but over a long, a very long, period so that it is bound to seem, in a sense, spun out ..." And he added: "Darling, how hard it was for me to write the play!" [17]

Two days later, he sent a list of casting notes:

> I. Lyubov Andreyevna will be played by you, since there is no one else. She is dressed with great taste, but not gorgeously. Clever, very good-natured, absent-minded, friendly, and gracious to everyone, always a smile on her face.
> II. Anya. Absolutely must be played by a young actress.
> III. Varya. Perhaps Marya Petrovna will take this part.
> IV. Gaev is for Vishnevsky. Ask Vishnevsky to listen to people playing billiards and to note down as many of the terms as he can. I don't play billiards, or rather I did play once, but have forgotten it all, and it is all put down at random in my play. We'll talk it over with Vishnevsky later, and I will put in all that is necessary.
> V. Lopakhin. Stanislavsky.
> VI. Trofimov, the student. Kachalov.
> VII. Semeonov-Pishchik. Gribunin.
> VIII. Charlotta—is a question mark. I will put in some more of her sayings in the fourth act. Yesterday I had a bad stomach-ache while I was copying Act IV, and I could not put in anything fresh. Charlotta plays a conjuring trick with Trofimov's galoshes in the fourth act. Rayevskaya could not play it. It must be an actress with a sense of humor.
> IX. Epikhodov. Perhaps Lazhsky.
> X. Firs. Artyom.
> XI. Yasha. Moskvin.

He added: "I confess I am awfully sick of the play... The house is an old mansion; at one time people lived in it in a very rich style, and this ought to come out in the staging. Wealthy and comfortable... Varya is rather crude and rather stupid, but very good-natured." [18]

It took some little time to get a report on the play from Nemirovich-Danchenko. Chekhov fretted. At last, on October 19 he received a very long and very reassuring telegram. The play, said Nemirovich, was his finest, but a little heavy in the second act and, in parts, a bit lachrymose. Chekhov wrote Olga, who had also written to congratulate him: "Many thanks. I was worried all the time, terrified. What most frightened me was the lack of movement in the second act, and a certain vagueness in the student Trofimov. You understand, Trofimov has been in exile repeatedly; he is constantly being expelled from the university; and how is one to say this?"

Two days later, Stanislavsky sent a ceremonial telegram. He had read the play. He was overcome with rapture. It was Chekhov's most beautiful creation. He was an author of genius. Chekhov was relieved, but he was not overly pleased. He detested having his work overpraised. He was particularly worried about the casting of Anya. Stanislavsky's choice, he feared, would play the part badly: "Anya is first and foremost a child, essentially light hearted; she knows nothing of life, and does not cry once, except in Act II, and even then she only has tears in her eyes." [19] He disapproved strongly of Stanislavsky's intention of casting himself as Gaev. He wanted him for Lopakhin. "You see, Lopakhin is the central character... Lopakhin must not be played as a loud, noisy man; there is no need for him to be a typical merchant. He is a soft man."

The real ground of contention, however, involved the basic interpretation of the play, and once again the two men found themselves opposed on a question of mood. Chekhov had written the play as a comedy. Stanislavsky took a completely different view of it: "This is not a comedy or a farce, as you wrote; it is a tragedy, no matter what solution you may have found in the second act for a better life." To make matters worse, the growing estrangement between Nemirovich and Stanislavsky threatened to prejudice the entire repertory.

In spite of everything, the casting progressed satisfactorily, and Stanislavsky announced that *The Cherry Orchard* would go into rehearsal on November 10. The censor passed the play with only a few minor corrections, mainly in Trofimov's lines. On December 4, 1903, Chekhov came to Moscow. He spent a good part of the next six weeks attending rehearsals, while Stanislavsky did what he could to control his temper in the face of the author's intrusions into what was considered the unquestionable dictatorship of the regisseur. Stanislavsky wrote a friend on December 26 that *The Cherry Orchard* was no longer blooming: "The blossoms had only just begun to appear when the author arrived and spoiled everything for us . . . only now are the new buds beginning to show themselves." He thought the end of the second act was long, and must be cut. It was a thought that had already occurred to Chekhov, but now he paled at the suggestion. Nevertheless he complied. The production was heavy with disagreements, arguments, misunderstandings. Chekhov, with *The Betrothed* still fresh in his mind, stressed the happiness of the young couple. It was his idea that Anya, like Nadya in *The Betrothed*, would consider the passing of the old order a trifling thing in comparison with the consequences for the future happiness of mankind, and that therefore she would hardly be affected by the destruction of her home. Stanislavsky, however, felt the pathos of its passing very deeply, and was determined that the production should reflect this sadness. In any case, as Nemirovich had already pointed out, there was a good deal of weeping in the play, far too many tears for comedy.

Indeed, it is inconceivable that Chekhov was insensible to

the tragic implications of the situation he had created. He himself was a gardener. He was accustomed to watch over his plants and trees with the solicitude of a father. Everything indicates that the orchard as a symbol had exceptional significance for him, and that its destruction touched him deeply when he first wrote the play. In the circumstances, his insistence that these scenes be played comedically must seem eccentric, or, at the least, defensive. He was, none the less, perfectly serious in this. He told Yakovlev: "I cannot fathom it; either the play is no good, or the actors don't understand me . . . As it is being done now, *The Cherry Orchard* is impossible to produce."

The play went through its rehearsals amid general misgivings. Stanislavsky braced himself for disaster. The opening was announced for January 17, 1904, the date of Chekhov's forty-fourth birthday. On that occasion it was planned to celebrate also the twenty-fifth anniversary of his debut as a writer, and the theatre had secretly arranged for a jubilee performance. Stanislavsky wrote: "Our idea was simple. If the actors were not able to put the play across, their lack of success could be blamed on the unusual conditions of the jubilee evening; this could not fail to draw the audience's attention to the author and away from the play."

Chekhov evidently had some suspicion of what had been planned. He refused to attend the opening. But at the end of the second act, Nemirovich dispatched an urgent note asking him to come at once to the theatre. Chekhov arrived in the interval before the fourth act, and was conducted solemnly to the stage where all the cast and a group of dignitaries were assembled and waiting. The curtain was then raised, and the audience, quite taken by surprise, gave Chekhov an ovation. Wreaths and gifts were presented. There were interminable speeches. Chekhov stood up through it all in the glare of the lights, pale, and terribly ill at ease, trying as best he could to smother his fits of coughing. Somehow he survived this ordeal, but later he wrote his friend Batyushkov that he had been so thoroughly honored that he had not yet recovered from it.

The Cherry Orchard was not a success. The press was, on the whole, favorable, but the reviewers were not enthusiastic, and both the production and the acting were criticized. As to the play, the consensus appeared to be that it was no great thing; the theme was dated; the vein had been worked to death. The play was taken to be a portrayal of the passing of the old order. Nobody suggested that there was anything in the least funny about this. Nevertheless Chekhov persisted in his notion that Stanislavsky had ruined his comedy by playing it tragically. On April 10, he wrote Olga: "Why is it that my play is persistently called a *drame* in the posters and newspaper advertisements? Nemirovich-Danchenko and Stanislavsky see in my play something absolutely different from what I have written, and I am willing to stake my word that neither of them has read it through attentively even once. Forgive me, but I assure you that this is so." [20]

It is strangely ironical that Chekhov never saw his play produced as a comedy, as he intended, nor has anyone, apparently, ever ventured to produce it in this manner. *The Cherry Orchard* has many comic passages, some of them so broad as to approximate farce but, generally speaking, directors have been unable to fathom the author's comedic intention. The reason is not far to seek. The play, on the whole, is not funny. The characters have their comic side, but the situation is sad. No rationalization has ever succeeded in giving it a comic bias.

The Cherry Orchard is somewhat less obvious in its structure than *The Sea Gull* or *Uncle Vanya,* and it is far less complex than *The Three Sisters.* Nevertheless, its formal pattern is much the same as in the other plays: an arrival, a sojourn, and a departure. After *Ivanov,* all Chekhov's plays are designed after this principle. But, as in the case of *The Sea Gull*, the plot of *The Cherry Orchard* is actually quite extensive. In full development it would provide ample material for a long novel.

The principal action of *The Cherry Orchard* is not dramatized. What is played is a minor episode, ancillary to the main line of the action, but distinct from it. The technique is not a technique of retrospection, as in *Rosmersholm;* nor does the singularity of the design result from the lateness of the point of attack as in plays arranged after the classic mode. The movement of *The Cherry Orchard* depends upon a theme external to the play which is developed entirely through exposition and allusion, very much as in the analogous case of Strindberg's *Ghost Sonata.*

Since the author puts on the stage only the consequences of the primary action, the play makes the effect of a chess game played by invisible hands, and the characters seem to move without any will of their own, like characters in a dream. For this reason, *The Cherry Orchard* is likely to make a less spirited impression on the stage than *Uncle Vanya* or *The Three Sisters* and, in consequence, directors have a tendency to stress its melodramatic aspects much beyond the author's evident intention. Just as *Hedda Gabler* is always in danger of being played in terms of the vampire-woman, so *The Cherry Orchard* may come somewhat closer than one might wish to the stock-formula of the cold-hearted scrooge and the mortgage on the old homestead.

The ostensible action of *The Cherry Orchard* is very simple. It describes in somewhat desultory fashion the forced sale of the Ranyevsky property, and the consequent eviction of the hereditary proprietors by the son of one of their former serfs. The play must, therefore, be considered a demonstration of the workings of poetic justice in the evolutionary process. Simplified to this extent, *The Cherry Orchard* is virtually unrecognizable; yet it is undeniable that this formula is the basis of the narrative, and the source of its power and its irony.

Behind this simple action is a very complex story, the outlines of which are by no means certain. This story not only makes Ranyevskaya's extraordinary inertia with relation to the sale of her estate comprehensible, it also gives this unlikely material its lyric quality. The story is told in snatches, first by Anya, then by Lyubov Andreyevna herself. Nobody dwells on it. It is known to all the characters, and they have no desire to hear it again from anyone. It is an exposition without the slightest urgency.

What is conveyed in this manner is that Lyubov Andreyevna was a beautiful girl, thoughtless and extravagant by nature. She inherited a large estate from her father, married a penniless lawyer who drank himself to death, and, soon after her husband died, fell in love, and went abroad with her lover. A month after her departure, her little boy Grisha was drowned in the river near the cherry orchard. Lyubov took this to be a punishment from heaven. In her contrition, she once again left her home, presumably never to return, and bought a villa near Mentone, where for three years she nursed her lover through an illness. When he recovered, she sold the villa to pay her debts, and went with him to live in Paris. Her lover robbed her of what money she had left, and then cast her off. Lyubov poisoned herself; but she did not succeed in dying. It was at this point that Lyubov's seventeen-year-old daughter was sent to Paris to fetch her mother home.

Anya, with her German governess Charlotta, left in Holy Week. It is now late spring. They have all come back together. But Lyubov's former lover has fallen ill again in Paris, and he is peppering her with telegrams imploring her to come back. Though she realizes his worthlessness, she cannot resist his pleas, and is certain to squander the last of her fortune on him. And, now that she has come home, she is asked to cheapen herself even further by parceling out her lands to strangers from the city who will build themselves *dachas* where once her beautiful orchard stood. It is obvious that in the circumstances she cannot even consider the idea.

Most of this story is told in the second act, in a single speech to which nobody listens. Like many of the speeches in this play, it has a curiously tangential relation to the context, though it appears to be quite irrelevant to the question under discussion. In this scene, Lopakhin is begging Lyubov to lease the orchard in accordance with his plan of development, since this is the only way to save it:

LYUBOV ANDREYEVNA: Cottages! Vacationers! It's all so vulgar, forgive me.
GAEV: I agree with you completely.
LOPAKHIN: I'm either going to burst into tears, or scream, or faint! I can't stand it any more. You're killing me! (*To Gaev*) You're an old woman!

Lopakhin is about to fling off in a rage. Ranyevskaya stops him.

LYUBOV ANDREYEVNA: We've sinned too deeply.
LOPAKHIN: Sinned? In what way have you sinned? [21]

It is at this point that Ranyevskaya tells the story of her life. It explains quite clearly why it is that she cannot save her fortune by committing what she considers a vulgarity. It is not at all that she suffers a paralysis of the will, nor is she too flighty to understand, nor too absent-minded to make a sensible decision. But by character and background she is precluded from acting like a merchant in this crisis. The psychic impotence and the economic bankruptcy of her class at this period of history are aspects of the same illness. The nobility is at the end of life. It remains only to die nobly, if that is possible. She herself is full of guilt, and greatly desires to suffer. With regard to her estate, she has a deep sense of *noblesse oblige*, and prefers to lose it honorably rather than to degrade it as she herself has been degraded. Thus Lopakhin's very sensible proposal seems to her completely preposterous, and it seems so much rubbish also to her brother.

They are, after all, gentry. Even in their utmost need they do not compromise. They do not haggle; and therefore in the new age which has overtaken them they do not survive. There is, consequently, the same magnificent and ridiculous gallantry about these people which we admire in the more flamboyant figures of the nineteenth-century theatre, in characters like Hernani and Cyrano; they die, but they do not bedraggle their *panache*.

The Cherry Orchard, like *The Three Sisters*, describes a world in transition. It depicts the terminal stages in the disintegration of a nest of gentlefolk, and the end of their way of life. From a descriptive viewpoint, it covers the situation quite thoroughly. It composes on a single canvas all the elements that bridge the gap between the old order and the new, and includes a gallery of unforgettable portraits, some of them familiar through the works of Turgenev, Goncharov, and Pisemsky, some of them original. It would hardly be possible in a play of this sort to avoid the inclusion of certain stereotypes of the social novel of the period. Ranyevskaya, for example, makes no effect of novelty. Pishchik, the perpetually astonished man; Gaev, with his imaginary game of billiards; the congenitally clumsy Epikhodov; Jean, the Frenchified valet; Dunyasha, the pretty soubrette—these were all vaudeville types; and both Firs, the faithful retainer, and Trofimov, the perpetual student, were by now conventional in Russian fiction. What was new in *The Cherry Orchard* was not the characters, nor the situation, but the way in which these were treated. It was precisely that blend of comedy and pathos with which, as it seemed to Chekhov, Stanislavsky was ruining his play, that gave *The Cherry Orchard* its originality and freshness.

The tendency toward portrait-painting which is a chief characteristic of Russian drama in the nineteenth century is nowhere so well exemplified as in *The Cherry Orchard*. None of the people represented is entirely simple. Chekhov evidently meant them all to seem at least a little ridiculous, but he treated them all with courtesy, and one suspects that he liked these characters very much, particularly Trofimov and Lopakhin, the theorist and the practical man.

Lopakhin is by way of becoming a millionaire, though he can hardly write his name. He is strong and shrewd, but he cannot summon up the courage to propose marriage to Varya, who is a member of the upper class, if only by adoption. Obviously, Varya is quite a handful. She is said to have the soul of a nun; and Lopakhin cannily prefers to torture her a little rather than to be tortured by her. In the scene by the chapel in the fields, when Lyubov congratulates her on her coming marriage with Lopakhin, Varya bursts into tears. He has not asked her yet. But instead of taking advantage of this golden opportunity to make her a definite proposal, Lopakhin pokes fun at her cruelly, playing a clownish Hamlet for her benefit:

> LOPAKHIN: Okhmelia, get you to a monastery!
>
> GAEV: Oh, look how my hands are shaking: it's a long time since I had a game of billiards.
>
> LOPAKHIN: Okhmelia, nymph, remember me in your prayers!
>
> LYUBOV ANDREYEVNA: Come, gentlemen. It's nearly supper time.[22]

Lopakhin is not a kindly man, after all, and though Chekhov described him to Olga as a soft man, he is not soft. He has the brutality of the *muzhik*, and he plays sadistically with the woman who wishes to marry him, much as Chekhov once played with his women, though with less subtlety. From time to time, we catch a glimpse of the steel in Lopakhin, and we understand how it is he has become so rich so quickly. He is brisk with the servants, and pitiless with Gaev; and he prods

Trofimov mercilessly, though it is clear he likes him. He worships Lyubov, and can refuse her nothing, though he has given her up for lost. It is clear that she is the secret love of his life, his ideal of womanhood, and perhaps the true reason why he will not compromise by marrying Varya.

Lopakhin is, above all, a workman. There is an unspoken sympathy between him and Trofimov, though they belong to different camps, and cannot communicate, and perhaps are fated to destroy one another:

> TROFIMOV: Your father was a *muzhik*, mine was a druggist —what has that to do with it? (*Lopakhin takes out his wallet*) Stop, stop . . . Even if you offered me two hundred thousand, I wouldn't take it. I'm a free man. And the things that mean so much to people like you—rich and poor alike—have no more power over me than a bit of fluff floating about in the wind. I am strong and proud. I do without you, I pass you by. Mankind is marching toward the highest truth, the greatest happiness possible on earth, and I march in the van of the column.
>
> LOPAKHIN: Will you reach it?
>
> TROFIMOV: I will reach it. (*Pause*) I will reach it, or I'll show others how to reach it.
> (*The sound of an axe striking a tree is heard in the distance*)
>
> LOPAKHIN: Well, goodbye, *galuvchik*. Time to go. We look down our noses at one another, but life goes on just the same. When I work a long stretch without rest, my mind seems clearer, and sometimes I even think I know why I'm here. But there are so many people in Russia, brother, who are here for no reason at all . . . [23]

This passage recalls the discussion between Tusenbach and Vershinin in *The Three Sisters*, and its predecessors as far back as *Ward No. 6*, but it is by no means the same discussion. Vershinin is a dreamer. Tusenbach represents the Tolstoyan type of enlightened aristocrat. But Lopakhin is a practical man of business, whose manifest destiny it is to become a magnate like Suvorin or Saava Morozov, while Trofimov is a version of Sasha, the socialist student in *The Betrothed.* Trofimov was originally intended to be an agitator, as we see from Chekhov's correspondence, several times expelled from the university, and several times exiled. It was evidently impossible to get such a character past the censor. Chekhov did not try. On the contrary, he went to some pains to give Trofimov a comic coloring, and it is strongly hinted that he is, for all his earnestness, merely another passionate drifter in the universities, a member of that intelligentsia which he himself derides at some length in the second act for its laziness and lack of purpose.[24] The scene between Trofimov and Anya in act two is certainly reminiscent of the analogous scene between Sasha and Nadya in *The Betrothed*, and doubtless must be understood in the same way:

> TROFIMOV: . . . to free ourselves of all that is petty and ephemeral, all that prevents us from being free and happy, that's the whole aim and meaning of life. Forward! We march forward triumphantly toward that bright star that shines there in the distance. Forward! Don't fall back, friends! [25]

This was the sort of rhetoric which made Chekhov smile. There can be no question that in inflating Trofimov to this point, he meant to make him out an ass, though likeable, and here Trofimov reminds one very much of Ivan Dmitrich in *Ward No. 6*. Anya, however, though she cannot bear the slightest hint of rhetoric from Gaev, thinks Trofimov is really wonderful:

> ANYA (*raising her hands*): How beautifully you speak! (*A pause*) It's wonderful here today!
> TROFIMOV: Yes, the weather is marvellous!
> ANYA: What have you done to me, Petya? Why don't I love the cherry orchard as I used to? I loved it so

much that I thought there was no place in all the earth so beautiful as our orchard.

TROFIMOV: All Russia is our orchard. The earth is broad and beautiful, and there are many wonderful places in it. (*Pause*) Think, Anya: your grandfather, and your great-grandfather, and all your ancestors were serf owners, they owned human souls. Don't you see that from every tree in the orchard, from every leaf and every trunk, human beings are watching you, don't you hear their voices? . . . They owned human souls—that's what made them different from other people, those who lived before you, and those who are living now—so that your mother, and you, and your uncle, don't even notice that you're living on credit, at the expense of others, at the cost of people you don't even admit into your house beyond the kitchen. We are at least two hundred years behind the times here, we have no true values, and no sense of history; we just talk, and complain of boredom, and drink vodka. But it's clear that if we're ever going to catch up with the present, we must first atone for the past, and make a clean break with it, and we can only atone by suffering, by working, by continual work and effort. You must see that, Anya!

ANYA: The house we live in hasn't really been ours for a long time. I'll leave it, I give you my word.

TROFIMOV: If you have the keys, throw them down the well, and go away. Be free of it, free as the wind.

ANYA (*enraptured*): How beautifully you put things! [26]

But Trofimov, like Sasha, has his less engaging side. He is slovenly, and superficial, and though not yet 30, he is beginning to look old and ugly. There is no suggestion that, like Ivanov, he will wear out in a few years; he does not belong to the upper classes. But Chekhov is almost always ironic at the expense of the activist, and he makes Trofimov less impressive than Vershinin. There is some question about Trofimov's sexual development. He has grown no beard. He is, as he says a little fatuously, above passion; he does not believe in such trivialities. He has, moreover, a strong inclination to speak in stereotypes and, in comparison with Lyubov, he seems pathetically pedantic, thin, and lacking in dimension. The scene they play together is one of the masterpieces of modern drama:

TROFIMOV: Whether the estate is sold today or not—what difference does it make? It was gone long ago. You can't turn back now, that path is lost. You mustn't worry; but above all you mustn't deceive yourself. For once in your life you must face the truth squarely.

LYUBOV ANDREYEVNA: What truth? You seem to see so clearly what is true and what is not true, but I have lost my power of seeing, I don't see anything. You are able to solve all your problems so neatly; but tell me, *galuvchik,* isn't that because you are young, because life is still hidden from your eyes, so that you can't believe anything horrible can ever happen to you, and don't expect it will? You're braver, and more honest and more serious than we, good; but put yourself in our place, try to be generous, if only a little, have pity. I was born here, you know, and my father and mother lived here, and my grandfather too, and I love this house—I can't imagine life without the cherry orchard, and if it really must be sold, then sell me along with it... (*She embraces Trofimov, and kisses him on the forehead*) My little boy, you know, was drowned here... (*She weeps*) Have pity on me, my good, kind friend.

TROFIMOV: You know you have my entire sympathy.

LYUBOV ANDREYEVNA: But how differently, how differently, that should be said! (*She takes out her handkerchief. A telegram falls to the floor*) My heart is so heavy today, you can't imagine! It's so noisy here that my heart trembles, I can't stop trembling, yet I can't go to my room; when I'm alone the silence frightens me. Don't blame me, Petya... I love you as if you were my own son. I'd gladly let Anya marry you, honestly I would, only you must study, my boy, you must complete your course. You don't do anything, you're merely tossed about from place to place, it's so strange—isn't that so? Isn't it? And you should do something about your beard, make it grow or something . . . (*She laughs*) You look so funny!

TROFIMOV (*picks up the telegram*): I have no desire to look beautiful.

LYUBOV ANDREYEVNA: That telegram is from Paris. I get one every day. One yesterday; one today. That madman is ill again, and he's in a terrible mess . . . He begs me to forgive him, he wants me to come back and, really, I suppose, I should go to Paris and stay with him a while. You're frowning, Petya, but what else can I do, dear boy, what else am I to do? He's sick and lonely and unhappy, and who is to look after him there, who is to stop him from making a fool of himself, and give him his medicine at the right time? And after all, why should I hide it, why make a secret of it? I love him, I love him. He's a millstone round my neck, and he's dragging me to the bottom, but I love this stone, and I can't live without it. (*Presses Trofimov's hand*) Don't think I'm bad, Petya, don't say anything to me, don't say anything . . .

TROFIMOV (*with tears in his eyes*): Please—forgive my frankness—but this man is robbing you . . .

With this, Trofimov touches the hidden spring. Lyubov flashes out at him with all the fury that her gentleness conceals. The scene recalls the quarrel between Treplev and his mother in *The Sea Gull*. It is a masterly emotional transition:

LYUBOV ANDREYEVNA (*angry, but restraining herself*): You're twenty-six or twenty-seven years old, but you're still a sophomore.

TROFIMOV: Nonsense!

LYUBOV ANDREYEVNA: At your age, you should be a man, you should understand what it is to be in love. And you should be in love yourself . . . why aren't you in love? (*Angrily*) Yes! Yes! You're not so pure and innocent as all that, you're a ridiculous prude, a prig, a pervert . . .

TROFIMOV (*horrified*): What is she saying?

LYUBOV ANDREYEVNA: "I'm above passion!" You're not above passion, you're simply what Firs calls "useless lumber." Imagine anyone your age who's never had a mistress!

TROFIMOV (*horrified*): This is awful! What's she saying! (*He rushes toward the ballroom clutching his head in his hands*) This is awful! I can't bear it! I'm going . . . (*Goes out and comes back immediately*) It's all over between us! (*Goes out into the hall.*)

LYUBOV ANDREYEVNA (*calls after him*): Petya, wait! Silly man, I was only joking! Petya! [27]

There is a crash. Petya has fallen down the stairs. The girls scream, then burst into laughter. A moment or two later, Lyubov is dancing with Petya, and all is forgiven.

It would be a mistake to conclude from a scene of this sort that the degree of seriousness with which such characters must be taken is gravely compromised by the clownishness of their behavior. These lapses from dignity serve to accentuate the humanity of the characters, but they change nothing. Lyubov is volatile. She passes easily from tears to laughter, and from tenderness to anger. She rails bitterly; she stabs seemingly to the heart; what she says is unforgivable; but Trofimov is fundamentally as good-humored as she, and he forgives her readily; he understands.

Gorky, in his autobiography, marvels at the Russian character: people who are at one another's throats one moment, sit down comfortably together to dinner the next. But whether or not this sort of volatility is a national characteristic, it is certainly universally understandable, and a scene of this sort makes an extraordinarily vivid effect. There is nothing in the least abstract about Trofimov. Unlike the characters of tragedy, it is possible for him to fall down a flight of steps, and to survive the fall, completely intact in every aspect of his personality. Indeed, it is by putting his characters through the ordeal of laughter that Chekhov proves their validity. Lyubov is no less tragic for having played a comic scene, nor is Trofimov any the less significant for having tumbled down the stairs. The stiff-necked Belikov, however, in Chekhov's story *The Man in a Case*, cannot survive a fall of this sort. Trofimov is elastic; Belikov is brittle. Trofimov can stand a good deal of laughter; he is indestructible. But bigots like Belikov are another matter. They make one angry. Chekhov literally laughs Belikov to death; and, as the narrator remarks, "it must be confessed that to bury people like Belikov is a great pleasure." [28]

The Cherry Orchard is another example of the type of drama which acquires magnitude by virtue of its relation to a conflict external to the theatre. It belongs to the tradition of modern tragedy initiated by Hebbel with *Maria Magdalena*, and developed, principally by Ibsen, into a primary pattern for serious drama. Its characters were all conceived comedically. They fall readily into more or less absurd poses; some are very broadly caricatured. In general, everything is done in this play to minimize the scale, and to bring the action down to a colloquial level. In the middle of a dialogue which threatens to become serious, for example, Lopakhin suddenly sticks his head into the scene, and moos like a cow. At the height of the suspense in the third act, he comes in, the bearer of important tidings, a little drunk, just in time to receive a knock on the head intended for Epikhodov. Then he proceeds to give a lamentable exhibition of bad taste and low breeding. Chekhov spares nobody. He is at pains to show his characters in the round, with all their faults and absurdities in plain view, and the effect is necessarily funny. But behind this comedy is a sense of disaster. For all the clownishness of their behavior, these characters are profoundly affected by events, and it is impossible to forget that their actions, absurd as they may seem, reflect the cosmic drama which is properly the subject of the action.

Conceivably, the cosmic drama also has its absurd side, though the order of its magnitude precludes its being treated, as a rule, with less than complete solemnity. But to the eye of a dying man life, even at its most majestic, may reveal a degree of absurdity which is not readily apparent to those who expect to live forever. It is, very likely, this sense of the ultimate stupidity of the whole performance, on all its levels from the individual to the cosmic, that gives *The Cherry Orchard* its unique place in the social drama of our time. It is very arguable that at this stage of his career, Chekhov had expanded his sense of the comic to quite unusual proportions —he was writing something in the nature of a cosmic *vaudeville*. If this was his viewpoint, his impatience with Stanislavsky over the production of *The Three Sisters* and *The Cherry Orchard* becomes comprehensible, and it is also apparent that nobody in the Moscow Art company could possibly have understood in what way he intended these plays to be performed as comedies.

What *The Cherry Orchard* involves is the economic and social reorganization of a continent, a vast process of which its action constitutes an infinitesimal fraction. This minute complex, nevertheless, suggests and measures the scale of the whole phenomenon; it is a module from which the whole may be, in some degree, conceived. In comparison with the magnitude of the forces which move them, these characters may be thought to dwindle into insignificance; but they are not isolated from nature. Their plight is universal. Their heartbreak is resonant. It echoes from the uttermost confines of the universe.

Obviously, it is not the foolishness, or the profligacy, of the landowners that brings about the catastrophe of *The Cherry Orchard*. They are by nature neither thrifty nor resourceful, but this is in itself no more than a sign of their passing, a detail; it is not its cause. The economic order in which once they were necessary has decayed. Another order is at hand, and these people have no longer any function in the world. Like the characters in *Ghosts*, they are vestiges of a past which must be cleared away before the future can take its proper form. The cherry orchard was once useful. In its day, it was a source of revenue and employment; therefore it was maintained. But the market long ago dried up. The secret of preserving the fruit was lost. The trees are old and will not bear. Now the orchard is merely beautiful. And–such is the intimation–the class it symbolizes is equally beautiful and equally useless. In the nature of things, both are ripe for the axe.

For Trofimov, their destruction is no disaster; it is merely a transitional episode to be observed with detachment. For Lopakhin the destruction of the orchard, and the expropriation of its owners, is largely a matter of business, regrettable, perhaps, but inevitable. But for Chekhov it was not so simple. He could not record with detachment the passing of a lovely thing; as he arranged his play, the ruin of Ranyevskaya, and the cutting down of her orchard, are alike a source of grief. In consequence, *The Cherry Orchard* has a very full modal development. Even in its lightest moments we are aware of the magnitude of the conception, of the dynamic upsurge of force from the depths of society, the immense potency of the emancipated peasantry, the ambition of the newly moneyed class, the psychic disintegration of the gentry. The process doubtless has its amusing aspects; but it is grim. In the grip of inexorable circumstance, these people can assert, at the most, their nobility of character, their breeding, and that rigidity of class which at the same time commands admiration and ensures their destruction. They have no flexibility; they insist on being themselves to the end. There is, certainly, something vaguely ridiculous about this display, and their manners are parodied to some purpose by Yasha and Epikhodov, who have not yet quite got the hang of things. But it is impossible not to sense their heroism also, and it is this blend of the heroic and the absurd that sets the mood of the play.

The Cherry Orchard fills a narrower canvas than *The Three Sisters*, and has less obvious poignancy, but its technique indicates a considerable advance in Chekhov's dramatic method. It seems clear that in his last years he was working toward a concept of drama that departed further and further from the conventions of the well-made play and, had he lived, he might have liberated himself completely from that tradition.

Chekhov's method differs from that of such writers as Ibsen and Hauptmann not so much in the shape of the plot, or the intricacy of the narrative, as in the extent to which he frees his characters from its service. He permits them, for example, an extraordinary degree of freedom in the association of ideas, so that the dialogue constantly strays from the line of the play. Simple as Ibsen's plots often are, his characters are in every case chiefly employed in developing the narrative, and in this respect they are remarkably efficient. Chekhov's characters do not serve the plot at all. At best, they accommodate themselves to it, like unwilling passengers on a train which is taking them where they have no desire to go.

In *The Cherry Orchard*, as in *The Three Sisters*, Chekhov's dialogue is barely responsive. Sometimes the speeches make the effect of an interrupted revery, as if they are the external signs of an inward dialogue, the details of which are only partially suggested. The characters communicate through innumerable pauses and silences; these silences are often singularly meaningful. The speeches themselves, on the other hand, are often insignificant. The lines of thought converge, but soon part company; quite often, they seem to run parallel to one another without making any contact.

The result is a scenic climate that is curiously different from the traditional atmosphere of the stage. In these plays, a good deal more is suggested than is said. The characters sometimes make the impression of being isolated from one another beyond the possibility of communication; yet occasionally they appear to be in far more intimate communication than words can achieve. In act three of *The Three Sisters*, for example, Vershinin and Masha play their love scene musically, without benefit of language. In the last act of *The Cherry Orchard*, Lyubov and Gaev have a moment by themselves shortly before their departure. They embrace and weep quietly, with restraint, so as not to embarrass the others. They say practically nothing:

> GAEV (*in despair*): Sister, sister . . .
> LYUBOV ANDREYEVNA: Oh my orchard, my beloved, my beautiful orchard! My life, my youth, my happiness . . . good bye! Good bye!
> ANYA (*calls gaily offstage*): Mamma!
> TROFIMOV (*offstage, gaily, excited*): Hi!
> LYUBOV ANDREYEVNA: I must look once more at these walls, these windows . . . How mother loved this room!
> GAEV: Sister . . . sister . . .
> ANYA (*offstage*): Mamma!
> TROFIMOV (*calling, as before*): Hi!
> LYUBOV ANDREYEVNA: We're coming.
> (*They go out.*) [29]

The poignancy of this scene in the dilapidated nursery is positively overwhelming. The leavetaking breaks Lyubov's heart. It marks the end of her world. But for Anya it marks the beginning of life. Anya is full of joy at the thought of the wonders that are in store for her, and her mother is exquisitely tactful in sparing her the sight of her sorrow, or any intimation of her foreboding for the future. For the first

…lay we see Gaev without any trace of his protec- …on, and his closeness to Lyubov is demonstrated …y need for words. The scene is obviously a master- …oncision. It takes but a moment, and makes use of virtual… no rhetoric; yet in this moment is recapitulated the entire theme and all the mood of the play.

In the case of *The Cherry Orchard*, the question of mood is troublesome. Nothing is sustained. The variations are kaleidoscopic. With the possible exception of Lyubov Andreyevna, all the characters are in some way comic, and some, as we have seen, are comic types. The bank manager in *The Jubilee*, the overburdened commuter in *A Tragedian in Spite of Himself*, the naval officer in *A Wedding with a General*, even the orator in *The Evils of Tobacco*, all have that blend of comedy and pathos which was Chekhov's specialty as a caricaturist; but such characters offer no particular difficulty in interpretation, since they play in situations which are primarily funny. *The Cherry Orchard*, however, is a tragic play composed almost entirely of comic scenes.

In these scenes the pathetic element is necessarily quite close to the surface. It crops out constantly. As we have seen, Chekhov was deeply concerned lest his play be presented as a *comédie larmoyante*. The danger was all too evident, and, as he feared, Stanislavsky's production did nothing to avert it. It is difficult, indeed, to see how, short of a dramatic miracle, the pathos of the situation could be disguised or diluted. With all its jokes, its slapstick, and comic flourishes, with all its expressions of hope for the future, *The Cherry Orchard* centers upon the sound of the breaking string.

This effect is played twice. The first time the sound is heard, it is in the scene near the abandoned chapel in the fields. After Trofimov's long tirade against the intelligentsia, and Lopakhin's answer regarding the people and the wealth of Russia, there is a pause. Epikhodov crosses upstage, playing his guitar. The rest are silent. There is nothing left to say:

LYUBOV ANDREYEVNA (*pensively*): There goes Epikhodov.
ANYA (*pensively*): There goes Epikhodov.

Neither of them is particularly interested, but, clearly, they are thinking different things about Epikhodov. For Lyubov, he represents the half-emancipated peasantry, clownish, intractable, useless, and seemingly unteachable—a cogent argument for doing nothing. For Anya, he is an argument for redoubling one's efforts in behalf of the lower classes. But for Gaev, he is all that is left of the old life, a vestige of the former times, and the thought inspires him with romantic melancholy:

GAEV: The sun has gone down, my friends.
TROFIMOV: Yes.

For Gaev the sun has gone down in more ways than one, and the association of images, perhaps unrealized, motivates his next speech. He declaims softly, like a chorus in Sophoclean tragedy:

GAEV (*in a subdued voice, as if reciting a poem*): Oh nature, glorious nature, shining with eternal light, so beautiful and so indifferent . . . you whom we call Mother, you unite within yourself both life and death, you create and you destroy . . .
VARYA (*imploringly*): Uncle, dear!
ANYA: Uncle, you're at it again!
TROFIMOV: You're better off with the red to the middle.
GAEV: I'll be quiet. Quiet.[30]

There follows a silence. Suddenly there is a sound in the sky, a far-off sound, the sound of a breaking string. They wonder what it is and what it means.

This scene marks the very zenith of Chekhov's art. Gaev has been presented as an old windbag, a foolish man given to inappropriate oratory, an aging dandy who has taken refuge from life in an imaginary game of billiards. But the moment is magical, and quite unexpectedly this empty vessel is inspired. In his apostrophe to nature is said all that can be said of the mystery of life, and in this moment Gaev gives voice to what all those present must feel in their hearts. It is the essential theme of the play. But the young people find his words unbearable, and they force him to be silent. It is at this point that we hear the sound of the breaking string in the sky.

It is indicative of the nature of humanity that the young and the old are seldom on speaking terms. Each generation is self-enclosed; as distinct from its forebears as the egg from the hen that laid it. It is impossible for Gaev to communicate his feelings. The young cannot apostrophize nature in this manner. They must wait until they are old; and then, in their turn, they will find no listeners. And so, even though at this moment Gaev speaks with the tongues of men and of angels, though the whole of the heavenly choir is ranged behind him, and all the universe crowds forward to listen, these people who are nearest to him will not listen, cannot listen. To them he seems an utter fool, the relic of a bygone age. His frustration brings about a moment of inexpressible sadness. A string breaks in the sky.

The effect is repeated at the very end of the play, so that the author's intention is unmistakable. In the last scene, after the carriage bell is silent and the family has gone, the shutters are fastened, and the doors are locked for the winter. Nothing is heard but the ring of the axe in the orchard. Then old Firs comes shambling into the deserted room. He is ill. He was to have been sent to the hospital, but somehow in the bustle of departure he has been left behind:

FIRS (*he walks to the door and tries the handle*): Locked. They've gone . . . (*He sits on the sofa*) They forgot me . . . Never mind . . . I'll sit here a while . . . I'll bet Leonid Andreyevich hasn't put on his furs; he's gone off in his

> topcoat. (*He sighs anxiously*) I should have kept an eye on him. When they're young, they're green... (*He mumbles something unintelligible*) My life's gone by as if I'd never lived. (*He stretches out*) I'll lie down a while. There's no strength left in you, old boy, nothing left, nothing... Ah you... useless lumber! (*He lies still. A distant sound is heard. It seems to come from the sky, the sound of a breaking string mournfully dying away. Then all is silent once again, and nothing is heard but the sound of the axe on a tree far away in the orchard.*)[31]

The sound of the breaking string remains mysterious, but it has finality. The symbol is broad; it would be folly to try to assign to it a more precise meaning than the author chose to give it. But its quality is not equivocal. Whatever of sadness remains unexpressed in *The Cherry Orchard*, this sound expresses.

Doubtless the worlds to come, the worlds of Lopakhin and Trofimov, will be better than the world in which Firs and Gaev were not yet useless lumber. It is perhaps necessary and proper that the cherry orchard be cut in order that all Russia should become a garden. But it is inevitable that these pruning operations should elicit an occasional pang. If the world is an organism, a living thing, perhaps it too has its moments of heartbreak.

In February of 1904, Chekhov left Moscow once more for Yalta, again in defiance of his doctor's orders. The early winter months had passed amid the excitements attending the outbreak of the war with Japan. Chekhov was still depressed about *The Cherry Orchard*. He insisted on every occasion that Stanislavsky was responsible for its failure. But in April Stanislavsky wired him that the play had enjoyed a great success in Petersburg, "incomparably greater than in Moscow."

The war, meanwhile, was much on Chekhov's mind. He declared more than once that he was going to the front as a doctor. Early in May he returned to Moscow and at once fell ill. He was sufficiently recovered by the beginning of June to be able to travel to Badenweiler in the Black Forest, which was medically recommended, but he was very low in his mind. He was sure now that he was going away to die. Yet in a few days he was in Berlin with Olga in excellent spirits, sightseeing and shopping—he complained chiefly of the plainness of the German women. The following week he was comfortably installed in a private pension in Badenweiler, and, shortly after, he moved to the Sommer Hotel. His health was much improved, and once again his letters were full of hope and cheer.

At the end of June he suffered a severe attack. Again he seemed to recover; but soon after midnight on July 2, he felt ill. His doctor, Schwöhrer, came about two in the morning, found his pulse weak, and gave him an injection of camphor. He was gasping for breath. The doctor sent for a flask of oxygen. Chekhov remarked dryly that before it came he would be dead. The doctor then ordered up a bottle of champagne. Chekhov, with a bright smile, took a glass and drained it with relish. Then he lay on his side and closed his eyes. A few minutes later, he was dead.

In a letter to his wife written in July 1904, Gorky described with characteristic bitterness the arrival of Chekhov's body in Moscow in a refrigerated railway car marked "Fresh Oysters." The sordidness of the funeral was obviously much harder for Gorky to bear than for Chekhov: "They were talking about everything in the crowd of 3000, maybe 5000, people; they were thinking of their lunch, of what friends they were going to visit, but about him, about Chekhov, not a word was said. Not one, I assure you. An overwhelming indifference, an unbreakable wall of vulgarity—there were even smiles . . . We waited in the hope of hearing something beautiful, or sad, or sincere. There was nothing . . ."

The Sound of the Breaking String

CHEKHOV'S drama, like Ibsen's, represents a world in transition. In Ibsen's Norway, wherever that might be, the impact of modern thought in the latter half of the nineteenth century brought about a relatively peaceful revolution. In Russia the idea of the state was formulated along particularly rigid lines, and the transition from the old to the new was accompanied by impressive rites of passage. In his *Autobiography*, Gorky speaks with something like awe of an old policeman's description of the invisible thread that issued from the heart of the Tsar and wound through his ministers down to the least of his soldiers in a web that encompassed the nation.[1] To many, life under these conditions seemed intolerable; but the thought of breaking the tie caused much uneasiness.

One of the constant complaints of the time centered on the breakdown of communication between fathers and sons, and the abyss that divided the older generation from the younger. This is, no doubt, a universal complaint in all periods, but the social and economic situation of Russia in the latter half of the nineteenth century made the break particularly sharp and deep. The golden string that connected man with his father on earth and his father in heaven, the age-old bond that tied the present to the past, was not to be broken lightly. When at last it snapped, the result, we have discovered, was both world-shaking and soul-shaking.

It was on the threshold of this cataclysm that Chekhov set his stage. He was primarily an ironist, and his plays were, on the whole, comedically conceived. But Chekhov was taking the pulse of a dying world. It died well, with courage and gayety; nevertheless, the description of its agony could not be altogether funny. His plays are full of laughter, but in each we hear the sound of the breaking string; and from the contrast between what seems, from one viewpoint, comic, but tragic from another, Chekhov developed a form of drama, a dramatic polyphony, which is unparalleled in the history of the theatre.

The technique of suggestion and implication through which this result was achieved had been fully worked out in his stories before Chekhov attempted to employ it on the stage. The short story called *The Wife*, for example, concerns the relations of a husband and his estranged wife with regard to the relief of a neighboring village in time of famine. In the behavior of these two people is implied the whole story of their past, what amounts virtually to a novel. None of this is actually related. But by the end of the story, what has not been said has become completely clear, and one realizes that two stories have been told simultaneously, the one related directly, and the other altogether implied. Similarly, *About Love* is the story of an adulterous relationship that does not take place. It results in an intimate characterization of the narrator, Alekhin, who is understood mainly by reference to what he does not do and does not say. It would be an error to conclude from such examples that Chekhov was primarily concerned with novel forms of narration. He was, on the contrary, much inclined to a very simple and unaffected style, and disliked anything that smacked of trickery. But the things that most interested him as a writer were often too intangible for direct communication. In consequence, he developed a curiously tangential method of approach.

The difficulty of representing on the stage anything that cannot be directly stated is enormous. Unlike the novelist, the playwright relinquishes control of his material the moment it is played, and the audience is at liberty to do with it what it pleases. The theatre therefore inclines one to an uncompromising frontality of approach, and its conditions are generally unsuitable for any but the simplest and most unambiguous effects. This is particularly true of characterization. In the theatre it is usually assumed that the audience will be briefed quite precisely as to the nature of the characters by the end of the first act—such was the Scribean practice. Anything that changes this impression is then in the nature of a major effect, a surprise, or a recognition.

None of Chekhov's plays follows this prescription. His characters do not announce themselves, nor do they lend themselves readily to definition. Like real people, they are the subject of surmise and inference, and the author furnishes only the barest clues as to his intention. When the Moscow Art Theatre presented *The Sea Gull*, its directors went to great lengths to explore the personality of the principal characters in the interests of a truly realistic production. Chekhov's approach to these problems was characteristically oblique. Stanislavsky had been playing Trigorin in the elegant costume of a successful writer. When he managed in time to elicit from Chekhov a judgment of his interpretation, Chekhov's only comment was: "Excellent. Only he wears checked trousers, and his shoes have holes." He was somewhat more expansive with Kachalov, who also undertook this role for a time: "His fishing-rods are homemade, you know, all crooked and bent; he makes them himself with a penknife. His cigar is a good one, perhaps even a very good one; but he never removes the cigar band." And after a moment's earnest thought, he added: "But the main thing is his fishing rods." Similarly, during the rehearsals of *Uncle Vanya*, he wrote to Stanislavsky to explain Astrov's last scene: "He whistles, you know. Whistles. Uncle Vanya cries, but Astrov whistles."

These were, in fact, very useful clues to the characterization in each case, though willfully—one might even say mischievously—enigmatic. Even in the interests of his own production, Chekhov did not trouble to spell out for his cast the process of reasoning through which the character of Trigorin might be deduced from the holes in his shoes or the crudeness of his fishpoles. Here, as elsewhere, he contented himself with pointing to the external fact, the superficial manifestation of the inner situation.

That this epigrammatic mode of representation was learned rather than innate can hardly be doubted. Experience had taught him the futility of long explanations. In 1888, he had written copious notes analyzing the characters of *Ivanov*, and he had coached Davydov for hours in connection with the Petersburg production, all to no avail. Even toward the end of his life, in his letters to Olga Knipper he furnished from time to time detailed analyses of character and action, which nobody in the acting company understood or heeded. But he had his special magic, and used it to good effect. He knew that a moonlit landscape could be evoked by the highlight on the neck of a bottle; and in a man who whistled while others wept one could divine the depths of the soul's despair.

Until the last years of the nineteenth century, only the greatest dramatists had attempted anything on the stage beyond the depiction of the obvious. Traditionally, a play was an acted story, an observable pattern of events, but it was considered necessary in the course of a dramatic action for the author to reveal something of the secret life of his characters. This was accomplished in the simplest manner. Even in the nineteenth century, we find the characters of drama eager to explain themselves to us verbally in soliloquies or, more subtly, in the relation between what they do and what they say. Until the advent of symbolism, drama was an art that made things clear. Only the greatest plays preserved their mystery.

Impressionism was the great innovation of the later nineteenth century. The impressionists declined to look below the surface and, in the novel as on the stage, impressionist art was primarily concerned with the definition of external experience. For the impressionists, and their semi-scientific brethren, the naturalists, a character was what he seemed to be, and nothing more. The reaction was inevitable. Long before 1891, the year Huret published the results of his *Enquête* on the future of literature, it had become evident that a literary art which declined to look beyond appearance could have no great future.

The immediate result of the reaction to the school of Médan was a renewal of interest in symbolism and psychology, both of which attempted to probe the surface in order to discover what lay beneath the external tissue of experience. Chekhov had no taste for the metaphysical; but the workings of the human psyche interested him very much. His attitude from first to last remained staunchly impressionistic. He was concerned primarily to describe the face of nature; but its physiognomy fascinated him and, like all the major writers of his day, he came readily under the influence of symbolism.

Maeterlinck's essay *Le Tragique quotidien* was not published until 1896, the year of *The Sea Gull;* but Chekhov had been reading him for some time in French, and in the summer of 1897 he wrote Suvorin of the great impression Maeterlinck's plays had made upon him. Maeterlinck had written of the need for a quiet drama, the drama of every day, which would convey the true sound of life:

> Here we no longer live with barbarians, nor is man now fretting in the midst of elementary passions, as though these were the only things worthy of note; he is at rest, and we have time to observe him. It is no longer a violent, exceptional movement of life that passes before our eyes—it is life itself.[2]

It must have occurred almost as readily to Chekhov as it had to Maeterlinck that in "life itself" there is something other than the obvious component, and that, consequently, naturalism, even at best, is a needlessly shallow evaluation of experience. People are primarily visible to the sensual eye, but only in their solidity, their opacity; the eye sees them and understands nothing. If they are to be understood, they must be perceived with the eye of the mind, armed with all the perceptive powers of which the mind is capable. Chekhov was unwilling to speculate, and refused to predicate anything of a general nature with regard to the substrate. Nevertheless, he was very much aware of the invisible life. He noted the outward detail of his world with the vigilant eye of the impressionist, but the result was valuable to him chiefly insofar as the outer world furnished a basis for the exploration of the world within, and it was in the relation of the two worlds that he found the true substance of his art.

In *The Lady with the Little Dog* the contrapuntal nature of the double life is demonstrated in a very elementary form. Gurov, the hero of the story,

> had two lives, one open, seen and known by all who cared to know it, full of conventional truth and conventional falsehood, exactly like the lives of his friends and acquaintances, and another life that ran its course in secret. And through some strange, perhaps accidental combination of circumstances, everything that was of interest and importance, and essential to him, everything about which he felt sincerely and did not deceive himself, whatever constituted the core of his being, was

> hidden from other people; while all that was false in him, the shell in which he hid in order to conceal the truth . . . all that life went on in the open. And, judging others by himself, he believed nothing that he saw, and always considered that every man led his real, and most interesting life under the cover of secrecy, as under the cover of night . . . [3]

It was Chekhov's special gift as an artist that he was able to penetrate to the core around which the outer life is shaped; but it was characteristic of his native reticence that beyond a certain point he did not betray his characters. With Chekhov, the revelation of truth was a matter involving the greatest circumspection. He never pretended to understand what he did not understand, and he scrupled to make a display of what he knew. In *The Black Monk*, Kovrin lives his true life in the company of the mysterious apparition he has called forth from within himself. His well-meaning wife and her father, by means of diet and bromides, succeed in driving away the phantom which absorbs his attention, and are surprised when the excitement and the joy of his life vanish also. Once he is cured of his hallucination, the man is ruined, and his resentment knows no bounds. When the phantom monk returns at last, Kovrin is happy once again, and it is now that he suffers the hemorrhage that puts an end to him.

This is all Chekhov tells. But the intimation is clear. Kovrin's secret life, his essential life, is inseparable from the disease he hides in his breast, his tuberculosis, which works silently and secretly within him, and at last appears before his eyes as his dearest friend and greatest solace, his sincere admirer, the black monk. Such is the compensation he has invented for his mediocrity; and the fantasy is more than merely compensatory. It is a work of art precisely suited to his psychic needs, realized step by step until it destroys him. This growing death which he nourishes is, in short, his life, the illusion of greatness which at once sustains and consumes him. In the same way, in *The Sea Gull*, Treplev cannot endure the thought of his mediocrity. For him also the idea that he is a genius is his link with the vital principle; when this link snaps, his life comes to an end.

The art of Chekhov is, seemingly, limpid, a more or less humorous representation of the life of his time. In fact it is the art of the incomprehensible, the half-surmised, the enigmatic. It elicits, not a feeling of satisfaction but a revery, a mood that is very often disturbing. Chekhov speaks not to the mind, as perhaps he intended, but to the soul, reaching inward through a train of associations over which he exercises only a partial control. There is certainly something in this method that suggests the poet, or better still the composer; and Chekhov's work has, in consequence, often been called poetry, and compared with music. But if this art is musical, it is, on the whole, a discordant music that it makes. Chekhov was often compassionate, but more often brutally ironic. His was not a gentle art.

It is perhaps for this reason that Chekhov seems to us in our day so astonishingly modern. He was no ordinary realist. Had he been, his work would very likely have withered with his age, as he feared it might. In his own day, and in his country, he was admired for things that no longer seem important; and even now there is surely a tendency among Russian critics to exaggerate his role as a precursor of the Revolution. Tolstoy admired him greatly as an artist; but he thought his plays were pointless. Of all his stories, Tolstoy liked *Dushechka* best—*The Darling*—which he considered a beautiful portrayal of womanhood, completely overlooking the irony of the characterization.[4]

The truth of "life as it is," which Chekhov thought it the function of the artist to reveal, was not, indeed, a truth perceptible to the realist. The life with which he was concerned was not the life which people exhibit. His was another order of realism. For those who are mainly aware of the external life, it is Chekhov's comic tales which are primarily valuable, and the works of his later period seem to them the product of a mind which ceased at a certain point to be amusing.[5] But after half a century of earnest psychologizing, we tend to look beyond the jester in Chekhov, beyond the ironist, and for the first time, perhaps, we become aware of his terrifying insight into the guarded depths of the personality, the dark continent of the mind which only the artist can enter without intrusion.

Chekhov's characters are never wholly detached from the matrix. They stand out in various degrees of relief, never wholly in the round, physically and psychically a part of their environment, something to be contemplated along with the other things of nature, rivers and trees, the sky, the flight of geese, the lightning. For Chekhov all such manifestations of life were equally animate and equally mysterious, a source of wonder in themselves and in their mutual relations. Chekhov never ceased to be the boy traveling across the steppe toward the distant city, and he transmitted best of all the sense of surprise, the feeling of awe that life can arouse in a fresh and receptive mind. Perhaps because death was so near to him, he had no strong terminal sense. Man ends; but his story is endless. Chekhov's plays are not finished. When the curtain has fallen, the play goes on; there is still the sense of flux. We say farewell, and the brigade moves on toward other horizons. With Chekhov the story is soon told; but behind the story there is an eternity of stories, there is the eternal story:

> Yalta was hardly visible through the morning mist; white clouds stood motionless on the mountain tops. The leaves did not stir on the trees, cicadas chirruped, and the monotonous, hollow sound of the sea, rising from below, spoke of peace and the eternal sleep that awaits us. So it must have sounded when there was no Yalta, and no Oreanda; so it sounds now, and so it will sound,

> indifferent and hollow, when we are no more. And in this permanence, in this complete indifference to the life and death of each one of us, there is hidden perhaps a pledge of our eternal salvation, of the unceasing movement of life on the earth, of the unceasing movement toward perfection.[6]

It is in such passages that we sense the nature of the Chekhovian "Beyond," the strangely unreal atmosphere in which the realities of his later plays are suspended. It is an atmosphere less mysterious and less explicit than the Maeterlinckian *au-delà*, and certainly more intelligible. Like many of Chekhov's stories, his plays, *The Sea Gull*, *The Three Sisters*, and *The Cherry Orchard*, are presented with utmost realism, but they are presented *sub specie aeternitatis*, so that everything in them seems provisional and ephemeral in its nature, and the action seems curiously insignificant, a trifle in comparison with the vast process of which it forms a part.

Men live and suffer and die and are forgotten; the wave piles high on the beach, recedes, returns, endlessly repeating its monotonous cycle. It is perhaps quite aimless and meaningless; yet we are permitted to see in it the symbol of our salvation. The doubt, the question, is at the bottom of all. It is the true source of the unity of these plays, and the ultimate principle of their form. In consequence of the doubt which shaped them, they have a dream-like quality which is emphasized by somnambulistic characters for whom the borders of reality seem blurred. And, indeed, beyond the action of these plays we are made aware through dubious signs of another and more questionable reality to which these symbols barely reach; and which is perhaps not there.

Late in his life, it is said, Chekhov came to the conclusion that his works were essentially of exemplary and didactic character. Tikhonov recalls that in the course of a discussion in Moscow Chekhov remarked: "You say that you have wept over my plays. Yes, and not you alone. But I did not write them for that; it is Alexeyev who has made such cry-babies of my characters. I wanted something else. I wanted to tell people honestly: 'Look at yourselves. See how badly you live and how tiresome you are!' The main thing is that people should understand this. When they do, they will surely create a new and better life for themselves. I will not see it, but I know it will be entirely different, not like what we have now. And so long as it does not exist, I will continue to tell people: 'See how badly you live, and how tiresome you are!' Is that what makes them weep?" [7]

Evidently, at this stage of his career, the work of preparing the future of humanity, of which Vershinin speaks so vaguely, was taking a more definite form in Chekhov's mind, and he was willing to present his work primarily as social criticism. Unquestionably Chekhov said things of this sort from time to time, and especially when he found it necessary to defend himself against the charge, often repeated, that his writings made no point and carried no message. But while such statements are understandable in the circumstances, and even perhaps to his credit, the truth is that, as a dramatist, he was a very minor social critic, but a very great artist. It is doubtful that anyone will wish to read *Uncle Vanya*, *The Three Sisters*, or *The Cherry Orchard* for purposes of edification, and it seems quaint that Chekhov should have suggested the possibility; but they have the universal validity of the highest art.

It seems altogether unlikely that Chekhov ever wrote with a particular point in mind. His work is never argumentative, seldom demonstrative. It is descriptive, representational. When he found a subject to his liking, he proceeded, apparently, to set it down as a painter might, filling in his canvas with broad, and often seemingly unrelated, touches which in the end are seen to make a *Gestalt*. Chekhov was certainly concerned with meaning, but not often with message. His works leave one with a sense of a deeply felt and complex experience, in part emotional, and in part intellectual, but never with the feeling of having digested a sermon or an *exemplum*. Apart from his often-expressed faith in the future of humanity, it is quite impossible to say what Chekhov believed. He affirmed life. He gave to the transitory a permanent form, an intimation of eternity; and he fixed the cultural elements of his time in patterns that are beautiful in themselves, and universally intelligible. It is the traditional role of the artist. His work comes as close to life as the work of Gogol and, since like him he was inclined to caricature, he strove for a likeness. But from the intellectual standpoint he was never precise: he displayed mainly his ambivalence. His plays are never definite in function or in aim and, as works of art, they seem as irrelevant to such concerns as the paintings of Brueghel or Vermeer.

It was evidently Chekhov's idea that the elemental forces of the universe express themselves most clearly in the individual, and that it is by observing the behavior of individuals that we become aware of the great tides that sweep the world. All of Chekhov's plays are small in subject matter, plays of the drawing-room and the garden. Yet no one has painted a broader canvas, or unfolded a deeper perspective. It was his aim to write simply and accurately. No modern dramatist is more complex; and few have elicited more diverse interpretations. In the belief that a representation of life involves everything that can be truly said about it, he noted in detail the symptoms of the world's malaise. So far as he could see, his world was a tissue of absurdities. It made no sense, and was probably no longer viable. He had only general therapeutic measures to suggest. Perhaps it could be nursed back to health. If not, it would die; and a new world would rise from its ashes. The question of how precisely this was to happen seemed, at the moment, unanswerable. But in two or three hundred years at the most, he was certain, the answer would be clear, and perhaps even the question. In the meantime, there was nothing for it but patience. Life was painful, but it was amusing; on the whole, an interesting and exasperating experience that one would not willingly forego. There was no more to be said on the subject. "You ask, what is life?" he wrote Olga some months before his death. "That is just the same as asking what is a carrot. A carrot is a carrot, and nothing more is known about it." [8]

Chekhov expressed no great faith in his chances of survival on the literary scene. In 1901 he remarked to Ivan Bunin that he did not expect his works to live over seven years. "But even though they read me only seven years more," he added, "I have less than that to live. Six."

He exaggerated. He had only three years more to live, barely that; but he would surely be read for centuries. He was not like other writers of his age, who spoke well, but only for their time, and were certain to pass away with it. Better than any among his contemporaries he expressed the transition between the old world and the new; his viewpoint was universal, his insights were at the same time Olympian and intensely human, he saw the jest where others saw only the injustice, and sensed the pain where others were moved chiefly to laughter. It is much to his credit that he saw life in the round, and also that he was not much concerned to formulate it philosophically. After all, he was soon to die, and for him the word *nichevo*, which his characters speak so often, had a special connotation.

In a noisy age, Chekhov greatly cultivated the gift of understatement. Therefore his words come to us softly and clearly through the hubbub of his time, and in this manner he is emphatic beyond any of his contemporaries, more convincing than Tolstoy, more effective than Gorky. Occasionally in his world there arises a scream of anguish or a shriek of laughter; but not often. His world, in general, is quiet, so quiet that when a string breaks in the sky, we hear it.

Notes

THE BASIC TEXT for Chekhov's works and his letters is *Polnoe sobranie sochinenii i pisem A. P. Chekhova,* edited by S. D. Balukhatyi, V. P. Potemkin, and N. S. Tikhonov, in 20 volumes, Moscow, 1944-51. In the following notes, I have occasionally referred to this magnificent edition (*Complete Works*), but more often to the modest three-volume edition of the *Selected Works* (*A. P. Chekhov, Izbrannie proizvedeniya v trekh tomakh*) published in Moscow, 1964, which is very easily come by, and contains much of the material under discussion. The English translations to which I have referred the reader are those which at the present time are most readily available. Since it may be of some interest occasionally to compare the readings, I have in most cases cited more than one. Translations of Chekhov's letters, where I have not specifically cited the source, will be found in E. J. Simmons's *Chekhov,* and in the various collections by Garnett, Friedland, Koteliansky, and Josephson. In general these references are intended mainly to assist the reader in locating the context of the quotations. Unless they are specially credited, the translations in the text are my own.

CHEKHOV'S THEATRE

1. Cf. Ernest J. Simmons, *Chekhov, A Biography,* Boston, 1962, pp. 42, 65; V. I. Nemirovich-Danchenko, *My Life in the Russian Theatre,* translated by John Cournos, Boston, 1936, p. 20.

2. See B. V. Varneke, *History of the Russian Theatre*, New York, 1951, pp. 293 f., and Chekhov's letter to Suvorin, 22 December 1902.

3. For comparable government regulation in England, see W. N. M. Geary, *The Law of Theatres and Music Halls*, London, 1885; W. Nicholson, *The Struggle for a Free Stage in London*, London, 1906; and the summary of anti-theatre activity in W. J. Courthope, *A History of English Poetry*, London, 1875-1910, II, 381. For the history of the French law relating to the theatre, see A. Lacan and C. Paulmier, *Traité de la législation et la jurisprudence des théâtres*, 2 vols., Paris, 1853; G. Maugras, *Les Comédiens hors la loi*, Paris, 1887. For the Italian law: V. Rivalta, *Storia e sistema del diritto dei teatri*, Bologna, 1886; N. Tabanelli, *Il Codice del teatro*, Milano, 1901.

4. Alexander Griboyedov, *Letter to P. A. Katenin*, 14 February 1825, in A. Griboyedov, *Works*, Moscow, 1953, letter 39, p. 527.

5. A. W. Schlegel, *Vorlesungen über dramatische Kunst und Literatur*, Lecture III. Translated in B. Clark, *European Theories of the Drama*, New York, 1929, p. 344.

6. Quoted in Varneke, op. cit., p. 215.

7. Cf. Marc Slonim, *Russian Theater from the Empire to the Soviets*, New York, 1961, pp. 40 ff., 47 ff.

8. For the varied fortunes of this literary character, see Mario Praz, *The Romantic Agony*, Chap. 2, New York, 1960, pp. 53 ff.

9. In *Man and Superman*, Tanner explains this metamorphosis of the Byronic hero. Tanner says: "I am ten times more destructive now than I was then. The moral passion has taken my destructiveness in hand and directed it to moral ends. I have become a reformer, and like all reformers, an iconoclast. I no longer break cucumber frames and burn gorse bushes: I shatter creeds and demolish idols." Shaw, *Man and Superman*, Act 1. In *Collected Works of Bernard Shaw*, New York, 1930, X, 36.

10. Cf. Marc Slonim, *Russian Theater*, pp. 41, 48 f.

11. W. K. Bruford's very informative work, *Chekhov and His Russia, A Sociological Study*, London, 1947, is based on the contrary assumption. See pp. 35 ff.

12. Quoted by D. V. Averkiyev, cited in Varneke, *op. cit.*, p. 342. Cf. Slonim, *Russian Theater*, pp. 75 ff.

13. Cf. Stendhal, *Le Rouge et le noir*, Chapter 8. The situation is interestingly similar to that in Turgenev's play, and the characters are much the same: the noble lady, the obtuse husband, the young tutor. The young ward corresponds to the chambermaid Elisa in Stendhal's novel. Instead of Rakitin we have Monsieur Valenod. Stendhal's novel was published in 1830, but its great vogue began about 1865. In 1850 it would not have been widely known in Russia. The resemblance may, of course, be coincidental. See *Le Rouge et le noir* in Stendhal, *Oeuvres*, Paris, 1959, Vol. I, pp. 484 ff.

14. For Chekhov's opinion of Turgenev as a novelist, see his letter to Suvorin, 24 February 1893. In *A. Chekhov, Letters on the Short Story, the*

Drama and Other Literary Topics, ed. Friedland, New York, 1924, p. 242.
15. Both Nemirovich-Danchenko and Meyerhold saw the relation of Chekhov to Turgenev. See V. Meyerhold, *O teatre*, Petersburg, 1912, p. 112.

PLATONOV

1. See S. Danilov, *An Outline of the History of the Russian Theatre*, Moscow, 1948. Cf. D. Magarshack, *Chekhov the Dramatist*, New York, 1960, p. 68. See also his translation of *Platonov*, New York, 1965.
2. Letter to A. N. Leikin, 20 August 1883; to the same, 10 December 1883. Both translated in Simmons, *Chekhov*, pp. 59, 60.
3. Letter to V. V. Bilibin, 28 February 1886.
4. Letter to D. V. Grigorovich, 28 March 1886. Quoted in full in Simmons, *Chekhov*, pp. 95 ff., and in *Letters on the Short Story, etc.*, pp. 55 f.
5. Cf. letter to Suvorin, 26 April 1893.
6. Letter to Maria Kiseleva, 29 September 1886. In Simmons, *Chekhov*, p. 125.
7. For example see his letter to Suvorin, 24 February 1893. Cf. his letter to the same, 11 July 1894, in which he writes of evoking the spirit of Turgenev in the course of a séance. And cf. Chekhov's story, "A Terrible Night" (1884).
8. Letter to A. F. Lazarev-Gruzinsky, 4 February 1888.
9. Letter to Alexander Chekhov, 10 May 1886.
10. Letter to D. V. Grigorovich, 28 March 1886.
11. See Chekhov's letters to Leontiev-Shcheglov in *Letters on the Short Story, etc.*, pp. 106 and 217-223.
12. Letter to Alexander Chekhov, 10 May 1886.
13. Letter to D. V. Grigorovich, 12 January 1888.
14. Letter of 14 January 1887.
15. Letter to Maria Kiseleva, 29 September 1886.
16. Letter to A. N. Pleshcheyev, 4 October 1888.
17. To the same, 7-8 October 1888.
18. Letter to Suvorin, 30 May 1888.
19. To the same, 27 October 1888. In *Letters on the Short Story, etc.*, pp. 59 f.
20. "The Lights" (*Ogni*, 1888) in *The Tales of Chekhov*, translated by Constance Garnett, Vol. XIII: *Love and Other Stories*, New York, 1931, pp. 19 ff.
21. M. Gorky, *Autobiography*, translated by Isidor Schneider, New York, 1949, p. 393. His translation.
22. "The Lights," p. 68.
23. Letter to Leontiev-Shcheglov, 9 June 1888.
24. Stendhal, *Le Rouge et le noir*, Chapter 24; Chapter 33. In Stendhal, *Oeuvres*, Paris, 1959, I, 589 ff., and 629 ff.
25. Gorky, *Autobiography*, p. 159.

26. "Gooseberries" (*Kryzhovnik*, 1898) is translated in Garnett, *Tales*, Vol. V: *The Wife and Other Stories*, New York, 1918, pp. 269 ff. Cf. Thomas G. Winner, "Chekhov and Scientism," in *Anton Čechov, Some Essays*, edited by Tom Eekman, Leiden, 1960, pp. 325 ff.
27. Gorky, *Autobiography*, pp. 448 f.
28. "The Beauties" (*Krasavitsky*, 1888). In *Tales*, translated by C. Garnett, Vol. IX: *The Schoolmistress and Other Stories*, New York, 1921, p. 283.
29. Cf. Bruford, op. cit., p. 208; A. Kuprin in S. S. Koteliansky, *Anton Tchekhov: Literary and Theatrical Reminiscences*, London, 1927, pp. 52, 53; Vershinin's speech in *The Three Sisters*, Act 2, translated in Ronald Hingley, *The Oxford Chekhov*, Vol. III, London, 1964, p. 98.
30. Bruford, op. cit., p. 209. His translation.
31. Cf. "The Beauties," "The Bishop" (*Arkhierey*, 1902); "The Black Monk" (*Cherny monakh*, 1894); "The Lady with the Little Dog" (*Dama s sobachkov*, 1899).
32. Letter to Suvorin, 27 December 1889.

IVANOV

1. Letter to Maria Kiseleva, 13 September 1887. In Simmons, *Chekhov*, p. 135.
2. To Alexander Chekhov, 10-12 October 1887.
3. To the same, 23 October 1887.
4. Strindberg, *Miss Julie*, "Author's Foreword." In *Strindberg, Seven Plays*, translated by Arvid Paulson, New York, 1960, pp. 62 ff. My translation.
5. Letter to N. M. Yezhov, 27 October 1887. In Simmons, *Chekhov*, p. 136.
6. Letter to N. A. Leikin, 15 November 1887. On Davydov's performance see letter to Suvorin, 7 January 1889, in *Letters on the Short Story, etc.*, p. 142.
7. Letter to Alexander Chekhov, 20 November 1887, in *Selected Letters*, ed. Hellman, New York, 1955, pp. 40 ff.
8. To the same, 24 November 1887.
9. Letter to Mikhail Chekhov, 3 December 1887.
10. Letter to Suvorin, 23 December 1888.
11. Letter to Pleshcheyev, 23 January 1888.
12. Letter to Suvorin, 19 December 1888. *Bolvan* means blockhead.
13. To the same, 30 December 1888.
14. Letter to Pleshcheyev, 15 January 1889.
15. Letter to Shcheglov, 18 February 1889.
16. Letter to Suvorin, 30 December 1888.
17. Letter to Bilibin, 18 January 1886.
13. Letter to Alexander Chekhov, 10-12 October 1887.
19. *Ivanov*, Act 4. In *Selected Works of A. P. Chekhov*, Moscow, 1964, Vol. III, p. 338; translated in Corrigan, *Six Plays of Chekhov*, New York,

1962, p. 60. Cf. David Magarshack, *Chekhov the Dramatist*, New York, 1960, p. 113.
20. Letter to Suvorin, 30 December 1888. In *Letters on the Short Story, etc.*, p. 135.
21. Barbey d'Aurevilly, *Le Cachet d'Onyx*. In *Oeuvres*, Paris, 1964, Vol. I, p. 16.
22. Cf. Émile Tardieu, *L'Ennui*, Paris, 1903, pp. 81 ff.; E. von Sydow, *Die Kultur der Dekadenz*, Dresden, 1921, pp. 24 ff.
23. Gorky, *Autobiography*, p. 330.
24. Baudelaire, "*La Destruction*" in "*Les Fleurs du mal.*" *Oeuvres*, Paris, 1954, p. 181.
25. *Ivanov*, Act 3. In *Selected Works*, III, p. 321; translated in Corrigan, *Six Plays*, p. 43.
26. Letter to Suvorin, 7 January 1889.

THE WOOD DEMON

1. Letter to Suvorin, May ... 1889. In Simmons, *Chekhov*, p. 183.
2. Letter to Suvorin, 4 May 1889.
3. Ibid.
4. Letter to Pleshcheyev, 21 October 1889.
5. Letter to Suvorin, 27 December 1889.
6. *The Wood Demon (Leshiy)*, Act 1, sc. VIII. In *Complete Collected Works and Letters of A. P. Chekhov*, Moscow, 1944-51, Vol. XI, pp. 385 f.; translated in Hingley, *The Oxford Chekhov*, III, 221.
7. To Alexander Chekhov, 10 May 1886.
8. *The Wood Demon*, Act 2, sc. X, *Collected Works*, XI, 400 f.; Hingley, *Chekhov*, III, 236.
9. *The Wood Demon*, Act 3, sc. III, *Collected Works*, XI, 403 f.; Hingley, *Chekhov*, III, 239.
10. *The Wood Demon*, Act 3, sc. XI, *Collected Works*, XI, 414; Hingley, *Chekhov*, III, 249.
11. *The Wood Demon*, Act 4, sc. VI, *Collected Works*, XI, 425; Hingley, *Chekhov*, III, 260.
12. Evidence has been adduced, far from conclusive, that *Uncle Vanya* was in fact finished in the spring of 1890. See N. I. Gitovich, *Chronicle of the Life and Works of A. P. Chekhov*, Moscow, 1955, pp. 282 ff. Cited in Simmons, *Chekhov*, p. 200, note.
13. *The Wood Demon*, Act 4, sc. VIII, *Collected Works*, XI, 429; Hingley, *Chekhov*, III, 264.
14. Ibid., sc. IX, *Collected Works*, XI, 430; Hingley, *Chekhov*, III, 265.
15. Ibid., sc. IX, *Collected Works*, XI, 431; Hingley, *Chekhov*, III, 266.
16. Letter to A. I. Urusov, 16 April 1900. In *Letters on the Short Story, etc.*, p. 128.

THE SEA GULL

1. See letter to Suvorin, 7 December 1889.
2. Letter to Shcheglov, 22 March 1890.
3. Letter to Suvorin, 30 August 1891.
4. Letter to Suvorin, 17 March 1892.
5. Letter to Suvorin, 16 August 1892.
6. Letter to Suvorin, 2 August 1893.
7. "Ward No. 6" (*Palata No. 6*, 1892). In *Selected Works*, II, 233; translated in *Seven Short Novels of Anton Chekhov*, by Barbara Makanowitzky, New York, 1963, p. 129. I am indebted to her excellent translation, but I do not follow it.
8. "In Exile" (*V sosilke*, 1892). In Garnett, *Tales*, Vol. IX: *The Schoolmistress and Other Stories*, New York, 1921, p. 100.
9. Ibid.
10. "Ward No. 6," op. cit., p. 120.
11. Letter to Suvorin, 25 November 1892.
12. Letter to Suvorin, 2 January 1894.
13. Letter to Suvorin, 11 July 1894; to the same, 24 August 1893.
14. Letter to Suvorin, 13 January 1895.
15. "The Murder" (*Ubiystvo*, 1895). Translated in *Peasants and Other Stories*, edited by Edmund Wilson, New York, 1956, p. 157.
16. Letter to Suvorin, 5 May 1895.
17. Letter to Suvorin, 21 October 1895.
18. To the same, 21 November 1895.
19. To the same, 31 December 1895.
20. To the same, 16 December 1895.
21. To the same, 10 May 1891.
22. *A. P. Chekhov in the Remembrance of His Contemporaries*, Moscow, 1947, pp. 323 ff. For a full discussion of Avilova's relations with Chekhov see Simmons, *Chekhov*, pp. 207 ff., pp. 335 ff.
23. Letter to Lidiya Mizinova (Lika), July 1891.
24. To the same, 27 March 1892.
25. Letter to A. P. Chekhov, 7 October 1893.
26. Letter to A. P. Chekhov, 20 September 1894.
27. Letter to Lika, 2 October 1894.
28. *The Sea Gull*, Act 2. In *Selected Works*, III, 429; translated in Corrigan, *Six Plays*, p. 149.
29. Letter to Suvorin, 18 April 1892.
30. In Simmons, *Chekhov*, p. 504.
31. Letter to Alexander Vishnevsky, 7 November 1903.
32. *The Sea Gull*, Act 4. In *Selected Works*, III, 454; Corrigan, *Six Plays*, p. 174.
33. *The Sea Gull*, Act 2. In *Selected Works*, III, 430; Corrigan, *Six Plays*, p. 150.

34. Gorky, *Autobiography*, pp. 123 ff.
35. Letter to Suvorin, 14 December 1896.
36. Letter to Lidiya Avilova, 6 October 1897. In Chapter XV of Avilova's memoirs. In *A. P. Chekhov v vospominaniyakh sovremennikov*, Moscow, 1960. See Lydia Avilov, *Chekhov in My Life*, translated by David Magarshack, New York, 1950.
37. See Nemirovich-Danchenko, *My Life in the Russian Theatre*, Boston, 1936, pp. 80 ff.
38. Ibid., pp. 141 f.
39. Nemirovich writes: "At no time has he come forth as a champion of new forms, neither in disputes, nor in vehement conversation, nor in any article." *My Life in the Russian Theatre*, p. 18.
40. "A Tragic Actor" (*Tragik*, 1883). In Garnett, *Tales*, Vol. IX: *The Schoolmistress and Other Stories*, New York, 1921, p. 195.
41. V. I. Nemirovich-Danchenko, *My Life in the Russian Theatre* (*Iz proshlogo*), Leningrad, 1936, p. 37.
42. See, e.g., letter to Olga Knipper, 10 April 1904. Translated in Garnett, *Letters of A. P. Tchehov to Olga L. Knipper*, New York, 1924, p. 380.
43. Letter to Olga Knipper, 2 January 1900. In Garnett, *Letters*, pp. 32 f.
44. Quoted in Simmons, *Chekhov*, p. 430. On the much discussed question of Stanislavsky's method, see Stanislavsky, *My Life in Art*, New York, 1956; *Stanislavsky on the Art of the Stage*, translated by David Magarshack, London, 1950; N. Houghton, *Moscow Rehearsals*, New York, 1936, pp. 58 ff.
45. Nemirovich-Danchenko, *My Life in the Russian Theatre*, pp. 163 f.
46. Letter to Urusov, 1 February 1899.
47. Letter to Suvorin, 25 June 1899. The details of this transaction may be found in Simmons, *Chekhov*, pp. 453 ff., and in Hingley, *Chekhov, A Biographical and Critical Study*, London, 1950, pp. 187 ff.
48. Letter to M. Gorky, 9 May 1899.
49. Letter to Olga Knipper, 1 November 1899. In Garnett, *Letters*, p. 30.

UNCLE VANYA

1. See N. I. Gitovich, *Chronicle of the Life and Works of A. P. Chekhov*, Moscow, 1950, pp. 282 ff.
2. "The Beauties." Translated in Garnett, *Tales*, Vol. IX: *The Schoolmistress*, New York, 1921, p. 290.
3. "About Love" (*O lyubvi*, 1898). In Garnett, *Tales*, Vol. V: *The Wife and Other Stories*, p. 287.
4. See, e.g. Edmund Bergler, *Principles of Self-Damage*, New York, 1959, pp. 128 ff., and *The Basic Neurosis*, New York, 1949, pp. 75 ff.
5. Letter to Olga Knipper, 30 September 1899. In Garnett, *Letters*, p. 29.
6. *Uncle Vanya*, Act 4. In *Selected Works*, pp. 503 f.; translated in Hingley, *Chekhov*, III, 67; Corrigan, *Six Plays*, p. 233.

THE THREE SISTERS

1. Letter to Olga Knipper, 14 August 1900. Translated in Garnett, *Letters to Olga Knipper*, p. 40. The letter to Vishnevsky may be found in *Letters on the Short Story, etc.*, pp. 155 f., together with some of these letters to Olga.

2. To Olga Knipper, 18 August 1900. In Garnett, *Letters*, p. 41.

3. To Olga Knipper, 20 August 1900. In Garnett, *Letters*, pp. 42 f.

4. To Olga Knipper, 5 September 1900. In Garnett, *Letters*, p. 45.

5. To Olga Knipper, 15 September 1900. In Garnett, *Letters*, p. 49.

6. To Olga Knipper, 4 October 1900. In Garnett, *Letters*, p. 53.

7. To Olga Knipper, 6 January 1901. In Garnett, *Letters*, p. 68.

8. To Olga Knipper, 20 January 1901. In Garnett, *Letters*, pp. 72 f.

9. "On Official Duty." Translated in Garnett, *Tales*, Vol. IX: *The Schoolmistress*, p. 166.

10. "The Kiss" (*Potseluy*, 1887). In A. Yarmolinsky, *The Portable Chekhov*, New York, 1963, p. 171; in Garnett, *Tales*, Vol. IV: *The Party and Other Stories*, p. 173.

11. *The Three Sisters*, Act 1. In *Selected Works*, III, 516; translated in Hingley, *Chekhov*, III, 184; Corrigan, *Six Plays*, pp. 236 f.

12. "In the Ravine" (*V ovrage*, 1900). Translated in Makanowitzky, *Seven Short Novels by Chekhov*, New York, 1963, p. 409; in Garnett, *Tales*, Vol. VI: *The Witch and Other Stories*, New York, 1918, p. 177.

13. In Makanowitzky, *Seven Short Novels*, p. 431.

14. *The Three Sisters*, Act I. In *Selected Works*, III, 507; translated in Hingley, *Chekhov*, III, 78; Corrigan, *Six Plays*, p. 231.

15. Ibid., Act 3. In *Selected Works*, III, 545; Hingley, *Chekhov*, III, 115; Corrigan, *Six Plays*, p. 265.

16. *The Three Sisters*, Act 1. In *Selected Works*, III, 514; Hingley, *Chekhov*, III, 81; Corrigan, *Six Plays*, p. 234.

17. See conversation with Bunin in the spring of 1901, quoted in Simmons, *Chekhov*, p. 525.

18. *The Three Sisters*, Act 2. In *Selected Works*, III, 529 f.; Hingley, *Chekhov*, III, 98 f.; Corrigan, *Six Plays*, p. 250.

19. Ibid., Act 1. In *Selected Works*, III, 509; Hingley, *Chekhov*, III, 76; Corrigan, *Six Plays*, p. 229.

20. Ibid., Act 3. In *Selected Works*, III, 549; Hingley, *Chekhov*, III, 119; Corrigan, *Six Plays*, p. 269.

21. Ibid., Act 4. In *Selected Works*, III, 568; Hingley, *Chekhov*, III, 139; Corrigan, *Six Plays*, p. 287.

22. Ibid., Act 1. In *Selected Works*, III, 516; Hingley, *Chekhov*, III, 84; Corrigan, *Six Plays*, p. 237.

23. Ibid., Act 4. In *Selected Works*, III, 568; Hingley, *Chekhov*, III, 139; Corrigan, *Six Plays*, p. 287.

24. Ibid., Act 4. In *Selected Works*, III, 561; Corrigan, *Six Plays*, p. 281; Hingley, *Chekhov*, III, 132.
25. V. Feyder, *A. P. Chekhov, Literaturny byt i tvorchestvo po memuarnym materialem*, Leningrad, 1928, p. 160.

THE CHERRY ORCHARD

1. Letter to L. V. Sredin, 24 September 1901. Cf. letter to Olga Knipper, 13 February 1902.
2. Letter to Olga Knipper, 29 October 1901.
3. Letter to Olga Knipper, 17 March 1902.
4. Letter to Stanislavsky, 18 July 1902.
5. Letter to A. P. Chekhov, 28 August 1902. Cf. *Letters to Olga Knipper*, pp. 208 f. See Simmons, *Chekhov*, pp. 575 ff. for a full account of this correspondence.
6. Cf. Simmons, *Chekhov*, p. 576.
7. Letter to Olga Knipper, 20 January 1903. In Garnett, *Letters*, p. 261.
8. Letter to Olga Knipper, 16 March 1902. In Garnett, *Letters*, p. 184.
9. Letter to Olga Knipper, 29 August 1902. In Garnett, *Letters*, p. 205.
10. Letter to Olga Knipper, 23 January 1903. In Garnett, *Letters*, p. 262.
11. Letter to Olga Knipper, 5 February 1903. In Garnett, *Letters*, p. 270.
12. "The Betrothed" (*Nevesta*, 1903). Translated in Wilson, *Peasants and Other Stories*, p. 379; also in Garnett, *Tales*, Vol. XI: The *Schoolmaster and Other Stories*, London, 1921.
13. Letter to Olga Knipper, 20 September 1903. In Garnett, *Letters*, p. 305. Almost the whole of this correspondence may be found in Simmons, *Chekhov*, pp. 603 ff.
14. Letter to Olga Knipper, 21 September 1903. In Garnett, *Letters*, pp. 305 f.
15. Letter to Olga Knipper, 25 September 1903. In Garnett, *Letters*, p. 308.
16. Letter to Olga Knipper, 3 October 1903. In Garnett, *Letters*, p. 313.
17. Letter to Olga Knipper, 12 October 1903. In Garnett, *Letters*, p. 320.
18. Letter to Olga Knipper, 14 October 1903. In Garnett, *Letters*, pp. 322 f.
19. Letter to Olga Knipper, 21 October 1903. In Garnett, *Letters*, p. 327.
20. Letter to Olga Knipper, 10 April 1904. In Garnett, *Letters*, p. 380.
21. *The Cherry Orchard*, Act 2. In *Selected Works*, III, 590; translated in Corrigan, *Six Plays*, p. 310; Hingley, *Chekhov*, III, 166; A. Yarmolinsky, *Chekhov*, New York, 1963, p. 557.
22. Ibid., Act 2. In *Selected Works*, III, 596; Hingley, *Chekhov*, III, 172; Corrigan, *Six Plays*, p. 316; Yarmolinsky, *Chekhov*, p. 564.
23. Ibid., Act 4. In *Selected Works*, III, 612; Corrigan, *Six Plays*, p. 333; Hingley, *Chekhov*, III, 190; Yarmolinsky, *Chekhov*, p. 584.
24. Ibid., Act 2. In *Selected Works*, III, 593; Corrigan, *Six Plays*, pp. 313 f.; Hingley, *Chekhov*, III, 170; Yarmolinsky, *Chekhov*, p. 561.

25. Ibid., Act 2. In *Selected Works*, III, 596; Corrigan, *Six Plays*, p. 316; Hingley, *Chekhov*, III, 173; Yarmolinsky, *Chekhov*, p. 565.
26. Ibid., Act 2. In *Selected Works*, III, 597; Hingley, *Chekhov*, III, 173; Corrigan, *Six Plays*, p. 317; Yarmolinsky, *Chekhov*, p. 566.
27. *The Cherry Orchard*, Act 4. In *Selected Works*, III, 603 ff.; Corrigan, *Six Plays*, pp. 323 ff.; Hingley, *Chekhov*, III, 180 f.; Yarmolinsky, *Chekhov*, pp. 573 f.
28. "The Man in a Case" (*Chelovek v futlyare*, 1898). In Garnett, *Tales*, Vol. V: *The Wife and Other Stories*, 1918, p. 266; Yarmolinsky, *Chekhov*, p. 368.
29. *The Cherry Orchard*, Act. 4. In *Selected Works*, III, 620; Hingley, *Chekhov*, III, 197; Corrigan, *Six Plays*, p. 339; Yarmolinsky, *Chekhov*, p. 593.
30. Ibid., Act 2. In *Selected Works*, III, 594; Corrigan, *Six Plays*, p. 315; Hingley, *Chekhov*, III, 171; Yarmolinsky, *Chekhov*, p. 563.
31. Ibid., Act 4. In *Selected Works*, III, 620; Hingley, *Chekhov*, III, 198; Corrigan, *Six Plays*, p. 340; Yarmolinsky, *Chekhov*, p. 594.

THE SOUND OF THE BREAKING STRING

1. M. Gorky, *Autobiography*, New York, 1949, pp. 468.
2. Maeterlinck, *Le Tragique quotidien*. In *Le Trésor des humbles*, Paris, 1949, pp. 127 ff.; translated in part in B. Clark, *European Theories of the Drama*, p. 412.
3. "The Lady with the Little Dog." In *Selected Works*, III, 186 f.; translated in Yarmolinsky, *Chekhov*, pp. 430 f.; Garnett, *Tales*, Vol. III: *The Lady with the Little Dog and Other Stories*, New York, 1917, pp. 24 f.
4. See the fine study by Sophie Laffitte, *Chekhov et Tolstoy*, in Eekman, *Anton Čechov*, pp. 131 ff.
5. E.g. Prince Mirsky, *Contemporary Russian Literature*, New York, 1926, pp. 84 ff.
6. "The Lady with the Little Dog." In *Selected Works*, III, 178 f.; Garnett, *Tales*, Vol. III, p. 18; Yarmolinsky, *Chekhov*, 419.
7. "Chekhov v neizdannykh dnevnikakh sovremennikov" in *Literaturnoe nasledstvo*, LXVIII, Moscow, 1960, pp. 479 ff.
8. Letter to Olga Knipper, 20 April 1904. In Garnett, *Letters*, p. 386. For a good discussion of the various viewpoints, from the time of Skabichevsky and Shestov to that of Chukovsky, with regard to Chekhov's temperament, see Hingley, *Chekhov. A Biographical and Critical Study*, pp. 103 ff.

A Selective Bibliography

A LIST OF THE WORKS referred to in the text and notes, together with some other books which will be found useful in connection with this study. For more extensive bibliographical listings see E. A. Polotskaya, *A. P. Chekhov—Rekomendatelnyi ukazatel literatury*, Moscow, 1955, and N. I. Gitovich, *Letopis zhizni i tvorchestva A. P. Chekhova*, cited below. Anna Heifetz, *Chekhov in English*, edited by A. Yarmolinsky, New York, 1949, has a list of Chekhov's writings and works relative to them. David Magarshack, *Chekhov: A Life*, London, 1952, includes a list of Chekhov's works, their Russian titles, the English translations, and their dates. There is a chronological listing of Chekhov's stories in Ronald Hingley, *Chekhov*, and an excellent short bibliography in E. J. Simmons, *Chekhov*.

CHEKHOV'S THEATRE

Barbey d'Aurevilly, J. A., *Le Cachet d'Onyx. Oeuvres*, Volume I, Paris, 1964.

Baudelaire, Charles, *Oeuvres*, Paris, 1954.

Bergler, Edmund, *The Basic Neurosis*, New York, 1949.

———, *Principles of Self-Damage*, New York, 1959.

Clark, Barrett, *European Theories of the Drama*, New York, 1929.

Courthope, W. J., *A History of English Poetry*, 6 vols., London, 1895-1910, Vol. II, 1897.

Efros, N., *Moskovskii khudozhestvennyi teatr*, Moscow, 1923.

Evreinov, N., *Histoire du théâtre russe*, Paris, 1947.

Geary, W. N. M., *The Law of Theatres and Music Halls*, London, 1885.

Gobetti, P., *Paradosso dello spirito russo*, Turin, 1926.

Gogol, N. V., *Sochineniya N. V. Gogolia*, ed. N. Tikhonravov, 7 vols., Moscow, 1889-1896.

Gorchakov, N., *Stanislavsky Directs*, New York, 1954.

Gorky, Maxim, *Autobiography*, translated by Isidor Schneider, New York, 1949.

Gourfinkel, N., *Le Théâtre russe contemporain*, Paris, 1931.

Gregor, J. and Fülöp-Miller, *Das russische Theater, sein Wesen und seine Geschichte mit besonderer Berücksichtigung der Revolutions-Periode*, Zurich-Leipzig-Wien, 1927.

Griboyedov, Alexander, *Polnoe sobranie sochinenii A. S. Griboyedova* (*Complete Works*), ed. Piksanov, 3 vols., Petersburg, 1911-1917.

———, *Works*, Moscow, 1953.

———, *Gore ot uma*, ed. N. K. Piksanov and V. Filippov, Moscow, 1946.

Grube, Max, *Geschichte der Meininger*, Berlin, 1926, translated by A. N. Koller, as *The Story of the Meininger*, Coral Gables, 1963.

Gukovskii, G., "Racine en Russie au XVIIIe siècle" in *Revue des études slaves*, VII (1927), pp. 75 ff. and 241 ff.

Houghton, Norris, *Moscow Rehearsals*, New York, 1936.

Kara-Murza, S. G., *Malyi teatr*, Moscow, 1924.

Lacan, A. and C. Paulmier, *Traité de la législation et la jurisprudence des théâtres*, 2 vols., Paris, 1853.

Lermontov, M. J., *Dramy i tragedii*, ed. B. M. Eichenbaum, Moscow-Leningrad, 1935.

Lo Gatto, E., *Storia del teatro russo*, 2 vols., Florence, 1952.

Maeterlinck, Maurice, *Le Trésor des humbles*, Paris, 1949.

Maugras, G., *Les Comédiens hors la loi*, Paris, 1887.

Maurois, André, *Tourgeniev*, Paris, 1931.

Meyerhold, V., *O teatre*, Petersburg, 1912.

Mioni, Ada, *Il "Boris Godunov" di A. Pushkin, studio storico-critico*, Rome, 1935.

Mirsky, D. S., *Contemporary Russian Literature*, New York, 1926.

———, *Modern Russian Literature*, London, 1925.

Nicholson, W., *The Struggle for a Free Stage in London*, London, 1906.

Patouillet, J., *Le Théâtre des mœurs russes des origines à Ostrovskii*, Paris, 1912.

———, *Ostrovskii et son théâtre de mœurs russes*, Paris, 1912.

Praz, Mario, *La Carne, la morte e il diavolo nella letterature romantica*, translated as *The Romantic Agony*, by Angus Davidson, 2nd ed., New York, 1956.

Pushkin, Alexander, *Dramatisheskie proizvedeniya*, Leningrad, 1937.

Rivalta, V., *Storia e sistema del diritto dei teatri*, Bologna, 1886.

Schlegel, August Wilhelm, *Vorlesungen über dramatische Kunst und Literatur*, 3 vols., Heidelberg, 1817. Translated as *A Course of Lectures on Dramatic Art and Literature*, by John Black, revised by A. J. W. Morrison, 2 vols., London, 1846.

Slonim, Marc, *Russian Theater from the Empire to the Soviets*, New York, 1961.

Sobolev, J., *Vl. I. Nemirovich-Danchenko*, Moscow, 1929.

Stanislavsky, K. S., *Rabota aktera nad soboi*, translated by E. Provoledo as *Il lavoro dell'attore*, Bari, 1956.

———, *Stanislavsky on the Art of the Stage*, translated by David Magarshack, London, 1950.

Stendhal, *Le Rouge et le noir*, in *Oeuvres*, Vol. I, Paris, 1959.

Strindberg, August, *Seven Plays*, translated by Arvid Paulson, New York, 1960.

Tabanelli, N., *Il codice del teatro,* Milan, 1901.

Tardieu, Émile, *L'Ennui,* Paris, 1903.

Turgenev, Ivan, *Polnoe sobranie sochinenii I. S. Turgeneva (Complete Collected Works),* 7th ed., 10 vols., Petersburg, 1915.

Varneke, B. V., *Istoriye russkogo teatra,* 3rd ed., Moscow-Leningrad, 1939, translated as *A History of the Russian Theatre* by Boris Brasel and Belle Martin, New York, 1951.

———, ed., *A. N. Ostrovsky, 1823-1923,* Odessa, 1923.

Von Sydow, E., *Die Kultur der Dekadenz,* Dresden, 1921.

Vsevolodsky-Gerngross, V. N., *Istoriya russkogo teatra,* 2 vols., Moscow-Leningrad, 1929.

Wiener, L., *The Contemporary Drama of Russia,* Boston, 1924.

CHEKHOV: WRITINGS

A. P. Chekhov, *Polnoe sobranie sochinenii i pisem A. P. Chekhova (Complete Collected Works),* 20 vols., Moscow, 1944-51.

———, *Izbrannie proizvedeniya v trekh tomakh (Selected Works),* 3 vols., Moscow, 1964.

———, *Works of Chekhov,* translated by Constance Garnett, 15 vols., London and New York, 1916-23.

———, *The Oxford Chekhov,* translated by Ronald Hingley, Vol. III, London, 1964.

———, *Ivanov,* translated by David Magarshack, New York, 1966.

———, *Peasants and Other Stories,* ed. by Edmund Wilson, New York, 1956.

———, *Platonov,* translated by David Magarshack, New York, 1965.

———, *The Portable Chekhov,* ed. by Avrahm Yarmolinsky, New York, 1947.

———, *Seven Short Novels by Chekhov,* translated by Barbara Makanowitzky, New York, 1963.

———, *Chekhov, Six Plays,* translated by R. W. Corrigan, New York, 1962.

———, *Letters of Anton Tchehov to his Family and Friends,* translated by Constance Garnett, New York, 1920.

———, *The Letters of Anton Pavlovitch Tchehov to Olga Leonardovna Knipper,* translated by Constance Garnett, New York, 1924.

———, *Letters on the Short Story, the Drama, and other Literary Topics,* edited by L. S. Friedland, New York, 1924.

———, *The Life and Letters of Anton Tchekhov,* translated by S. S. Koteliansky and Philip Tomlinson, New York, 1925.

———, *The Notebooks of Anton Tchekhov,* translated by S. S. Koteliansky and Leonard Woolf, London, 1921.

———, *The Personal Papers of Anton Chekhov,* introduction by Matthew Josephson, New York, 1948.

———, *The Selected Letters of Anton Chekhov,* ed. by Lillian Hellman, translated by S. K. Lederer, New York, 1955.

CHEKHOV: BIOGRAPHY AND CRITICISM

Avilov, Lydia, *Chekhov in My Life*, translated by David Magarshack, New York, 1950.

Balukhatyi, S. D., *Chekhov-dramaturg*, Leningrad, 1936.

Brisson, Pierre, *Tchékhov et sa vie*, Paris, 1955.

Bruford, W. K., *Chekhov and His Russia, A Sociological Study*, London, 1947.

Bunin, I. A., *O Chekhove. Nezakonchennaya rukopis*, New York, 1955.

Chukovsky, K., *Chekhov the Man*, translated by Pauline Rose, London, 1945.

Eekman, Tom, ed., *Anton Čechov 1860-1960. Some Essays*, Leiden, 1960.

Elton, O., *Chekhov. The Taylorian Lecture*, Oxford, 1929.

Feyder, V., *A. P. Chekhov, Literaturny byt i tvorchestvo po memuarnym materialem*, Leningrad, 1928.

Gerhardi, W., *Anton Chekhov, A Critical Study*, London, 1923.

Gitovich, N. I., *Letopis zhizni i tvorchestva A. P. Chekhova (Chronicle of the Life and Works of A. P. Chekhov)*, Moscow, 1955.

——, and Fedorova, I. V., editors, *A. P. Chekhov v vospominaniyakh sovremennikov (A. P. Chekhov in the Recollection of his Contemporaries)*, 4th ed., Moscow, 1960.

Hingley, Ronald, *Chekhov, A Biographical and Critical Study*, London, 1950.

Koteliansky, S. S., translator, *Anton Tchekhov: Literary and Theatrical Reminiscences*, London, 1927.

Laffitte, Sophie, *Tchékhov par lui-même*, Paris, 1960.

Magarshack, David, *Chekhov: A Life*, London, 1952.

——, *Chekhov the Dramatist*, New York, 1960.

Nemirovich-Danchenko, V. I., *Iz proshlogo*, Leningrad, 1936, translated as *My Life in the Russian Theatre*, by John Cournos, Boston, 1936.

——, *Teatralnoe nasledie (The Legacy of the Theatre)*, Vol. I, Moscow, 1952.

Shestov, L., *Anton Chekhov and Other Essays*, translated by S. S. Koteliansky and J. M. Murry, London, 1916.

Simmons, Ernest J., *Chekhov, A Biography*, Boston, 1962.

Stanislavsky, K. S., *My Life in Art*, translated by J. J. Robbins, New York, 1956; translated by G. Ivanov-Mumiyev, Moscow, 1958.

Stroeva, M., *Chekhov i khudozhestvennyi teatr*, Moscow, 1955.

Tumanova, A. N., *Anton Chekhov, The Voice of Twilight Russia*, New York, 1937.

"Vospominaniya o Chekhove" in *Literaturnoe nasledstvo*, LXVIII, Moscow, 1960, pp. 531 ff.

Yermilov, Vladimir, *A. P. Chekhov* (Moscow, 1954), translated by Ivy Litvinov, Moscow, n.d.

Zaitsev, Boris, *Chekhov: Literaturnaya biografiya*, New York, 1954.

Index

U

V

W

Y

Z